News and Journalism in the UK

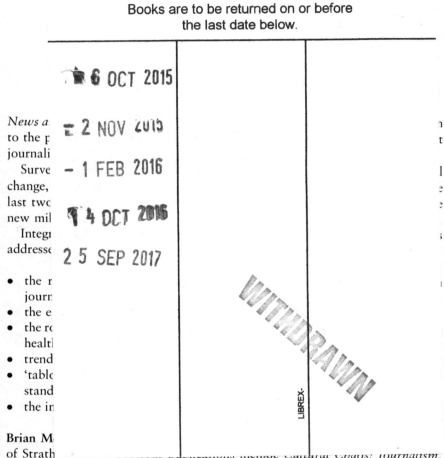

Books are to be returned on or before
the last date below.

News a n
to the p t
journali
Surve l
change,
last two e
new mil e
Integr
addresse s

- the r
  journr
- the e
- the r(
  healtl
- trend
- 'tabl(
  stand
- the ir

Brian M
of Strath ... publications include *Cultural Chaos: Journalism,
News & Power in a Globalised World* (2006) and *An Introduction to Political
Communication* (2007).

Communication and Society

Series Editor: James Curran

Glasgow Media Group Reader,
Volume 2
Industry, Economy, War and Politics
Edited by Greg Philo

The Global Jukebox
The International Music Industry
Robert Burnett

Inside Prime Time
Todd Gitlin

Talk on Television
Audience Participation and Public
Debate
Sonia Livingstone and Peter Lunt

Media Effects and Beyond
Culture, Socialization and Lifestyles
Edited by Karl Erik Rosengren

We Keep America on Top of the World
Television Journalism and the Public
Sphere
Daniel C. Hallin

A Journalism Reader
Edited by Michael Bromley and
Tom O'Malley

Tabloid Television
Popular Journalism and the 'Other
News'
John Langer

International Radio Journalism
History, Theory and Practice
Tim Crook

Media, Ritual and Identity
Edited by Tamar Liebes and
James Curran

De-Westernizing Media Studies
Edited by James Curran and
Myung-Jin Park

British Cinema in the Fifties
Christine Geraghty

Ill Effects
The Media Violence Debate,
2nd edn
Edited by Martin Barker and
Julian Petley

Media and Power
James Curran

Journalism After September 11
Edited by Barbie Zelizer and
Stuart Allan

Remaking Media
The Struggle to Democratize Public
Communication
Robert A Hackett and
William K Carroll

Media on the Move
Global Flow and Contra-Flow
Daya Kishan Thussu

An Introduction to Political
Communication, 4th edn
Brian McNair

The Mediation of Power
A Critical Introduction
Aeron Davis

Television Entertainment
Jonathan Gray

Western Media Systems
Jonathan Hardy

Narrating Media History
Edited by Michael Bailey

News and Journalism in the UK
Fifth Edition

Brian McNair

Routledge
Taylor & Francis Group

LONDON AND NEW YORK

First published 1994
by Routledge
This edition published 2009
by Routledge
2 Park Square, Milton Park, Abingdon, Oxon, OX14 4RN

Simultaneously published in the USA and Canada
by Routledge
711 Third Avenue, New York, NY 10017

Routledge is an imprint of the Taylor & Francis Group, an informa business

© 1994, 1996, 1999, 2003, 2009 Brian McNair

Typeset in Sabon by
Taylor & Francis Books

British Library Cataloguing in Publication Data
A catalogue record for this book is available from the British Library

Library of Congress Cataloging in Publication Data
McNair, Brian, 1959-
  News and journalism in the UK / Brian McNair. – 5th ed.
    p. cm. – (Communication and society)
  1. Journalism–Great Britain–History–20th century. 2. Journalism–Great
Britain–History–21st century. I. Title.
  PN5118.M35 2009
  072.09′049–dc22

                        2008037608

ISBN10: 0-415-41071-1 (hbk)
ISBN10: 0-415-41072-X (pbk)
ISBN10: 0-203-88141-9 (ebk)

ISBN13: 978-0-415-41071-7 (hbk)
ISBN13: 978-0-415-41072-4 (pbk)
ISBN13: 978-0-203-88141-5 (ebk)

To the Mugwump, for making it.

Contents

List of figures and tables

Preface to the Fifth Edition

The first edition of *News and Journalism in the UK* was published in 1994, and was based on research mostly undertaken in 1992–93. Three subsequent editions (published in 1996, 1999 and 2003) updated the book to take account of trends and debates around the British news media as they emerged through the 1990s and into the early 2000s. Material was added over time, reflecting emerging trends and issues for the British news media, such as sections on the feminisation of British journalism and the tabloidisation/dumbing down debate (1999), and discussion of the consequences of devolution for regional journalism in Scotland and other constituent parts of the UK (1999, 2003).

For this fifth edition, it has been necessary to do more than merely update the book. The first edition of *News and Journalism in the UK* was written long before the internet had become a widely-used platform for the delivery of news and other journalistic content; before the expansion of 24-hour real-time news in Britain to almost every household in the country; before digitisation, interactivity and participation had become buzzwords for print and broadcast news providers; before anyone had ever heard of analogue switch-off, blogging, participatory media, user-generated content or citizen journalism. 1994 was, in so many ways, a very different world from that which confronts the producers and consumers of news today.

Accommodating those differences has required a substantially revised book – updated, yes, as in previous editions, with the most recent available statistics on newspaper circulation, broadcast ratings, and, here for the first time, the increasingly important category of unique monthly usage of online journalism sites – but also extensively rewritten and restructured to reflect the transformed media environment of the times in which journalists and their readers, viewers, listeners and online users work. Where, in previous editions, the internet has appeared as a bit-player in the unfolding narrative of British journalism, in this edition an entire chapter has been devoted to the online news sector. As convergence between print, broadcast and online platforms has progressed, with major implications for established media organisations and those who work for them, it has been necessary to re-order and recalibrate the historical material that featured in previous editions, and to cut some sections to make room for the wealth of debate on the implications of new media for the future of British journalism, which now occupies so much of both scholarly and professional commentary. Chapters and sections have thus been merged, relocated, and in some cases renamed (although I retain some titles from the Fourth Edition). The key historical material on print and broadcast journalism in the UK that featured in earlier editions is concentrated in Chapters 6 and 7, covering print and broadcast journalism, respectively. Chapter 8 follows this material on the 'old' media with discussion of the online revolution.

The statistical updating for this edition focuses on the five-year period 2003–08, but I have taken the opportunity to undertake a broader assessment of trends in British journalism over the 15 years between completion of this edition and that of the First. Over that period there have been many concerns expressed by politicians, academics, journalists, regulators and audiences about the direction of trends in British journalism. There has been recurrent grumbling about dumbing down, tabloidisation, commodification and Americanisation (the terms have often been conflated). There have been laments for the death of print and the decline of current affairs and investigative reportage, and criticism of the corrosive cynicism of what Tony Blair, just before his resignation as Prime Minister in June 2007, called the 'feral beast' of the British news media. There has been much commentary on the corrupting impact of public relations and spin on British journalism; speculation on the future of the BBC's news and current affairs operation (and that of the commercial public service sector), and of regional broadcast journalism throughout the UK, faced with the challenge of digitisation and the end of half a century of 'analogue subsidy'. These and many other issues were not high on the agenda when *News and Journalism in the UK* was first published – if they were considered issues at all. Their presence on the agenda today reflects the impact on British journalism of hugely transformed political, economic and technological environments. In this edition, I take some distance from the various, often contradictory claims and counter-claims that have been made over those 15 years in order to present what I hope is a more nuanced assessment of what has really changed, and what it means for the quality of British journalism, as well as for British society, in the years to come.

Inevitably, the internet and online media feature heavily in this edition of what I hope will continue to be an accessible and user-friendly overview of news and journalism in the UK. An important and welcome consequence of the emergence of the internet since the early 1990s has been the dramatically expanded availability, online and often free of charge, of much of the information and research materials required to understand and evaluate trends in the British news media. Once upon a time, academics undertook research, wrote it up, and published the results in book and scholarly article form. Years would elapse between the start and finish of this process, and published work would normally retain its 'shelf life' for a good number of years after that. Meta-journalism – media about media – has always been available to the researcher as a source, and successive revisions of this book have relied heavily on the data and evidence of trends provided by ongoing journalistic commentary. But access to information about the media, as well as the pace of media change, was much reduced by comparison with the present time. Things have speeded up considerably, and the academic researcher must struggle to keep pace.

Fortunately, the source of that acceleration is also the source of dramatically enhanced access to the data required to make sense of it. In preparing this edition of *N&JUK*, I have benefited from research commissioned and published – usually online and free of charge – by the regulator Ofcom. Organisations such as ABC, RAJAR and the Newspaper Readership Survey have also established themselves online. Research undertaken by parliamentary bodies such as the House of Lords Select Committee on Communication's *Report on Media Ownership*, published in June 2008 (at the very last moment of the research phase for this writing), has been made available online. Media organisations themselves, and associated bodies – Channel 4, the BBC Trust – have undertaken research on issues of particular relevance to them, such as impartiality and the future funding of public service broadcasting.

If the task of the academic media researcher has been made harder by the accelerating pace of media change, it has also been made easier by online access to sources that would once have required time-consuming and expensive visits to libraries, interlibrary loans or expensive purchases of government papers and other documents. Much of this research – produced as it often is by luxuriously resourced organisations such as the BBC and Ofcom – contains data of the type once delivered by academics engaged in isolated and slow work. That it is now much more readily available does not obviate the need for independent academic analysis and overview of these data, and originally produced data of our own. Their availability does, however, mean that they need not be duplicated by time- and cash-poor academics. My approach here has been to use this material where appropriate to refresh data sets that I prepared myself in an earlier, pre-internet environment. Students and teachers who use this book on courses are encouraged to access this treasure trove of online sources for more detailed information on topics and trends necessarily covered in outline or summary form here.

Brian McNair, Glasgow, January 2009.

1 Why journalism matters

This chapter contains:

- An outline of the organisational structure of the British news media, including details of current ownership patterns, trends in newspaper and periodical circulation, TV and radio ratings and online usage.

In the twenty-first century the production of news, and journalism of all kinds, is big business, and getting bigger all the time. The supply of information (whether as journalism or as rawer forms of data) occupies an industry of major economic importance, employing vast human and financial resources, and enjoying high status. According to a 2007 report by the World Association of Newspapers (WAN), there are more than 10,000 newspaper titles in existence, employing some two million people and generating US$180 billion of revenue. Notwithstanding concerns about the impact of the internet on print journalism (see below, Chapters 5 and 7), for WAN these figures indicate that the global print industry is 'healthy and vigorous'.[1] Across the world, top newsreaders, anchormen and women, bloggers and newspaper columnists acquire the glamour of movie stars and exert the influence of politicians. Media companies such as the BBC, CNN, Sky and Reuters judge themselves, and are judged, by the perceived quality of their news brands in an increasingly competitive and globalised marketplace.

Journalism is also an expanding business. At the beginning of the 1980s there were just two organisations supplying televised news and current affairs to the UK: the British Broadcasting Corporation and Independent Television News. Each provided around two hours of news per day. Now there are three UK-based providers of television journalism accessible to the British audience (BBC, ITN, Sky), transmitting on five free-to-air terrestrial channels, and several satellite and cable channels operated by these and other providers. The number of hours of television news available to the dedicated viewer has increased exponentially as 24-hour services have come on air, and the established free-to-air channels have steadily over the years augmented their services with breakfast news, round-the-clock bulletins and coverage of Parliament. A

2002 Broadcasting Standards Commission/Independent Television Commission (BSC/ITC)-commissioned study found that the provision of TV news had expanded by 800 per cent between 1986 and 2001, from an average of 30 hours per week to 243 hours, including 24-hour channels (Hargreaves and Thomas, 2002).

Radio journalism is also expanding as more national and local channels have been set up, benefiting from the expansion of spectrum provided by digitisation. Radio journalism remains principally the preserve of the BBC, and its Radio 4 and Five Live channels in particular. These compete with talkSport and other commercial channels, which provide varying amounts of news, mostly supplied in bulletin form by Independent Radio News and Sky News Radio.

In print, there are, if one counts such upstarts as the *Daily Sport*, *Sunday Sport* and *Sunday Star* (launched in September 2002), more national newspapers available in the UK than there were 20 years ago. At local and regional level, a large 'free sheet' sector exists alongside the 'paid-fors'.

Last, but certainly not least, Britain has seen an explosion of online news and journalism-based websites. Some of these are produced in the UK, many others overseas. The point about the internet – to which we will return below – is that regardless of where they are produced, online media are global by nature insofar as they are accessible to anyone, anywhere on the planet, who has access to a networked computer (state censorship exists in some countries but becomes ever more difficult to sustain as populations become more skilled at evading it). Thus the *Guardian*, which had a print circulation in the UK of around 310,000 as this edition of *N&JUK* went to press, had more than 25 million regular users of its *guardian.co.uk* online site globally. Many established news organisations, in the UK and elsewhere, have 'gone global' in this sense, a fact with significant implications for how they produce and market their content. Since the late 1990s, when the number of journalism-based websites was numbered in the hundreds worldwide, online journalism has emerged as a major news platform in the UK, accessed on personal computers and mobile phones. We will examine both trends – what we might call the globalisation and mobilisation of news, respectively – and their implications for the future of print and broadcast journalism in detail below.

A news map of the UK

Producing all this journalism for print broadcast and online platforms, respectively, is an industry employing some 50,000 journalists in the UK, generating billions in revenue from various sources, including sales and subscriptions, advertising, syndication and other services. The next chapter examines current thinking on how these proliferating journalistic media might affect individuals and social processes. Most of us assume that journalism matters: but does it really, and if so, in what ways?

Before that, however, and as a prelude to the more detailed discussion of trends and issues which make up Chapters 5–9, we begin with a description of the British journalism industry as it was at the time of writing: the types and structures of organisation that provide us with journalistic information; who owns them; the extent of their reach and the size of their audience. In this way, we can draw a news map of the UK (Figure 1.1), beginning with what remains for now at least, despite the migration of readers to new platforms such as the internet and the mobile phone, one of the most popular and pervasive of our news media, as well as the oldest – the press.

The national press

In the UK, as of June 2008 there were 12 national 'paid-for' daily newspapers (including the *Daily Sport* and the *Morning Star*) with a combined circulation of around ten million (Table 1.1). The largest circulations were achieved

Table 1.1. Circulation of British national newspapers, 1988–2008

	1988	*1998*	*2008*
Daily			
Daily Express	1,679,438	1,133,000	694,260
Daily Mail	1,792,701	2,312,000	2,042,453
Daily Mirror/ Daily Record	3,850,579	3,006,000	1,715,130
The *Sun*	4,146,644	3,701,000	2,884,987
The *Daily Telegraph*	1,138,673	1,067,000	813,346
The *Financial Times*	286,774	362,000	131,807
The *Guardian*	470,023	400,000	302,636
The *Times*	450,626	770,000	576,444
The *Independent*	375,317	225,000	176,785
Daily Star	1,013,688	664,000	606,331
Daily Sport	–	–	82,920
Morning Star			
Total	15,204,463	13,640,000	10,027,099
Sunday			
Mail on Sunday	1,932,799	2,192,000	1,947,444
News of the World	5,213,901	4,165,000	2,908,392
Sunday Express	2,143,374	1,033,000	625,193
Sunday Mirror	2,778,435	1,971,000	1,243,042
People	2,749,246	1,712,000	580,948
The *Independent on Sunday*	–	256,000	162,832
The *Observer*	749,644	403,000	386,140
The *Sunday Telegraph*	716,044	834,000	598,493
The *Sunday Times*	1,362,743	1,320,000	983,767
Sunday Star	–	–	304,927
Sunday Sport	–	–	78,576
Total	17,646,186	13,886,000	9,819,754

Source: Audit Bureau of Circulation.
*Average figures for January–June in each year.

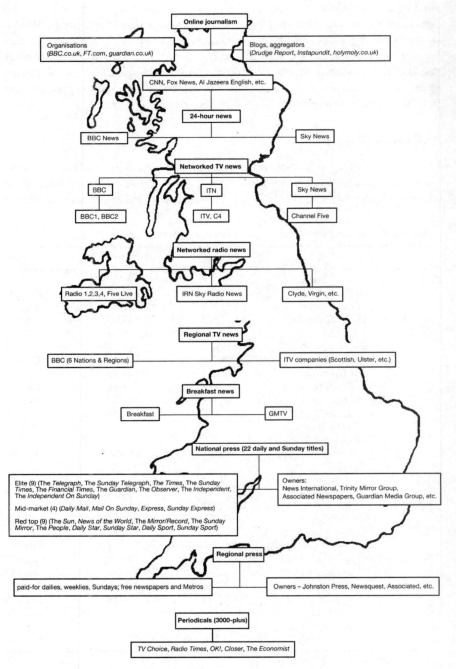

Online journalism

Organisations
(*BBC.co.uk, FT.com, guardian.co.uk*)

Blogs, aggregators
(*Drudge Report, Instapundit, holymoly.co.uk*)

CNN, Fox News, Al Jazeera English, etc.

24-hour news

BBC News

Sky News

Networked TV news

BBC

ITN

Sky News

BBC1, BBC2

ITV, C4

Channel Five

Networked radio news

Radio 1,2,3,4, Five Live

IRN Sky Radio News

Clyde, Virgin, etc.

Regional TV news

BBC (6 Nations & Regions)

ITV companies (Scottish, Ulster, etc.)

Breakfast news

Breakfast

GMTV

National press (22 daily and Sunday titles)

Elite (9) (The *Telegraph*, The *Sunday Telegraph*, *The Times*, The *Sunday Times*, The *Financial Times*, The *Guardian*, The *Observer*, The *Independent*, The *Independent On Sunday*)

Mid-market (4) (*Daily Mail*, *Mail On Sunday*, *Express*, *Sunday Express*)

Red top (9) (The *Sun*, *News of the World*, The *Mirror/Record*, The *Sunday Mirror*, The *People*, *Daily Star*, *Sunday Star*, *Daily Sport*, *Sunday Sport*)

Owners:
News International, Trinity Mirror Group,
Associated Newspapers, Guardian Media Group, etc.

Regional press

paid-for dailies, weeklies, Sundays; free newspapers and Metros

Owners – Johnston Press, Newsquest, Associated, etc.

Periodicals (3000-plus)

TV Choice, Radio Times, OK!, Closer, The Economist

Figure 1.1 A news map of the UK.

by what used to be known as the tabloids, with the *Sun* enjoying a significant lead over the *Daily Mirror/Daily Record*, and the *Daily Mail* in second place.

Until quite recently, 'tabloid' in the UK context referred both to a particular size and layout of newspaper, and also to a particular type or style of popular journalism on either print or broadcast platforms (Engel, 1996; Conboy, 2000). There were 'red-top' tabloids such as the *Sun* and the *Daily Star*, read largely by socio-economic groups C2DE and notorious for their sensational, often salacious content; and 'mid-market' tabloids such as the *Daily Mail* and the *Daily Express*, reaching higher socio-economic categories (ABC1 – generally more affluent, better educated sectors of the reading public, estimated to number just over 50 per cent of the population). All other newspapers were defined as 'broadsheets', being larger in size and containing more demanding content. In 2003 the fourth most popular daily newspaper in the UK was a broadsheet title – the *Daily Telegraph* – at that time the only daily broadsheet with a circulation above one million. In January–June 2008 the *Daily Telegraph* averaged over 800,000 daily sales, and was still the fourth most popular newspaper title. By then, not only was it the most popular broadsheet in the UK, it was the *only* broadsheet title remaining on the market, all other ex-broadsheets having moved for economic and competitive reasons to a smaller print format (the familiar tabloid as in the case of *The Times* and the *Independent* or, in the case of the *Guardian*, the Berliner format).

The collapse of the traditional tabloid/broadsheet distinction is reflected in the British Newspapers Online website (www.britishpapers.co.uk), which divides newspapers into 'heavy-weight', 'mid-market' and 'red-top'. I have previously used 'elite', 'mid-market' and 'mass' circulation categories to describe the three sectors of the UK newspaper market (McNair, 2000).

Red-tops and mid-market titles also dominated the Sunday market in 2008. Of 11 national Sunday newspapers available to the British reader (including the *Sunday Star*, launched in September 2002), four of the five most popular in terms of sales were in these categories.

The 2008 figures provide only a snapshot of the national newspaper market as it was during the six-month period of January–June that year, and thus tell us nothing about longer-term trends. Over the 20-year period between 1988 and 2008, there has been a consistent decline in the circulation of many British newspapers, particularly those popular titles, like the *Sun* and the *Daily Star*, which operate at the more sensationalist end of the market, although the latter was showing signs of resilience as this edition went to press (Table 1.1). The mid-market *Daily Mail* has bucked the trend of tabloid decline, and is one of the few titles actually putting on daily sales (some 200,000 extra by 2008) over the period.

The elite titles, or heavy-weights, have done better on the whole, with *The Times* up by more than 20 per cent over the period. the *Financial Times* shows a circulation increase of 63 per cent in two decades, when one includes over 300,000 overseas sales (not shown in Table 1.1, which is UK only).

While total UK newspaper sales have fallen by around one-third over two decades, and many commentators have identified a circulation crisis (see Chapter 6), this has not affected all newspapers, nor all equally. What emerges, looking at 20 years of circulation figures, is that decline of newspaper circulation in the UK has averaged around three per cent per year for ten years and more, and that combined daily circulations in 2008 are around 66 per cent of what they were in 1988. The circulation of Sunday titles is around 56 per cent of 1988 levels. This is bad news for some titles, such as the *Daily Mirror*, which has slipped to below the *Daily Mail*, and the *Daily Express*, which lost more than half of its circulation in that period. But decline should be seen in the context of broader trends in the media environment. Newspapers now compete with many more information outlets than was the case 20 years ago, and just as the big free-to-air terrestrial TV channels have seen their audiences whittled away by the proliferation of new cable and satellite channels as well as the growth of online services (see Chapters 7 and 8), the UK press, like that of other countries, has had to deal with a reduced share of the overall media market. Against this background, it would have been surprising had they not experienced some loss of audience share. What matters for the UK press in the coming years, as we shall see, is how they meet the challenge to old-established business models that is posed by the rise of online and real-time 24-hour journalism, and if they can retain their traditional presence in that world.

For now, many UK newspapers remain profitable, as business managers have exploited new technologies to cut costs and improve margins (regional newspapers were working to 30 per cent profit margins on titles as recently as 2008, when the 'credit crunch' and global financial crisis of that year began to affect bottom lines everywhere), and few observers believe that the newspaper in print form is doomed to extinction any time soon, given its uniquely user-friendly properties as a platform for the distribution of journalism. For all that, audiences for news are migrating to PC and mobile platforms, especially younger audiences – the convenience and tactility of print, rolled up and placed in one's pocket on the underground or the bus, or spread out on the coffee table on a Sunday morning, will not easily be matched by laptops, e-readers or mobile devices, at least not in the professional lifetime of most journalists working today (nor indeed of readers of this book).

Ownership of the British press

Ownership of the British national press continues to be concentrated in the hands of a few publishing organisations (Table 1.2). The largest, News International, is owned by Rupert Murdoch's News Corporation, whose two daily and three Sunday newspapers accounted in 2008 for 34 and 39.6 per cent of total UK circulation, respectively. The Trinity Mirror Group, formerly owned by the late Robert Maxwell and now administered by a consortium of banks and other financial institutions, accounts for a further 17 and 18.5 per cent of

Table 1.2 Ownership of the British National Press, 2002–08

Company	2002		2008	
	Daily	Sunday	Daily	Sunday
News International the *Sun*, the *News of the World*, *The Times*, *The Sunday Times*	32	39	34	39.6
Mirror Group *Daily Mirror/Daily Record, People, Sunday Mirror*	21	27	17	18.5
Associated Newspapers *Daily Mail, Mail On Sunday*	19	17	20	22
Northern & Shell *Daily Express, Sunday Express, Star, Sunday Star*	12	6	13	9
Hollinger the *Telegraph*, the *Sunday Telegraph*	8	6	8	8.5
Guardian Media Group the *Guardian*, the *Observer*	3	3	3	3
Financial Times Ltd the *Financial Times*	4	-	1.3	-
Indepependent Group the *Independent*, the *Independent On Sunday*	1.2	2	1.7	1.6

Source: Audit Bureau of Circulation.

daily and Sunday circulation, respectively (substantially down on the 2002 figures used in the previous edition of this book).

Other major owners include Richard Desmond's Northern & Shell, which in 2000 purchased the *Express* and *Star* titles for £125 million; the Barclay brothers, who bought the *Daily* and *Sunday Telegraph* from the disgraced Conrad Black's Hollinger group in 2006; and Associated Newspapers (the *Daily Mail* and *Mail on Sunday*).

The *Guardian* and the *Observer* remain 'independent' insofar as they are owned by shareholders organised in such a way – through the non-profit-making Guardian Media Group and the Scott Trust – as to guarantee the editorial integrity and financial independence of the paper 'in perpetuity'. In 1991 the *Independent* and its sister publication, the *Independent on Sunday*, having struggled since the 1980s to retain the independence that inspired their launch, found themselves in such financial difficulties that they were required to modify their constitutions and allow foreign investors to purchase substantial stakes in the papers. In 1998 the *Independent* titles passed into the control of Irish entrepreneur Tony O'Reilly and his Independent News & Media group, where they remain as of this writing. The *Morning Star* (formerly the paper of the Communist Party of Great Britain) struggles on in the post-communist world, owned by its readers and relying on them, rather than on advertising revenue, for funds to sustain its print run of about 13,000 copies.

By comparison with figures for ownership cited in previous editions of this book, there has been no fundamental change in the degree of concentration that has historically existed in the UK. Rupert Murdoch's News Corporation remains the (marginally more) dominant force among five big players and a few smaller, but still substantial owners such as the Guardian Media Group, and with roughly the same share of circulation as its four titles had in the 1990s. Some big owners – Conrad Black, most notably – have gone (in his case, to a US prison, convicted of fraud), to be replaced by others (the Barclay brothers who, having sold the *Scotsman* titles to Johnston Press in 2005, purchased Black's *Telegraph* titles for £700 million). Their share of national circulation, three per cent, remains as it was in 2002. Associated's share has gone up, as has that of Northern & Shell.

The regional press

For the regional press in Britain, the past two decades have seen a period of expansion, particularly in the market for small, community-based papers funded entirely from advertising revenue – the 'free sheets'. There are now dozens of companies publishing hundreds of these newspapers across the country (nearly 600 in 2006). Although their main function is to advertise local businesses and services, most contain a certain amount of local news with which to attract the attention of potential readers, and so can legitimately be included in any discussion of British journalism. Local newspapers are also a major employer of the UK's journalists.

In the late 1990s, a network of *Metro* publications, owned by Associated Newspapers,[2] was established in several British cities, including London, Glasgow and Manchester. By 2008 there were *Metros* in 16 UK cities, reaching millions of what marketing experts call 'young urbanites' going to work between the hours of 6:30 and 9:30 am. Their success has inspired the launch of competing free titles by companies such as News Corporation (*thelondonpaper*). In August 2006 Associated launched another free title, *London Lite*, to run alongside *Metro*. I discuss the implications of this trend below. Here, we note that the growth of the free newspaper has added further to the challenges facing the traditional print journalism industry in the UK, and is certainly a factor in the declining circulation of paid-for newspapers, especially those in the regions (see Chapter 9).

In addition to the free sheets, of course, there are hundreds of paid-for newspapers being produced outside London, ranging from the large-circulation Scottish and regional titles such as the *Daily Record* and *Sunday Mail*, to smaller-circulation titles targeted on small towns and rural communities the length and breadth of the UK. To the Scots the aforementioned newspapers are not 'regional' but 'national', as is *Wales on Sunday* to the Welsh, and the *Belfast Telegraph* to the Northern Irish.

The British regional press, including that of the nation-regions, has until quite recently been in what one commentator calls 'boisterous health'.[3] Indeed, as Bob Franklin puts it, it has been 'booming' (Franklin, 2006: xvii), with 84 per cent of UK adults reading a regional newspaper (compared with 70 per cent who read national titles). Northern Ireland, with a population of 1.6 million people, supports 18 daily papers. Scotland's five million people support some 80 titles. These data were gathered some time ago, before the 'credit crunch' and the associated recession, since when the economic climate for all media organisations has worsened, and the technological challenge posed by the internet and other emerging platforms intensified. Circulations have declined, as with the national press, but the regional/local press remains an important feature of the UK news map.

Like the national press, ownership and control of the regional newspaper industry in Britain is concentrated in the hands of a small number of companies, predominant among them the Trinity Mirror Group, the US-based Newsquest Media Group, and Johnston Press (which purchased the *Scotsman* titles from the Barclay brothers in 2005 for £216 million, and in the summer of 2008 owned some 284 regional titles across the UK). Some national proprietors are also significant owners at regional level, such as Associated Newspapers and the Guardian Media Group.[4] Until 1995, Thomson Regional Newspapers was a major regional proprietor. In July that year, however, the parent Thomson Corporation announced that it was selling its British newspaper interests in order to raise investment capital. The English and Irish TRN titles were taken on by Trinity International Holdings, the Scottish titles by the enigmatic Barclay brothers (the *Scotsman*) and Associated Newspapers (the *Aberdeen Press and Journal*). To this extent the ownership structure of the regional press has changed significantly in the lifetime of this book, as formerly major proprietors like Thomson have been replaced by companies, such as Johnston Press and Newsquest, dedicated to regional publishing.[5]

The periodical press

No overview of the British print media would be complete without some reference to the periodical sector – those weekly, fortnightly and monthly publications that straddle the boundaries between journalism, leisure, entertainment, and business. Some periodicals, such as *Private Eye* and the *Economist* (both among the most successful publications in the country, if measured by circulation and advertising revenue), have a clearly journalistic emphasis. The satirical *Private Eye*, in particular, has investigated and uncovered many political and business scandals in its five-decade history, which have subsequently gone on to make the mainstream news agenda. The *Economist*, as its name suggests, provides background, analysis and commentary on the domestic and international economic situation. As a UK periodical with a global reach, it sells over 180,000 in the UK and around 460,000 worldwide, as compared with *Prospect*'s circulation of 27,700.

The great majority of UK periodicals operate in what the Audit Bureau of Circulation classifies as the 'specialist consumer and business markets'.

This includes such titles as *Exchange & Mart* and *What Car?*, dedicated to providing practical information for buyers and sellers of goods and services; magazines such as *House & Garden* and *Good Housekeeping*, containing ideas for DIY and home decoration enthusiasts; *i-D* and *Dazed & Confused*, which cover style trends and fashion in clothes, music and popular culture; listings and review magazines such as *Radio Times* and *Sight & Sound*; *Cosmopolitan* and *Woman's Own*, addressing the female audience; *FHM* and *Loaded*, for men; and *Management Today*, which attempts to keep professional managers informed of issues relevant to them.

There are some 3000 periodical titles published in the UK, with new titles launched regularly, indicating that periodicals comprise a relatively healthy segment of the print industry as a whole. Indeed, as the print sector generally suffers a slow decline in circulation, the magazine sector has been buoyant. A sample of the leading titles by circulation at the time of going to press is shown in Table 1.3, and includes TV listings magazines such as *Radio Times*, celebrity culture titles such as *Glamour* and *Closer*, and current affairs magazines such as the *Economist* (these are not the top ten as listed by the Audit Bureau of Circulation (ABC), which include give-away magazines distributed by media companies such as Sky and chain stores such as Asda, Tesco and Sainsbury). Men's magazines such as *Loaded*, which flourished in the 1990s and early noughties with circulations approaching the half-million figure, have declined to around 100,000, suggesting that the heyday of the 'lad's mag' has passed.

Ownership of periodicals is concentrated, like that of national and regional newspapers, in large companies such as IPC and Bauer, but the sector is one in which many relatively small, independent companies are thriving. Some, like Pressdram, which publishes *Private Eye*, are well established. Others are recent entrants who have exploited the changing technology and economics of publishing ushered in by the 'Wapping revolution' and subsequent waves of changing fashion.

Table 1.3 Top ten UK periodicals by circulation, July 2008

Title	Circulation
TV Choice	1,403,512
What's on TV	1,385,840
Radio Times	1,051,746
Take a Break	988,056
OK! Magazine	608,638
Reader's Digest	649,131
Saga Magazine	649,400
The Economist	190,762
Glamour	497,928
Closer	536,186

Source: Audit Bureau of Circulation.

Broadcast journalism in the UK: television

The earliest provider of television journalism in the UK, the British Broadcasting Corporation, began life in 1922 as the Broadcasting Company. Originally a cartel of radio manufacturers, the Broadcasting Company was financed by a licence fee, and by a share of the royalties on the sale of radio receivers. The Broadcasting Company was nationalised and became the British Broadcasting Corporation in 1926, from which time it has been licensed to serve as 'a cultural, moral and educative force for the improvement of knowledge, taste and manners' (Scannell and Cardiff, 1991: 8).

Operating under the provisions of a Royal Charter, the BBC was constituted as a public service, funded by public taxation. It will continue to play this role for the foreseeable future, subject to periodic charter renewal (the next is due in 2017). From the outset, the BBC interpreted its public service role to mean that it should be a major provider of journalistic information to the British people, devoting a large proportion of its resources to news and current affairs broadcasting, first on radio, and then on television, the latter of which has, over time, expanded to five channels with journalistic output, including BBC News (formerly BBC News 24; the channel was renamed in May 2008 as part of a larger rebranding exercise for the corporation's news output).[6] In 2006–07, according to the BBC's annual report for that year, the main free-to-air terrestrial channel BBC One devoted 1149 hours to news and current affairs. For BBC Two the equivalent figure was 831 hours, while the digital channels BBC Three and BBC Four also transmitted journalism. The Directorate of News and Current Affairs – the department responsible for BBC journalism – had a budget in 1991 of £130 million (about 24 per cent of total TV costs). Journalism at the corporation had an annual budget in 2006 of £350 million and employed 2000 journalists.

Independent Television News

Until 1955, the BBC had a monopoly on British television news. That year a commercial network was launched, producing its own news and current affairs. The independent television (ITV) companies shared out the making of current affairs and documentary programmes, while their news was provided by Independent Television News (ITN). ITN was to be owned collectively by all the ITV companies, and run on a non-profit-making basis to supply them with news bulletins such as the flagship *News At Ten*. This it did very successfully, winning the contract to provide Channel 4 with news when it came on the air in 1981. By 1988, ITN employed more than 1000 people to produce over 25 hours of news per week (Dunnett, 1990: 132). In 1997, ITN won the £6 million contract to produce news for the new Channel 5. In 2001, despite vigorous competition from Rupert Murdoch's BSkyB, it won the contract to continue producing news for the ITV network, and in 2002 its long-standing Channel 4 news contract was renewed, at a value of £20 million per annum for five years. In 2007 ITN renewed its contract to supply news to ITV, worth £250 million. In January 2005, however, ITN lost the Channel 5 news contract to Sky, which thereby moved for the first time from the production of rolling news only (see below) to mainstream, free-to-air terrestrial TV journalism.

Regional TV news

The bulk of the BBC's news and current affairs, and all of ITN's, is produced in London and networked throughout the UK. But both the BBC and ITV also provide regional news services. Since the merger of Yorkshire TV and Tyne Tees TV in 1992 there are 15 ITV companies covering the country, most with their own locally produced magazines, news bulletins and current affairs output. As we will see below, the 13 distinct commercial regional TV news services are under considerable pressure as a result of the move to digital broadcasting in the UK, and in 2008 ITV chief executive Michael Grade described current levels of investment in regional news as 'unsustainable'.

The BBC has six 'Nations and Regions' (Scotland, Wales, Northern Ireland, and North, Midland and South in England) and 13 regional departments (such as BBC London, BBC South East) producing television news and current affairs at local level.

Breakfast TV

Breakfast television services, all of which include some news, were established in Britain in 1985, reflecting the trend throughout the 1980s towards more hours of news programming on television. The BBC was the first to provide a full three-hour breakfast programme, now known as *Breakfast News*, and was quickly followed by TV-am on ITV, owned by a consortium of banking and financial interests led by the Australian Bruce Gyngell, who had previously been chief executive of Australia's Channel 9. TV-am thus became the first new provider of national television journalism in the UK since ITN was established in 1955.

From the outset, TV-am, like the BBC, built its service around news and current affairs, although with a markedly 'lighter' touch than the latter's more analytical, in-depth coverage. Paralleling the distinction between the BBC's Birtian approach and that of ITN (see Chapter 6), TV-am attempted to construct a distinctive brand image for its product, which laid much more stress on human interest and lifestyle coverage than on 'hard' news. The TV-am formula, as described in its 1991 application for the ITV breakfast-time licence, was a 'live, fast-moving mixture of news, information and entertainment in short self-contained segments which viewers can dip in and out of, listen to as well as watch, as they start the day'. Its style was 'warm and friendly', with a 'human face', combining regional, national and international news feeds with cosy studio chats between casually dressed presenters and guests from the entertainment and political worlds.

Sixty-three per cent of TV-am's airtime and 75 per cent of its programme budget was devoted to news and current affairs, supplied by foreign bureaux in Washington, Moscow, Cyprus and Hong Kong, with local news coming from eight regional centres. Video material was supplied by Visnews.

TV-am was a highly popular service, achieving some 70 per cent of the national audience and making substantial profits for its owners. The company's finances were greatly helped by the successful outcome of its dispute with the broadcasting unions in 1988, making possible a reallocation of resources from the technical side of the production process to journalism. Jeff Berliner, TV-am's head of news, explained in 1991 that 'before the dispute we had 82 journalists. We've now got 120. Twenty-four per cent of TV-am's workforce are journalists. Most people at TV-am work on news and current affairs programming. Not finance, or management, or anything else.'

In this respect, TV-am was a pioneer and a mould-breaker in British television news. And having 'resolved the issue of who manages the industry' with the unions, the company looked set to go into the 1990s providing what Jeff Berliner called 'a fast, accurate, credible and creditable news service, within a sensible financial base'. Unfortunately for TV-am, and to the surprise of many in the industry, the company was destined to become the most prominent victim of the changes to the procedures for allocating franchises introduced by the 1990 Broadcasting Act.

The ITV breakfast-time licence was always going to be much sought after, given the profits it had generated for TV-am, and when invitations to tender were issued (competitive tendering was introduced for the first time by the 1990 Act), TV-am found itself competing with two rival consortia: Daybreak Television, consisting of ITN, Carlton Communications, the *Daily Telegraph* and NBC, among others; and Sunrise (now GMTV), the majority of which was owned by the Guardian and Manchester Evening News Group, Scottish Television, London Weekend Television and the Walt Disney Company.

Both Daybreak and Sunrise based their bids on the alleged weakness of TV-am's service. What to TV-am was 'warm and friendly' with 'a human face' was to Daybreak 'trite'. TV-am's 'soft approach' to news and current affairs would, it warned, lead in the future to a loss of ITV's breakfast audience and thus its advertising revenue.

Sunrise criticised TV-am for its poor regional service. Although TV-am took pride in having eight 'regional centres' feeding material into a national package, critics suggested that the centres – in reality remote-controlled studios on the premises of the regional companies – were 'cosmetic investments', with little input into the finished TV-am product. Sunrise proposed to farm out its regional news to the established regional companies, who would provide regular opt-out segments for viewers in different parts of the country, [7] while the resources of LWT and Visnews would be employed to produce national and international coverage.

When the ITC allocated the ITV breakfast licence in October 1991, Sunrise emerged as its favoured candidate to provide early morning television journalism in the 1990s. TV-am's application was deemed inferior to that of the Sunrise consortium, which began broadcasting on 1 January 1993 under the name Good Morning TV (GMTV). In 2008, GMTV continues to be the main free-to-air competitor to the BBC's *Breakfast News*. It also competes with Sky News's *Sunrise* breakfast show which, like other channels on satellite and cable, has steadily grown in importance as a UK news provider.

Rolling news

In 1989, Rupert Murdoch's News Corporation launched Sky News, Britain's first 24-hour television news channel, as part of its Sky Television service, transmitting from the Astra satellite. For a brief period of some six months there was another satellite provider of news – British Satellite Broadcasting – which launched 14 months after Sky on the direct broadcasting by satellite (DBS) system. Between April and October 1990, BSB and Sky fought an expensive battle for subscribers to their two completely incompatible systems, losing an estimated £1.25 billion between them. Neither Rupert Murdoch nor the consortium that owned BSB could sustain such losses for very long, and at the end of October 1990 it was announced that the two satellite networks would merge to form BSkyB, 50 per cent of which would be owned by News Corporation, 16 per cent by Pearson, 12 per cent by Granada Television, and 3.7 per cent by Reed International.[8] Today, BSkyB is one-third owned by News Corporation.

Although Sky News has been a critical success (perhaps surprisingly, given the widespread contempt in which the media establishment has traditionally held Rupert Murdoch's tabloid newspapers), its profitability was hampered for many years by the relatively slow initial take-up of satellite television by the British public, and the failure of cable services to penetrate the British media market to any significant degree until the end of the 1990s. Had it not been for the safety net provided by Murdoch's immensely profitable newspaper interests in the UK, Sky News's ongoing losses would, in the view of many industry observers, have been unsustainable. By the mid-1990s, however, BSkyB had entered a healthier phase, and with it Sky News. At the beginning of 1992, the *Observer* reported that the company was on the verge of profitability, with 100,000 dishes per month being sold, and 2.8 million homes by then being reached in the UK.[9] By 1998, BSkyB was available through satellite in 3.8 million homes, and through cable in another 2.4 million, generating profits substantial enough to make a significant contribution to such audacious moves as the attempted £620 million purchase of Manchester United football club in September 1998 (rejected by the British government on competition grounds). In early 2008, more than 8 million British households had access to Sky TV.

Sky News was Britain's first domestically-produced 24-hour television news service, although the US-produced Cable Network News, owned by American entrepreneur Ted Turner, had been available since 1985 to those with the appropriate receiving technology. Despite the global impact made by CNN with its coverage of such events as the 1991 Gulf War and the September 11 attack on the World Trade Center, its audience in the UK remains small.

The BBC has also firmly established itself in the 24-hour television news market. In November 1991, after years of planning, the World Service launched a global satellite television service – World Service Television News (WSTN) – which aimed to do for the global TV audience what the World Service has traditionally done for radio listeners. Moreover, the BBC hoped to make this service the base for its own 24-hour domestic TV news channel, which would compete with Sky News and CNN for the British audience. This plan came to fruition in November 1997 with the launch of BBC News 24 on cable (the service was also made available to terrestrial TV viewers on BBC One during the night). By that time, too, BBC's global television news service, BBC World, was transmitting to more than 100 countries. By 2002, BBC News 24 was reaching audiences of seven million viewers per week, and 33 million tuned in to the channel's coverage of the September 11 events, attracted by what were claimed by managers to be the BBC's 'hallmarks of authority, classic reporting and responsibility'. Benefitting from access to the substantial news-gathering resources of the BBC, News 24 claimed by 2002 to have overtaken Sky News, its main competitor, on the quality of, for example, its overseas and regional coverage, covering some 80–90 original stories on an average day.[10] Neither BBC News 24 nor Sky News achieved audiences anything like those enjoyed by terrestrial TV news (less than one per cent of the multi-channel audience, on average), except in times of crisis such as the September 11 attacks and the invasion of Iraq in 2003. Thirty-three million people in Britain watched BBC News 24's coverage of the September 11 attacks. When the Iraq war began in March 2003, BBC News 24 saw its audience rise by 500 per cent to 3.2 per cent and Sky News by 820 per cent to 8.3 per cent.[11]

In 2000, anxious not to be left behind in the UK rolling news market, ITV launched a 24-hour service of its own, ITV News Channel, although a lack of resources meant that it never matched either the reputation or the audiences of BBC News 24 and Sky News. On 11 September 2001, of the three UK-based rolling news services Sky News had most viewers, with 5.9 per cent of the multi-channel audience. BBC News 24 got 2.5 per cent and ITN's News Channel only 0.6 per cent. ITV closed the service at the end of 2005.

One further new service is worth noting – Al Jazeera English, which launched in November 2006 on the strength of the impact of Al Jazeera's main Arab-language service. Although intended as a competitor to CNN and BBC World for the global news market, it has been available to subscribers in the UK, and featured prominent British journalists among its presenters, including David Frost and Rageh Omar. By 2008 it had become established as a global 24-hour news player, although reports of management problems and culturo-ideological clashes between Arab and non-Arab staff were common, with many staff leaving the organization.[12]

Taking all the above together, and notwithstanding the significant challenges and issues to be explored later in this book, we can reasonably argue that the television journalism industry in the UK is in a state of relatively good health. News, current affairs and related information services have expanded both latitudinally, with new providers such as Sky News and CNN coming into the market, and longitudinally, with the time devoted to journalism on television increasing relentlessly. On an average weekday in 2008, the BBC produced some five hours of TV news and current affairs on its two terrestrial channels, ITN about the same across Channels 3 and 4, while Sky News serviced Channel 5. Viewers had access to another hour or so of local coverage on ITV, while those with satellite dishes or cable could watch Sky News, BBC News 24 (which in 2008, became simply BBC News), CNN and others for 24 hours per day, every day, if they wished. Audiences for individual television services were declining as more platforms for news delivery became established, but as is also true for print, this was to be expected in the face of growing competition from internet sites such as www.bbc.co.uk.

Teletext

Before leaving television, we should note the continuing importance of the electronic news and information services Ceefax (produced by the BBC) and Teletext (its commercial rival, owned by Associated Newspapers). These services enable the owners of television receivers to access electronic data about everything from current events to transport timetables and recipes. Although the view of some observers that teletext services functioned as 'electronic newspapers' and would eventually make redundant the more familiar paper-and-ink variety has been overtaken by the emergence of the internet, they have remained important as information sources, not least to the journalism industry itself, right up to the present time. As of 2004, it was estimated by the BBC that some 20 million people still used Ceefax each week. Ceefax and Teletext will be fully digitized with the end of analogue broadcasting in 2012.

Radio

Despite the expansion of television and other platforms in recent years, the oldest broadcast medium, radio, has retained a healthy share of the British audience and, in the commercial sector, of advertising revenues.[13] Despite recurring predictions of the imminent death of the medium, journalistic output on radio has been in a period of expansion since the early 1990s. In the ten years from 1992 to 2002, audiences for radio increased from 88 to 90 per cent of the population, with listeners tuning in for an average of 21.5 hours per week. Commercial radio's share of UK advertising revenue increased from 2 to 6.4 per cent by 2002. Radio Joint Audience Research (RAJAR) figures for the first half of 2008 (Table 1.4) showed commercial radio taking 41.1 per cent of the total market.

The dominant force in UK radio journalism remains by far the BBC, which reached 68 per cent of the adult population in early 2008 and achieved a 56.8 per cent audience share. The BBC broadcasts some 4000 hours per annum of national news, current affairs and documentary features across its five channels –

Table 1.4 Average audiences for UK radio channels*

Station	Reach (000s)	Reach (%)	Average hours per head	Average hours per listener	Total hours (000s)	Listening share in total survey area (TSA) (%)
All radio	45,397	90	20.5	22.8	1,033,308	100
All BBC	34,219	68	11.7	17.2	587,057	56.8
BBC Radio 1	11,067	22	2.2	9.9	109,824	10.6
BBC Radio 2	13,632	27	3.4	12.5	170,097	16.5
BBC Radio 3	1,795	4	0.2	5.4	9,764	0.9
BBC Radio 4	9,561	19	2.5	13.2	125,863	12.2
BBC Radio 5 Live	6,022	12	0.9	7.9	47,655	4.6
All commercial	31,019	62	8.4	13.7	424,396	41.1
talkSPORT	2,470	5	0.4	8	19,725	1.9
All local commercial	24,847	49	6.2	12.6	313,448	30.3

Source: RAJAR.
*Figures calculated as averages for December 2007–March 2008. Population = 5,033,400.

some 30 per cent of its total radio output.[14] In addition, regional stations such as Radio Scotland and Radio Ulster broadcast substantial quantities of their own news and current affairs output. The BBC also produces radio journalism, through the World Service, for an estimated global audience of 120 million people (see Chapter 7).[15]

At home, the BBC management in 1992 announced its intention to establish a 24-hour rolling news service on network radio.[16] Radio 5 Live is now firmly established in the UK journalism landscape, with a weekly reach of over six million people.

The supply of news to the commercial radio stations has traditionally been undertaken by Independent Radio News (IRN), the major part of which was until October 1992 owned by the Crown Communications Group. That month IRN merged with ITN and moved into the latter's headquarters in London's Gray's Inn Road. From here, a networked service of hourly news bulletins is transmitted to commercial companies across the country.

As a result of the 1990 Broadcasting Act, dozens of small community stations on the one hand, and several new national channels on the other, came into being, broadcasting news services as part of their programming. IRN continues to supply these stations, but has now been joined by rival providers such as National Network News and Europe FM. Sky Radio News supplies about 20 per cent of the UK's commercial stations. The larger (and richer) local stations, such as Radio Clyde in Glasgow, produce a large proportion of their own news and current affairs.

Online journalism

While access to teletext services is limited to conventional TV sets, computer and mobile phone users now have access to practically unlimited quantities of print-originated journalism, as well as audiovisual material and original news content distributed on the internet. This includes material made available on the online sites of established print and broadcast news organisations, such as the *Guardian* and the BBC; bulletin boards, gossip pages such as the *Drudge Report* (which famously placed the Monica Lewinsky scandal in the public domain early in 1998, and more recently broke the story that HRH Prince Harry was on active service in Afghanistan), and blogs, of which there are literally millions. While the majority of blogs are amateur sites of little journalistic value (see Chapter 8), a small number – the visible tip of the internet iceberg – have become influential and widely used platforms for distributing and accessing news, analysis and commentary. The blogosphere has become the site of what has been called a 'new commentariat' – a group of online writers who increasingly rival the traditional sense-making and news-filtering role of the press pundit (McNair, 2008b).

The precise number of online journalism sites is difficult to establish, but their growth has been exponential. When the first edition of this book was published there were none (although the internet was already being used to distribute information, including news). By 1998, and publication of my book on *The Sociology of Journalism* (McNair, 1998b), the number of internet news sites, although rising rapidly, numbered in the hundreds. Today we can talk of millions, from the well resourced sites of long-established print brands such as the *New York Times* and the *Guardian*, to the influential blogs of well known freelancers such as Andrew Sullivan, and the myriad more rough-and-ready blogs, social networking profiles and aggregator sites that collect and distribute news and news-based material.

The emergence of the internet, like television before it, has provoked speculation about the impending death of print, and one can easily see why online channels pose a threat to the traditional print and broadcast means of dissemination of news and journalism. The speed, interactivity and comprehensiveness of the internet as an information source are unprecedented in the history of communication media, and the implications of its introduction to the mass market (a development unforeseen two decades ago, and now unstoppable) are impossible to predict with certainty. In drawing our contemporary news map, however, it remains the case that online news media represent for the time being a complement to, rather than replacement for, traditional sources of broadcast and print journalism, accessed mainly by business, academic and journalistic users. Nearly all broadcast and print news organisations in the UK now have online versions, and some, such as *FT.com*, are able to charge for access to their specialist data and information services. As of May 2008, some 18 million people were recorded as 'unique monthly users' of the *guardian.co.uk* website (Table 1.5). The BBC has one of the world's leading news sites, with over 50 million users, competing for global domination with CNN, Yahoo! News, Fox.com and others seeking to establish themselves as online providers of choice for the discerning news junkie. But while virtually everyone in a country like the UK has a TV set, fewer as

Table 1.5 Leading online journalism sites, May 2008*

Website	Unique monthly users
BBC	50,358,061
Mail Online	18,712,533
Telegraph.co.uk	18,497,944
Guardian Unlimited	18,323,824
Times Online	15,877,693
The *Sun*	14,948,080
FT.com	7,113,132
The *Independent*	6,533,792

Source: ABCe.

yet have easy, unrestricted access to a computer terminal (although that number is increasing all the time, and computer access will soon be as commonplace within the average household as the TV and mobile phone). For that reason, among others, broadcast and print continue to be the main sources of news, in the UK and comparable countries. Research conducted in 2006 showed that TV remained the most important source of news for 55 per cent of the British population, followed by newspapers at 19 per cent, radio at 12, and the internet at 8 per cent.[17] Since then, the importance of the internet as a news source has undoubtedly increased, as has the economic challenge posed by internet competition for advertising revenue, although the most recent research conducted by Ofcom and others (see Chapter 8 below) confirms that TV and newspapers remain the main sources of news and journalism.

Conclusions

The journalism industry, taken as a whole, is a dynamic, growing sector of the economy in Britain, as elsewhere in the world. For that reason alone, it would be worthy of close study. But journalism is not just of economic importance, it is arguably one of the key social and cultural forces in our society. In Britain, 67 per cent of adults read at least one national newspaper, while 84 per cent read a regional title. A 1990 survey established that TV and newspapers come ahead of friends, family, politicians or other sources of information when it comes to influencing opinion, and that television journalism in particular is the main source of people's information about the world. Twenty-four categories of public issue were mentioned to respondents, and 'television news was shown to have the greatest influence among the largest number of people. And when it wasn't first as an influence it came second or third'.[18] 'On average', wrote Barrie Gunter in the 1980s, 'around two-thirds of the mass public of modern industrialised societies claim that television is their main source of national and international news' (Gunter, 1987: 7).

This remains broadly the case. Ian Hargreaves and the late James Thomas's *New News, Old News* study (Hargreaves and Thomas, 2002) found that TV was the main source of news for 65 per cent of the British audience (against 16 per cent for radio, 15 per cent for newspapers, and only two per cent for the internet). More recent research, conducted in 2006 by the UK broadcasting regulator Ofcom, demonstrated that viewers place high value on the continuing availability of TV news and current affairs, at both national and regional levels (Ofcom, 2007). I cited above a 2006 global survey of news consumers conducted for the BBC, Reuters and the Media Centre, which found that the most important sources of information for UK citizens were television, followed by newspapers, radio and the internet.

The same research further found that the most *trusted* news source in the UK was TV (cited by 86 per cent), followed by friends and family (78 per cent), newspapers (76 per cent) and radio (67 per cent). This was consistent with research conducted by the YouGov polling organisation in 2003, showing that broadcast journalists are trusted 'a great deal' by 81 per cent of those surveyed, compared with 65 per cent who trust broadsheet journalists, 36 per cent mid-market tabloid journalists, and 14 per cent red-top journalists.[19]

Further reading

To keep up-to-date on the ever-changing state of the British news media, see the industry periodicals *Press Gazette*, *Broadcast* and *British Journalism Review*. Reports by the BBC and Ofcom, usually available online, are useful sources of up-to-the-minute research data. Most broadsheet newspapers have weekly media pages, which cover ABC figures and current debates in the industry. The ABC now has figures for online usage, as well as print sales. *Journalism Practice* publishes recent scholarly research on the industry.

---

2 Journalism's social role

This chapter reviews the main approaches to the impacts and influences of journalism in society, including:

- the surveillance function of journalism
- agenda-setting
- social reproduction
- journalism and the social construction of risk.

Of wider importance than the relative efficacy of individual media as information sources is the issue of the effects of media communications on individuals and on society. What is the relationship between the products of journalism and wider social processes? If modern journalism's purpose is to supply information to a mass audience – or, as Niklas Luhmann and the systems theorists put it, 'the production and supply of topics for public communication' (Loffelholz, 2008: 20) – what social role does this information have?

Journalism as surveillance

At the simplest level, journalism presents us with an ongoing narrative about the world beyond our immediate experience. This narrative is asserted to be 'true'. The stories told to us by journalists are understood by their audiences to be factual, rather than fictional. For this reason, journalism performs a unique and essential social function. For most of us, most of the time, journalists are the main source of our information about the world beyond our own immediate environment. We may, on occasion, be participants in events that become the subject matter of journalism – in which case we may be better informed than any journalist about the event concerned – but this is exceptional (and most people would rather not be so close to a newsworthy event if they can avoid it). Journalism, consequently, is often said to be our 'window on the world', our means of contact with an external environment which, although shrinking because of evolving communication technologies such as the internet, is still largely beyond our direct, personal experience. It provides the information from which we draw our 'cognitive maps' of reality.

Beyond this basic social function, journalism is expected to perform an important political role in liberal pluralist societies, feeding and sustaining the democratic process by supplying citizens with the information they require to make rational electoral and economic choices. Journalism, according to this viewpoint, underpins democratic institutions by keeping voters informed about the things they need to know. The task of journalism is 'to make information publicly available' (Bruhn-Jensen, 1986: 31), this being 'one basic ingredient of the public sphere ... required for public participation in discussion and decisions' (McNair, 2000; Barnett and Gabor, 2001; Conboy, 2004; Lewis *et al.*, 2005; Anderson and Ward, 2007). Ofcom's *New News, Future News* study reaffirmed this view with the observation that 'news is important because it informs and educates citizens, helping them take part in the demo- cratic process' (Ofcom, 2007: 12). As we shall see in Chapters 3–5, many of the criticisms that have been directed towards British journalism in recent times have been inspired by the perception that it does not perform these functions adequately.

The view of journalism's social role as essentially benevolent is underpinned by the 'uses and gratifications' approach to media effects, which asserts that the media in general have only a limited impact on the audience, who 'use' their content to 'gratify' particular needs, such as 'surveillance of the environ- ment'. News is used for information purposes, but does not have significant power to tell us *what* to think.

A more complex analysis, but one that shares the basic optimism of the 'uses and gratifications' approach, is provided by the advocates of journalism's 'agenda-setting' role. In the words of one of the founders of this approach, agenda-setting asserts 'a direct, causal relationship between the [journalistic] content of the media agenda and subsequent public perception of what the important issues of the day are. This is an assertion of direct learning by members of the public from the media agenda' (McCombs, 1981: 211). The basic hypothesis of this approach is that 'through their routine structuring of social and political reality, the news media influence the agenda of public issues around which political campaigns and voter decisions are organised' (*ibid.*). In the agenda-setting hypothesis, journalistic news values act as a cue for the audience, alerting them to the importance of an issue, and encouraging them to place it on their personal agendas of important issues.[1]

The empirical evidence for this thesis is ambiguous, but since this is the case for all effects hypotheses, that is no reason to dismiss it. Denis McQuail notes that agenda-setting has the status of 'a plausible but unproven idea' (McQuail, 1987: 276). Iyengar and Kinder are more confident, expressing strong support for agenda-setting on the basis of their own audience research (which applies only to American TV news). They assert that 'the verdict is clear and unequi- vocal. ... By attending to some problems and ignoring others, television news shapes the American public's political priorities' (*ibid.*: 33).

More recent UK research on the link between media coverage of a story and public knowledge and understanding of it was conducted by Hargreaves *et al.* at Cardiff University. Their large-scale study of 'the public's knowledge, opinion and understanding of science-related issues reported in the media' found that:

> What people know [about science] usually corresponded with those aspects of the science story that received most persistent coverage. The details or subtleties of media coverage are, in this respect, much less important than the general themes of that coverage, in which certain ideas are repeated and associated with one another. While this does mean some information is communicated effectively to most people, it can also result in widespread misunderstanding – even if the reporting is generally accurate.
>
> (Hargreaves *et al.*, 2002: 2)

This research coincided with a period of intensive media coverage of the mumps, measles and rubella (MMR) issue, which spread to the general public the suggestion, subsequently discredited, that the rise of autism diagnosed in children in recent years was attributable in part to the effects of the triple-jab vaccine for MMR. This issue rose high on the public and political agenda in 2001–02, with parental concerns leading to a fall in take-up of the vaccine to a record low of 81 per cent. Then Prime Minister Tony Blair came under pressure to declare that his own newborn son had been vaccinated with MMR (although he refused to do so on the grounds of his family's personal privacy). Hargreaves *et al.* argued that media coverage of the MMR story had failed comprehensively or systematically to challenge the MMR-causes-autism theory, or to highlight the weaknesses of the scientific evidence underpinning it. As a result, members of the public who relied on news for their information formed a misleading impression of the risks associated with MMR, which then shaped the agenda confronting political and public health authorities. Here, and in many other cases, the presence of a story in the news agenda signals its importance to the audience, and initiates public and political debate based on the content of the news coverage.

That the agenda-setting hypothesis is taken seriously by policy-makers and other social actors is illustrated by the growth of public relations and news management as communicative practices in recent decades (McNair, 2007). Political parties, pressure groups and others with an interest in winning public opinion for their cause now routinely seek to shape the news agenda by headline-grabbing and other news management activities, from news conferences to spectacular demonstrations and the staging of pseudo-events. Election campaigns are built around efforts to shape the news agenda in ways that will favour a particular party or candidate, or to damage the opponent.

Journalism as social reproduction

Approaches that assert an essentially benevolent, or at least neutral, social role for journalism, such as the theory of agenda-setting, are challenged by 'critical' theorists, who draw on Marxist and other analytical frameworks to argue that journalism's function is essentially one of social reproduction, in the service not of society as a whole, but of its dominant groups and classes. From this perspective, the information media are viewed, like other cultural institutions in a class society, as producers of dominant ideology, representing the interests of an elite minority to the subordinate majority.

There are 'strong' and 'weak' variants of the social reproduction thesis, corresponding to wider disputes in materialist theory about the nature of ideology, the audience and the communication process. The structuralists, for example, inspired by the work of Jacques Lacan, Louis Althusser and others, would argue that the linguistic structure of journalism 'positions' the audience in a subordinate position *vis-à-vis* the dominant class of capitalism. This 'interpellation of the subject' operates at the level of the unconscious so that the individual member of the audience is, practically speaking, powerless to resist the ideological message. As Van Dijk puts it, 'the structures of news reports at many levels condition the readers to develop [dominant] interpretative frameworks rather than alternative ones' (Van Dijk, 1988: 182). Ideology, to put it another way, is 'produced' in language, at the level of the unconscious. The 'dominant ideology' thesis, as expressed in these terms, has come under some attack in recent years. On the one hand, it is argued that the hypothesis is primitive, underpinned by a mechanistic model of effects that has long been discredited.

Another position asserts that there is no such thing as a 'dominant ideology' or a 'ruling class', but rather a constantly shifting alliance of classes and social strata, which struggle to dominate ideologically but do not necessarily succeed. Even if there is a dominant ideology, those such as Umberto Eco in Italy and Stuart Hall in the UK draw on the theoretical concepts of semiotics and the political sociology of Antonio Gramsci to emphasise the possibility of oppositional and aberrant decodings of journalistic messages on the part of the audience. They would accept that there can be a dominant ideological message present in journalism, but that no inevitability attaches to its being transmitted successfully to the audience. For this group of theorists, ideological struggle is like a process of cultural negotiation, to which journalism contributes by 'reproducing consensus about social order' (Ericson *et al.*, 1990: 19). News organisations are said to play a strategic role in hegemonic struggle, functioning as 'a site of contest between competing social forces rather than as a conduit for ruling class ideas' (Curran, 1990: 142).

For John Fiske, journalism functions 'as discourse, that is, as a set of conventions that strive to control and limit the meanings of the events it conveys' (Fiske, 1987: 282). Starting from the assumption that news, like all texts, is polysemic – comprises a plurality of meanings – Fiske argues that the news text 'is engaged in a constant struggle to contain the multifarious events and their polysemic potential within its own conventions' (*ibid.*: 286). Journalists select aspects of the real world, then present them in a narrative form that allows them to be made sense of, but also prevents potentially disruptive readings of events being made by the audience. Journalism can thus be analysed in terms of the 'strategies of containment' which it deploys. More recently, Stuart Allan argues that 'news discourses help to *naturalise* a cultural politics of legitimacy so as to lend justification to modern society's distribution of power and influence' (Allan and Zelizer, 2004: 77, his emphasis), and that they 'effectively *depoliticise* the dominant meanings, values and beliefs associated with these inequalities'.

Regardless of the sophistication with which the social reproduction thesis is put, it is nearly always based on the assertion that members of the audience obtain from journalism information that will tend to support an ideologically loaded view of the world; one that will contribute to the reproduction of an unequal and fundamentally antagonistic social system without dysfunctional conflict.

Given the immense methodological difficulties attached to such a project, it is perhaps no surprise that attempts to demonstrate empirically such 'ideological effects' have been few. Those studies that have been undertaken are contradictory and inconclusive. Guy Cumberbatch's study of audience perceptions of television news coverage of the 1984–85 miners' strike appeared to show that viewers were generally apathetic or resistant to the 'dominant' message of the news, insofar as that message could be deduced from content analysis (Cumberbatch *et al.*, 1986). Greg Philo's audience research has claimed to demonstrate the opposite: that 'while differences in political culture and class experience have important influences on the interpretation of events ... the media are providing a major input of information which seems to relate very directly to the beliefs of some people' (Philo, 1990: 56).

The social reproduction thesis can at times veer close to the conspiratorial presuppositions of earlier 'mass society' theorists, who assigned to all media a direct and powerful role in the subjugation of the subordinate classes of capitalism. Paddy Scannell observes that 'for all its seeming sophistication the Theory of Ideology says something very simple indeed; something not very different from what Leavis was saying in the 1930s: the media are harmful and the function of theoretical critique is to expose them in that light' (Scannell, 1989: 158). The Frankfurt School's most important idea, as Richard Collins puts it, was to view the mass media – and journalism – as 'a "consciousness industry" propagating a "one-dimensional", "affirmative" culture in which the contradictions and barbarisms of capitalism are prematurely and falsely harmonised' (Collins, 1976: 49). In this form, with its view of news and journalism as instruments of thought control over passive mass audiences, it is clearly overly simplistic for contemporary purposes. The twenty-first century, as I and others have argued, is characterised by 'cultural chaos' rather than ideological thought control (McNair, 2006a); by what Tumber and Webster term the 'globalisation of consciousness' as the number and ideological diversity of news sources explodes on the internet (Tumber and Webster, 2007), contributing 'to what is now a remarkably rich and differentiated information environment' (*ibid.*: 72). Sarah Maltby argues similarly that stories such as the

Abu Ghraib torture scandal show how 'the multiple and diverse means of disseminating information in the public sphere have undermined the means by which states are able to control what is revealed, or concealed, about their activities ... The ability to produce information for mass dissemination is no longer restricted to those in power, nor limited to those who own the means of media production' (Maltby and Keeble, 2007: 3).

Rupert Murdoch himself, at the end of a long career providing much raw material for the critical theorists, has supported this assessment, by declaring that the age of the media baron is dead. In a speech given to the Worshipful Company of Stationers and Newspaper Makers in London in March 2006, he declared that 'power is moving away from the old elite in our industry – the editors, the chief executives and, let's face it, the proprietors. A new generation of media consumers has risen demanding content delivered when they want it, how they want it, and very much as they want it.' Journalism *does* have a socially reproductive function, comprising what the German sociologist Niklas Luhmann described as one of a society's 'recursively stabilised functional mechanisms' (Luhmann, 2000: 1), an 'autopoetic, self-reproducing system' for making sense of the world. This function is no longer realised – if it ever was – at the beck and call of ruling classes or power elites, but in conditions of fierce ideological rivalry and contestation, fuelled by the proliferation of online and user-generated media to be examined later in this book.

That said, variants of the social reproduction hypothesis remain influential, not only among Marxists, but feminists and others concerned with the sociology of culture, and the role of news and journalism in maintaining what they perceive to be structurally unequal societies. Chomsky and Herman's propaganda model, for example, still a prominent feature of many journalism studies courses in the UK and elsewhere, characterises the effects of western journalism in such terms as 'brainwashing under freedom' (Chomsky and Herman, 1979). The model – one variant of what I have termed elsewhere the *dominance* or *control paradigm* (McNair, 1998b, 2006a) – remains influential, as in a recent essay by Oliver Boyd-Barrett, which asserts baldly that 'news media are framed within an all-encompassing project of propaganda ' (Boyd-Barrett, 2007: 99) and that, by way of example, audiences are 'positioned' corresponding to the 'idealised role of the feminine in patriarchal society, whose features include passivity, trust and nurturing support for male authority'. Here, as in most such articulations of the propaganda model and its variants, the questions of who exactly does the positioning, and how, if at all, it is effective in duping the passive masses, are left unanswered.[2]

Journalism and the social construction of reality

A different approach to the social role of journalism asserts that it is not simply 'a vehicle for objective facts about remote events', but tells us 'something about the structure of the world' (Davies, 1990: 160). In particular, it constructs the world for us in terms of categories, such as 'normal' versus 'deviant', or 'militant' versus 'moderate', which are then used to police society, and to exclude or marginalise certain types of social actor. An early but still relevant study (in the era of perceived crime waves involving young people carrying knives, guns and drugs) informed by this perspective is Hall *et al.*'s *Policing the Crisis* (1978), which argues that news organisations do not merely report events, but are active agents in constructing the sociopolitical environment that frames those events in the public imagination. Journalists, as reporters of news, are at the same time social actors, with a key role to play in shaping our perception of what news is, and how to react to it. If a large proportion of news may be said to comprise the reporting of problematic social reality, then journalists contribute substantially to the process whereby 'problems' are defined.

Another exponent of this approach, which may be viewed as a variant of agenda-setting, suggests that journalism:

> can create social problems, can present them dramatically and over-whelmingly, and most important, can do it suddenly. The media can very quickly and effectively fan public indignation and engineer what one might call a 'moral panic' about a certain type of deviancy. Indeed, there is institutionalised into the media the need to create moral panics and issues which will seize the imagination of the public.
>
> (Young, 1971: 37)

Cohen's seminal study of the media sociology of moral panics was published in a new edition in 2004, indicating how relevant the concept remains to an understanding of journalism's social effects (see also Critcher, 2003; Jewkes, 2004). A recent example of moral panic in the British media would be the 2002 'naming and shaming' of paedophiles by the *News of the World* and other tabloids in the wake of a high-profile child murder case. In one infamous example of how the public can be led into mob rule by red-top tabloid journalism, a female paediatrician living in Bristol was chased from her home by an angry mob who thought that she was a child molester, as opposed to a doctor. Although the vast majority of child murders are committed by parents or family members and other carers, this wave of coverage created a moral panic about the prevalence of random child-killers and paedophiles in Britain that was entirely unrelated to the actual incidence of these crimes.

This approach, used in conjunction with what is known as the 'deviancy amplification model' developed by sociologists, views journalism as an active, if not necessarily directed social institution, working alongside other institutions such as the legal system and judiciary to regulate and negotiate morality. Examples of how journalism can lead to deviancy amplification have included the celebrated battles between mods and rockers that took place in the south of England in the 1960s; the mugging scare of the 1970s; and, in the 1980s football hooliganism, 'acid house' parties, and satanic child abuse. In all these cases, the media did not simply report events, but contributed to their emergence as problems in the public arena.

Journalism and the social construction of risk

If news media have the capacity to amplify deviance, they can have an analogous impact on public perceptions of risk. We looked earlier at the MMR case, in which media coverage of the alleged link between autism and MMR produced a substantial fall in vaccination rates, leading to the heightened possibility of epidemic. Other examples of this effect include the succession of health scares and food panics that characterised the 1990s in Britain. Typically, following news coverage of an incident (or series of incidents) involving a food product or a medicine, it would become associated in the public imagination with threats to health out of proportion to the actual risks involved. Consumption of the offending substance would plummet, leading to major problems for manufacturers, and sometimes unexpected negative consequences. For example, a 1997 BBC radio news report on the increased risk of thrombosis associated with a new contraceptive pill for women led, through a sudden decline in use of the pill, to an increased number of unwanted pregnancies. While the degree of risk associated with the contraceptive was, in statistical terms, minuscule, the health problems caused to at least some women by the reportage and its effect on their behaviour were substantial. It is estimated that several hundred women died in childbirth who would not have otherwise, simply because they were discouraged from taking the pill by exaggerated media coverage of its harmful effects.

Tumber and Webster consider the impact of what they call a 'chaotic information environment' on the global public's perceptions of the risk of terrorism post-9/11.

> The innocent deaths that come from terrorist attacks are minor compared to the great inter-state wars of the past ... Nonetheless, there appears to be an increased public perception of the threat of war ... This owes much to the increased awareness of wars around the world, particularly those involving Western forces, as well as to the dramatic and disconcerting character of terrorist attacks that come without warning and aim at maximising civilian casualties.
>
> (Tumber and Webster, 2008: 60)

On a day of terrorist 'spectaculars' such as 9/11 in New York, 7/7 in London, or 11/3 in Madrid, the news media's recently acquired capacity to provide real-time, round-the-clock coverage of events that, although horrifying, are in terms of their casualties small-scale by comparison with, for example, the Second World War in Europe or the atomic bombing of Japan, generates heightened and probably unwarranted collective anxieties about the risks of Islamic terrorism. There *are* risks, of course (the author's own locality, Glasgow, was subject to an attempted car bomb attack by Islamist terrorists in July 2007 – fortunately, no one but the terrorist himself died as a result of the incident), but the media may amplify and distort their scale, with real consequences for policy.

In 2008 the world was engulfed by economic anxiety – the sub-prime mortgage crisis, which began in the USA and then rippled outwards, and the ensuing 'credit crunch'. This global economic crisis was viewed by many as the worst since the Great Depression, fuelled not least by the speed of information flows and the resulting heightened propensity for panic among financial traders and over-hasty decision-making among policy-makers. As this edition went to press, no research had been done on the link, if any, between media coverage of the credit crunch and public perceptions of the state of the economy. It is, however, reasonable to assert that the hyperactive media of the twenty-first century played a role in the speed and intensity with which the crisis emerged.

Conclusions

The effects issue remains one of the most difficult and contentious in media studies, despite the vast resources and energies that have been expended in trying to resolve it. This is no less true for journalism than for any other category of media output. In the end, it can be stated with certainty only that journalism matters because we believe that it does. Whether or not the news and information media do indeed have the power to set agendas for the public at large, to reproduce ideology, to create moral panics, to spark runs on banks, or to influence what we think, the fact that politicians, pressure group activists, trade unionists, terrorists and other social actors think that they do some or all of these things means that they increasingly tailor their 'performances' to suit what their public relations and media advisers tell them are the requirements of the journalists (Davies, 2002, 2007). In today's world, public figures and organisations actively seek out the media, even if they cannot always guarantee that their coverage will be favourable. For Rodney Tiffen, in an observation that retains its insightfulness two decades later, this is the only thing about journalism that really matters. In his view, 'the impact of news [and journalism in general] must be sought in its effects on how political life is conducted, how news practices interact with political processes and outcomes' (Tiffen, 1989: 6). From this perspective, the important thing is not the effect of journalistic output on individual attitudes and ideas, but the effect of the widespread perception of journalism's importance on the social process as a whole.

The increasing importance of information media in the political process was illustrated during the Gulf War, when the leaders of the opposing sides used the news media, and the access it gave them to each other's populations, to communicate their diplomatic and military messages. The American news channel CNN functioned as surrogate diplomacy for Allied and Iraqi leaders in a conflict that was lived as it happened, not only by people in the firing lines in Israel, Baghdad and Bahrain, but by millions in Europe, Asia and America, through the medium of television. CNN, BBC World and the Arab network Al Jazeera have played important functions in managing public opinion about September 11 and its aftermath. The invasions of Afghanistan and

Iraq were examples of 'information war' (Maltby and Keeble, 2007) – conflicts fought in and through the news media, with journalists positioned not merely as objective reporters, but as conduits for competing propaganda messages. All conflicts in the modern world, whether violent or non-violent, are increasingly focused on efforts to shape public opinion through the globalised media of news and journalism.

In domestic politics, too, the ability to use and manipulate news media – to set agendas and shape debates with the aid of photo-opportunities, sound-bites and professional image consultants – is now generally accepted as a pre-requisite of success. Governments, political parties and pressure groups compete with equal vigour to manage the news, because they believe that, for the majority of the audience, news and current affairs is the key point of contact with the political process. For this reason, if for no other, journalism undoubtedly matters.

Further reading

The most recent academic research and writing on journalism can be found in such journals as *Journalism Studies, Media, Culture & Society, Journalism: Theory, Practice & Criticism*, and the *European Journal of Communication*. A full list of academic sources used in this and other chapters is contained in the Bibliography.

3 Journalism and its critics – (I) the view from the academy

This chapter contains:

- an overview of the governing principles of British journalism
- a discussion of the main criticisms of journalistic practice that have emerged from the academy, including the work of the Glasgow University Media Group, Noam Chomsky and Pierre Bourdieu.

To understand contemporary journalism, in the UK and in other liberal capitalist societies, one must first know something about the two concepts that have historically underpinned its organisation and production: liberal pluralism and objectivity. This and the following chapter discuss the origins of these concepts and the scholarly criticisms that have been made of them. Chapter 5 then reviews critical debates around current trends in journalistic form and content, as conducted in the public sphere by a range of commentators including academics and journalists.

Liberal pluralism and press freedom

The invention of printing – which represented the birth of mass communication, and was the precondition for the emergence of journalism as a media form – coincided with the upsurge of religious, political and social strife that accompanied the late-medieval period. Medieval societies were autocratic, in that they were dominated by an aristocracy and led by a monarchy with absolute power, in cooperation with the institutions of the Church. These institutions exercised strict control over politics, ideology and culture, powers that were claimed to derive from the divine will of God. The class structure and the privileges it conferred on the small minority were believed to be divinely ordained.

The authoritarianism of the late-medieval state was reflected in its control of the media. In sixteenth-century England, the state monopolised publishing and printing rights. All publications were strictly censored by Church and state. In 1529 the English Crown published its first list of prohibited books.

Books had long been suppressed on religious grounds, but Henry VIII and the Tudors 'worked on the principle that the peace of the realm demanded the suppression of all dissenting opinion' (Cranfield, 1978: 2).

Concern for 'the peace of the realm' derived from the fact that around the beginning of the fourteenth century, the feudal establishment began to be threatened by the rise of a new social class, whose wealth and claim to power derived not from 'God', but from trade, commerce and production. This rising capitalist class or bourgeoisie was, by the time of the invention of printing in the fifteenth century, becoming an important political influence in England and other European societies.

'News', in the sense of the dissemination of information about events, was already a familiar concept, dating back at least as far as ancient Rome. In the fifteenth century, public announcements about official occasions, public hangings and witchcraft became commonplace. But as merchant capitalism developed, the supply of information became an essential element of the wealth-creation process. The emergence of 'news' as a recognisably modern cultural form, and media to disseminate it, thus coincided not only with the invention of printing, but also with the development of capitalism.

News was not merely an aid to trade in a developing capitalist society, but an also important political instrument. Siebert notes that 'in most countries of western Europe the interests of the developing commercial class required limitations on monarchical powers and on the special privileges of the nobility. Capitalistic enterprise was incompatible with medieval notions of status and security' (Siebert, 1956: 42). The early news media served as a channel through which the rising capitalist class could articulate and express these interests. This was the context in which periodicals first appeared in England in the 1590s (Raymond, 1996), and the world's first weekly newspaper in English – *Curanto* – was published in Amsterdam in June 1618. In England, in 1622 a syndicate of publishers began to issue regular bulletins of internal and foreign news, known as newsbooks, described by Cranfield as 'a single sheet of small folio, printed in two columns, and bearing no title' (Cranfield, 1978: 2).

In response to the growing threat posed by the emerging bourgeoisie and its embryonic information media, the authorities intensified their control over the printed word. On 17 October 1632, a decree of the Star Chamber in London (one of the most important institutions for the suppression of opponents of the *status quo*) banned the publication of all newspapers and pamphlets. In 1637, another decree limited to 20 the number of newspapers allowed to be published in London.

Notwithstanding these authoritarian measures, the newsbooks survived by being circulated and read through informal networks, such as London's coffee house culture. The rising bourgeoisie, meanwhile, was increasing its economic strength *vis-à-vis* the aristocracy, developing and articulating further the ideological legitimation for its own political power. Enlightenment philosophers such as John Locke engaged in a philosophical critique of absolutism. The doctrine of divine right was incompatible with the rise of the bourgeoisie, which had to be 'free' from feudal authority. From this basic drive for power developed the political theory of liberalism and the bourgeois ideological concept of freedom: economic freedom, political freedom and intellectual freedom, advanced in opposition to medieval absolutism as the precondition for the ascendancy of the bourgeoisie as a ruling class.

John Milton articulated the concept of press freedom as early as 1644, and pioneered the concept of 'the open market of ideas', which played an important part in the rise of bourgeois economic and political power. This was the revolutionary ideology of a radical, progressive class fighting against a declining absolutist and authoritarian order. Applied to the media, liberal and Enlightenment principles meant, primarily, that the sole guarantee of the victory of reason and truth in the public sphere was the free competition of ideas and opinions between diverse viewpoints; and that only by the flourishing and encouragement of such intellectual diversity could the truth emerge.

These principles remain fundamental to the working of liberal democratic societies. Tolerance and diversity continue to be regarded as essential for servicing a democratic political system, since such a system depends on rational choice; for enlightening and informing the public, who make the choices; and for allowing the media to stand as a Fourth Estate over government, thus preventing dictatorship. As Altschull expresses it, 'in a democracy, it is the people who rule. The voice of the people is heard in the voting booth. The decisions made by the people in the voting booths are based on the information made available to them. That information is provided primarily by the news media. Hence the news media are indispensable to the survival of democracy' (Altschull, 1984: 19).[1] John Keane argues that 'the call for press freedom is a distinctive organising principle of the modern European and North American worlds ... the theory and practice of publicly articulating opinions through media of communication developed endogenously in no other civilization' (Keane, 1991: 7). It arose most vociferously in western Europe because it was here that the 'feudal components of the medieval *corpus politicum* relinquished their struggle against state builders only gradually and unwillingly' (*ibid.*).

Objectivity

If the term 'liberal pluralism' has defined the political environment within which journalism in capitalist societies has been practised, the concept of objectivity has become the key professional ethic; the standard to which all journalists should aspire. Gaye Tuchman famously called it a 'strategic ritual' (Tuchman, 1972: 661), which mobilises the society-wide credibility and legitimacy sought after by the journalistic profession. It is routinely 'used by journalists in warding off charges of bias or distortion, or other criticisms' (Schiller, 1981: 3). The concept of 'objectivity' is premised on the assertion that 'a person's statements about the world can be trusted if they are submitted to established rules deemed legitimate by a professional community' (Schudson, 1978: 7). The key assumption underlying the concept is that facts are assertions about the world open to independent validation. They stand beyond the distorting influences of any individual's personal pre-ferences. [By contrast,] values are an individual's conscious or unconscious preferences for what the world should be; they are ... ultimately subjective and so without legitimate claim on other people. The belief in objectivity is a faith in facts, a distrust of 'values', and a commitment to their segregation.

(*ibid.*: 6)

Objectivity in this sense, as Michael Schudson points out, is a relatively recent concept. In the early part of the nineteenth century, journalism was partisan, openly representing the interests of 'political parties and men of commerce'. Even by the 1920s, 'objectivity' 'was not a term journalists or critics of journalism used' (*ibid.*).

The precise origins of 'objectivity' as a professional standard in journalism remain a matter of contention. Some trace it back to the emergence of tele-graph agencies such as the Associated Press in the United States. These wire services supplied information to many clients simultaneously, so that their information had to be perceived as ideologically neutral if it was to be accep-table to all. Others have argued that objectivity was connected in some way with the process of commodification of newspapers that took place in the 1800s. In the USA in the 1830s, the expensive, partisan newspapers began to lose ground to what was called the 'penny press' (and what was sometimes called in Britain the 'pauper press') – a cheap, commercial press which set out to serve an expanding reading public. This public comprised not wealthy 'men of commerce', but small traders and artisans – the emerging urban middle class.

To attract and keep this readership (and thus to gain advertising revenue), newspapers began to report crime, human interest and other categories of news, which today's readers would recognise as modern and popular, even tabloid. Journalists became the spokesmen for what Schudson calls 'egalitarian ideals in politics, economics and social life [the ideals of their readers, by implication]. The penny papers expressed and built the culture of a democratic market society, a culture which had no place for social or intellectual deference' (*ibid.*: 60).

Dan Schiller argues that the penny press expressed the ideals of a small-tradesmen, republican public threatened by the encroachment of big business. It reflected the views of its readers that 'knowledge, like property, should not be monopolised for exclusive use by private interests'. While the elite press was widely perceived to be subservient and partisan towards the dominant economic class, the penny press successfully claimed to speak for the public as a whole, 'giving all citizens an equal access to knowledge and direct personal knowledge of impartially presented news' (Schiller, 1981: 48).

The impartiality and independence claimed by the penny press successfully ushered in its stewardship of the pursuit of enlightened reason in the public sphere. ... The pre-emptive claim staked by the cheap journals to the defence of natural rights and public good was ... the enduring foundation upon which the structure of news objectivity was built.

(ibid.: 75)

Another foundation stone of journalistic objectivity was the acceptance, by the late nineteenth century, of positivist epistemology and photographic realism, 'both of which claimed to reflect the world without reference to human subjectivity and selectivity' (*ibid.*: 11). The nineteenth century witnessed rapid technological progress, accompanied in the realm of philosophy by the beliefs in rationalism, realism, positivism and empiricism. These philosophies of science stressed the 'epistemological primacy of scientific knowledge' (*ibid.*: 87), and the possibility of an objective, 'knowable' universe. The social sciences, such as history, also adopted this view of the world, encouraging further 'a general cultural acceptance of a reportable, objective world' (*ibid.*).

To these intellectual trends in epistemology, Schiller then adds the invention of photography, the remarkable ability of which 'to represent reality – to depict, apparently without human intervention, an entire world of referents – bolstered the apparently universal recognition of it as a supreme standard of accuracy and truth' (*ibid.*: 92). These were standards to which journalism could also aspire.

Taking all these developments together, journalists at the end of the nineteenth century were encouraged to assume the existence of a world 'out there' which could be appropriated, or known, through journalism, with accuracy. The assumption was 'not that the media are objective, but that there is a world out there to be objective about' (*ibid.*: 2). Journalists now 'presumed a world prior to all imposed values, and the periodic construction of accurate and universally recognisable copies of events in this world became the newspaper's fundamental business' (*ibid.*: 87).

This concept of objectivity was challenged in the 1920s and 1930s by the emergence of fascist dictatorships, and the propaganda which came with them (and which was also used in the struggle to defeat them). This 'made journalists suspicious of facts and ready to doubt the naïve empiricism of the 1890s' (Schudson, 1978: 141). The new scepticism was reinforced by the emergence of the public relations industry, and the perception that absolute neutrality was unattainable. Facts were there to be manipulated: the only issue was, who did the manipulating, and to what end?

By the 1920s, then, reflecting the impact of a number of philosophical, scientific and epistemological trends towards relativism, journalists had come to accept that 'there were no longer facts, only individually constructed interpretations' (*ibid.*). They asserted that these interpretations could and should be constructed in a methodologically objective manner, using professionally agreed rules that could minimise the impact of subjectivity on reporting, but that a degree of subjectivity was inescapable. Eighty years later, a well known British journalist could write without fear of losing his professional credibility that 'objectivity doesn't mean that you don't have opinions, that you are without personal bias, and it doesn't mean neutrality. It means that the journalist's working method is objective – that you're independent, disinterested, and you're not going to let your interests determine the outcome of your journalism'.[2]

Thus, argues Schudson, the emergence of objectivity as a journalistic ideal came at the same time as a deeper loss of faith in ideas of rationality, absolute truth and progress; reflecting the need, as it were, to reassert the possibility of a transcending truth in the face of twentieth-century propaganda techniques. Today, the principle of objectivity is regarded by most journalists as not an absolute, but a relative term; something towards which professional journalists should aspire and work, but in the knowledge that absolute objectivity, like absolute zero in the world of physics, is in practical terms impossible to attain. The editor of one of Britain's (and the world's) leading journalistic organisations, the *Guardian*, put this pragmatism well when he noted that 'the newspaper that drops on your doorstep is a partial, hasty, incomplete, inevitably somewhat flawed and inaccurate rendering of some of the things we have heard about in the past 24 hours'.[3]

Broadcast impartiality: a special case

Closely related to, but distinct from, the concept of objectivity is that of 'impartiality', a notion of particular importance to any discussion of British broadcasting journalism. Chapter 1 referred to the specific technical and formal characteristics of broadcast journalism, which appear to make it more 'believable' as an information source. In the UK, the perceived legitimacy and 'truth' quotient of broadcast journalism is also founded on the broadcasters' assertion that they are 'impartial'.

The proclamation of impartiality as a guiding principle of British broadcast journalism goes back to the origins of the BBC in the 1920s, and to the distinctive role it was recognised to be playing in the developing 'mass society' of that period. By the early twentieth century, British society had become 'democratic'. Universal suffrage had been achieved and political rights extended to the masses. How, then, to ensure that these rights were exercised responsibly, in the national interest?

Part of the answer lay in the new medium of broadcasting, which was set up as 'a public utility to be developed as a national service in the public interest' (Scannell and Cardiff, 1991: 6). The Crawford Committee, which led to the establishment of the BBC in its present form, adopted this 'Reithian' notion of public service broadcasting (after the founder of the BBC, John Reith) and promoted the development of the BBC as 'a cultural, moral and educative force for the improvement of knowledge, taste and manners ... a powerful means of promoting social unity' and creating 'an informal and reasoned public opinion as an essential part of the political process in a mass democratic society' (*ibid.*: 8). Broadcasting was to take on the task of establishing a common culture amongst the national audience. Because 'the nation' was recognised to contain diverse elements (diverse politically, socially and geographically), the BBC would have to be an 'impartial arbiter' (*ibid.*), independent of commercial and political interests.

Impartiality is not absolute, however, any more than objectivity can be. Broadcasting was established as a public service by the state, in accordance with what were seen to be the interests of the state – or the 'national interest', as it is more often put. Consequently, the rules of impartiality are withdrawn whenever 'impartial' journalism is perceived to threaten the national interest. As the BBC puts it, impartiality 'does not imply absolute neutrality, nor detachment from basic moral and constitutional beliefs. For example, the BBC does not feel obliged to be neutral as between truth and untruth, justice and injustice, compassion and cruelty, tolerance and intolerance'.[4]

The concept of impartiality was also imposed on the commercial broadcasting organisations when they were established in 1954. Journalism on commercial television, like that of the BBC, would have to be impartial with respect to controversial issues and events. Rupert Murdoch's Sky News, in turn, chose to operate within the broad guidelines of impartiality when it was set up in the late 1980s, although as a satellite broadcaster at that time licensed in Luxembourg it was under no legal obligation to do so. It did so anyway because, to survive and compete effectively in the British TV news market, an organisation must be perceived to embrace impartiality, as opposed to the partisanship which is acceptable for, indeed expected of, the press. Different broadcast organisations have different styles or 'brands', and have developed different ways of defining and applying the principles of impartiality.

The coming crisis of impartiality?

As this edition went to press, British public service broadcasting was nearing the completion of another review of its operations and activities, against the background of digital switch-over (DSO – see below) and the continuing proliferation of TV channels and news sources. In its consultation document setting out the main issues around this review, the regulator Ofcom argued that now, as never before in British broadcasting history, there was a case for reviewing the way in which impartiality was defined and implemented by public service broadcasters. The old rules, argued Ofcom, established to defend pluralism and diversity in the era of analogue duopoly, may

> actually impede the expansion of genuine diversity of views ... they affect the way stories are told, and may have some influence on the selection of stories. This may have fostered a middle-of-the-road culture in mainstream news. Views that do not fit easily within a conventional, two-sided debate can struggle to be heard, resulting in a discussion around a narrow perceived fulcrum
> (Ofcom, 2007: 10)

There had been previous attempts to explore the relevance of impartiality in British public service journalism, when for example satellite and cable channels were becoming established in the 1990s, and in the Thatcher era. They had been resisted, however. By 2008, and with the imminence of DSO, the challenge to impartiality as a guiding principle of broadcast journalism in the UK was founded on fundamental transformation of the media environment, and could no longer be dismissed. One consequence of the emergence of a multi-channel TV marketplace has been the reassertion of an old argument favoured by the Thatcherite Conservatives in the 1980s – that impartiality is no longer required of public service broadcasting, nor is it desirable. Writing in the *Sunday Times* in 2002, commentator Andrew Sullivan argued for 'prejudiced television news' and condemned 'the suffocating liberalism of the pseudo-objective networks'.[5] Although this piece was directed at the USA, it is also applicable to the UK. As audiences grow more used to passionate, opinionated journalism on the internet, or on cable and satellite TV, the adherence of Britain's public service broadcasters to a model of impartiality established in the era of the 'comfortable duopoly' of BBC and ITV is viewed by some as counterproductive to the goal of maintaining audience share. In current affairs, as in news, it is argued, audiences are comfortable with, and increasingly expect the articulation of, viewpoint and opinion, and will shun the stoic adherence to balance and impartiality on which BBC journalism has rested for nearly a century (and to which commercial public service broadcasters must also sign up).[6]

One can see the logic of this argument. A journalistic approach premised on the scarcity of broadcasting provision, and the democratic necessity for audiences to hear both sides of a story from their most trusted sources of news and current affairs, looks less relevant when there is no such scarcity, and an unprecedented plurality of sources from which the audience may choose, just as he or she currently chooses his or her newspaper, usually aware of its editorial bias. There is a case for allowing more of the current affairs transmitted by public service broadcasting to have an editorial voice or position – a bias – on the basis that there will be counteracting biases of equivalent weight elsewhere in the schedule. There have in fact always been such spaces, exemplified by the passionate documentaries of John Pilger for ITV over many years. The argument for allowing more, as a means of retaining public support for public service broadcasting, is persuasive, and is likely to bear fruit. BBC1's *This Week* current affairs strand is presented by Andrew Neil, a stridently right-of-centre media executive who has been a key lieutenant of Rupert Murdoch and the Barclay brothers in his time. His opinions frequently intrude on his commentaries and questions of studio guests. But as long as there are counter-vailing or opposing views elsewhere on the programme, or at an equally prominent place elsewhere in the BBC schedule, Neil's opinionated journalism, formed in the ideological hot house of News Corporation, can add a valuable dimension to the BBC's current affairs output, and few viewers are likely to be unaware of his starting point on most of the issues which arise in his programme. Argument and heated debate can be very attractive to the viewer, and will increasingly have their place in the BBC's digitally enabled schedules.

On the other hand, the BBC remains the UK's most trusted source of journalistic information, and its current affairs, like its news, has a uniquely privileged place in the country's cultural life. For that reason, the gradual move toward more editorialising and polemic must be clearly signposted for the audience, and carefully balanced overall, even if individual programmes may in the future be more often weighted toward one side or the other. This view is accepted by the BBC's senior managers as part of the corporation's drive to 'make the important interesting'. At a speech in January 2005, the then-Director General Michael Grade insisted that 'due impartiality is, and must remain, one of the cornerstones of BBC journalism'. In September 2006 he again stressed that 'whatever the pressures, the BBC must remain a trusted supplier of impartial information on all its platforms'.[7] If the definition of 'due impartiality' is inevitably broadening to allow for more opinion and point of view, and if that can be judged a sensible adaptation to a changing media environment, the principle will retain its centrality in the BBC's current affairs output for as long as there is a public service broadcasting system. As the sources of journalism proliferate, and audiences find it harder to know what and who to trust, it will become more important, not less, for the BBC to retain this standard of quality control.

That said, Grade and his successor at the BBC have stressed the importance of formal innovation, creativity and excellence in the writing, narrativisation and visual presentation of current affairs. Due impartiality, it is accepted, will have to be achieved within programmes that are better at grabbing and holding the audience's attention than has (arguably) been the case. This is a competitive necessity for the commercial public service channels, and will become even more crucial in the post-analogue era. But it is also a political necessity for the BBC, which depends for its long-term future on being able to demonstrate some measure of popularity as well as civic value for its public service privileges.

The critique of objectivity

Objectivity, then (and for British public service broadcasters, impartiality), is the most important journalistic value. But it contains a fundamental contradiction. As Schudson puts it:

> while objectivity, by the 1930s, was an articulate professional value in journalism, it was one that seemed to disintegrate as soon as it was formulated. It became an ideal in journalism, after all, precisely when the impossibility of overcoming subjectivity in presenting the news was widely accepted and, I have argued, precisely because subjectivity had come to be regarded as inevitable. From the beginning, then, criticism of the 'myth' of objectivity has accompanied its enunciation.
>
> (Schudson, 1978: 157)

Criticism of objectivity can be divided into two broad categories. First, there is the criticism, usually based on empirical research (content analysis), that journalism is *biased*, that it falls short of the normative standard of objectivity. As we have seen, liberal pluralism accords journalism a key role in the orderly reproduction of democratic societies. Jeffrey Alexander, for example, defines the social role of the news media in the following terms:

> by daily exposing and reformulating itself *vis à vis* changing values, group formations, and objective economic and political conditions, the media allows 'public opinion' to be organized responsively on a mass basis. By performing this function of information-conduit, the news media provides society with the greatest degree of flexibility in dealing with social strains
> (Alexander, 1981: 21).

However, this flexibility (and thus the integrative social function of the news media) is threatened if journalists are not sufficiently autonomous from economic, political and other elites in society. As Alexander puts it, 'to the degree that the news media is tied to religious, ideological, political, or class groupings it is not free to form and reform public events in a flexible way. Without this flexibility, public opinion becomes 'artificial' and 'biased': it will be keyed to a part over the whole' (*ibid.*: 25). This approach is focused on 'how well or how badly the various media reflect the existing balance of political forces and the political agenda' (Collins, 1990: 37). The underlying assumption of such criticism is that there is a *possibility* of objective journalism, but that it is not being realised, and it is the role of the scholarly critic to point this out.

A more fundamental critique – shared, as we have seen, by many journalists – asserts that there can in fact be no objectivity; that the concept is nothing more than a mystification, a legitimising ritual with no real validity. From this perspective, there are a variety of potential journalistic accounts of events, corresponding to the plurality of viewpoints which exist in the world. More than one of these accounts may have validity.

The starting point of this critique is the acknowledgement that journalism is not, and never can be, a neutral, value-free representation of reality. As Paul Willis put it back in 1971, as well as anyone ever has: 'once an item of news has been selected for transmission to the public there is already bias, some selective principle, some value, quite apart from the way it is presented' (Willis, 1971: 9). Roger Fowler states that 'news is not a natural phenomenon emerging straight from reality, but a product. It is produced by an industry, shaped by the bureaucratic and economic structure of that industry, by the relations between the media and other industries and, most importantly, by relations with government and other political organisations' (Fowler, 1991: 222). Richard Hoggart argues that 'what its practitioners call 'objective news' is ... in reality a highly selected interpretation of events' (GUMG, 1976: x).

News and journalism, in short, are social constructions. This point (or something similar) has been made so often in the media studies literature that it has become a commonplace, but it remains central to the study of journalism: news is never a mere recording or reporting of the world 'out there', but a synthetic, value-laden account which carries within it the dominant assumptions and ideas of the society within which it is produced.

This view is rooted in the assertion that the categories by which we make sense of the world in consciousness are culturally specific. For example, in the UK, the USA and other liberal democratic societies, news tends to be about *conflict* and *negativity*. The negative – crime, industrial disputes, disasters – is more newsworthy than the positive. In the Soviet Union, on the other hand, journalists were taught an alternative conception of news values, which emphasised positive social phenomena. In Soviet news, until about 1986, crime was almost completely absent; there was no coverage of industrial disputes or of such phenomena as poverty, or of forms of social deviance from the officially sanctioned norm, such as homosexuality, although such things existed. There was no coverage of AIDS, none of aircrashes and other disasters, man-made or natural. Even the nuclear disaster at Chernobyl was hidden from the Soviet news audience until the last possible moment.[8]

These absences – strange and alien to the Western audience – were not simply the result of the authorities' wish to silence dissent and make invisible social and political problems. They were also a direct expression of Lenin's sincere view that journalism should perform a *constructive* social role: educating the masses with stories of exemplary production techniques; inspiring them with stories of industrial success; playing down crime and the deviant, rather than highlighting them. Instead of hearing about bad workers on strike, Soviet news audiences were told of the good workers who overfulfilled their production targets. The Soviet news media had no need to concern themselves with winning audience share or making profits, so they did not consistently have to outdo each other with exclusives and shock-horror headlines. Western news media, by contrast, are required to win audiences with entertainment as well as information. Entertainment is often about drama, and drama is, more often than not, about conflict and negativity.

Soviet socialism and Western capitalism represented two different political cultures, where different economic and ideological forces were at play, and where two very different concepts of what was newsworthy predominated. The question of which was the most appropriate is less important for our purposes than the recognition that news values can and do vary across cultures and, within a single culture, across media, so that in Britain *The Times*, the *Sun* and The *Sport* all have their own definition of what constitutes an important story. These definitions are value-laden.[9]

This is not the same thing as saying that journalism is 'biased', in the sense of 'deliberately shaping the content and presentation of the news so as to advance the cause of a particular party, candidate or ideology' (Ranney, 1983: 34). Bias in this sense is common in the media, particularly the press, but the social–constructionist argument is rather different: it is that journalism, regardless of the integrity of individual journalists and editors, is always a selective, partial account of a reality which can never be known in its entirety by anyone.

Notwithstanding the above, the 'objectivity assumption' remains powerful and prevalent among journalists.[10] Thus media sociologists have sought to 'prove' bias by means of content analysis. In this sense, the sociology of journalism has from the outset been concerned with 'establishing that [journalistic] information was produced: selected, organised, structured, and [therefore] biased' (Collins, 1990: 20).

Most work of this type has begun from the assumption that the media are inherently biased in favour of the powerful: the establishment, elite groups, the ruling class (or whatever one chooses to call those who occupy controlling positions in our society). An early example is contained in the work of Philip Elliot *et al.* (1970) on news coverage of student demonstrations in the late 1960s. This was the time of the Paris riots, which nearly brought down the French government; the shootings of students at Kent State University; and other manifestations of student unrest.

Elliot *et al.* asserted that the media play an important role in 'labelling' radical political action as deviant. When political groups (or other types of association, such as trade unions) go beyond the limits of normal parliamentary action (participating in demonstrations and strikes, for example), the media intervene to label these activities deviant or illegitimate, marginalising them and diverting public attention away from the root causes of social conflict towards its epiphenomenal forms. The case study used by these authors was the anti-Vietnam War demonstration, which took place in London's Grosvenor Square in 1968. They show that weeks before the event, media coverage built up an image of impending violence caused by 'foreign' Marxist extremists such as Tariq Ali (then a radical student leader). Although the organisers of the demonstration had made their peaceful intentions clear, the press nevertheless made sense of it in terms of the Paris riots – as a potentially violent, anarchical event. On the day of the demonstration itself, Murdock writes, 'there were relatively few incidents of confrontation between police and demonstrators, but having committed themselves to a news image based on this expectation, the newspapers proceeded as though the event had been characterised by street fighting' (Murdock, 1973: 165). Moreover, this construction of the event was reproduced in all the national daily newspapers, as well as on television news. In this way, 'the press played an indispensable role in the process of managing conflict and dissent, and legitimising the present distribution of power and wealth in British capitalism' (*ibid.*: 172). Murdock argues further that these features of news are present in other categories of coverage, including those of political, industrial and ethnic conflict, and of deviance.

The model employed by these authors is closely related to the 'deviancy amplification' framework of Jock Young and others discussed in Chapter 2. Hall *et al.*'s *Policing the Crisis* (1978), for example, attempted to do in the sphere of crime reporting what Elliot, Halloran and Murdock did in relation to political demonstrations: specifically, to show that 'law-and-order' news tends to label certain groups – in this case, the young black population of inner

London – as 'deviants', and in doing so, to contribute to the process whereby that labelling becomes a self-fulfilling prophecy (as measured in an increased incidence of the deviant behaviour). Scholarly work of this kind – aimed at proving or disproving bias, and the presence or absence of certain values and frameworks in news – has continued to feature prominently in journalism studies. Recent examples reflect currently newsworthy topics, and include media coverage of the post-9/11 'war on terror' and the invasion and subsequent occupation of Iraq (Miller, 2004; Tumber and Palmer, 2004); and media coverage of MMR and other public health issues (Hargreaves, Lewis, Speers, 2002).

The critique of television news

We have noted that television news is perceived to be the most important of all journalistic media, not least because of its reputation as an 'impartial' source of information. Consequently, a large number of studies within the critical tradition have been devoted to the 'demystification' of impartiality – the demonstration of television's 'bias'. The most ambitious of these to date has been the project begun by the Glasgow University Media Group (GUMG) in 1975 to analyse the output of British TV news over a six-month period. Their objective was to demonstrate, by means of quantitative content analysis and semiological techniques, that 'the news is not a neutral and natural phenomenon: it is rather the manufactured production of ideology' (GUMG, 1980: viii), a 'sequence of socially manufactured messages which carry many of the culturally dominant assumptions of our society' (GUMG, 1976: 1). To substantiate this hypothesis, the GUMG examined television news coverage of industrial relations at a time when this issue was at the top of the national political agenda.

Consistently, they concluded, in television news as a whole 'the ideology of one particular class is dominant and preferred' (GUMG, 1980: 415). During the period of their study, they argued, television journalists were presenting events and the issues that underpinned them in terms favourable to the British establishment. The journalistic emphases which the GUMG claimed to have documented – on wages as the cause of the inflation then gripping the UK; on strikes as the cause of Britain's economic crisis; on workers as the cause of strikes – made sense of these issues for the viewer in a manner that was biased towards capital and against labour.

The work of the GUMG was both influential and controversial. The broadcasters themselves rejected its findings (at least in public), while every anti-establishment group with a grudge against 'the meejah' used it as a weapon with which to beat the journalists. Consequently, it was the target of a sustained counter-attack, led by prominent members of the intellectual right such as Digby Anderson and Wes Sharrock. These authors set out to prove that it was members of GUMG who were ideologically biased, rather than the broadcasters; that they were Marxist left-wingers whose evidence could not, for that reason if for no other, be trusted.

> Media men [*sic*] are treated as if they have signed up to be professional
> sociologists and have fallen down on the job. They are alleged to distort
> events (if not Reality itself) in their reports, where the measure of distortion
> is precisely the extent of discrepancy between their account and that given by
> the favoured sociological theories of the media scholars. ... In effect, then,
> charges of distortion [or bias] could equally well be formulated as statements
> that the media men disagree with their sociologically-minded critics.
>
> (Anderson and Sharrock, 1979: 369)

Such studies do not prove bias, it was argued, 'they merely show that the
media do not accept the same theories that are presently fashionable within
sociology' (*ibid.*).

The methodological debates surrounding the content analysis of television
news have been pursued more fully elsewhere.[11] Here we might observe that
the ferocity and frequency of attacks on the GUMG's work, over a number of
years and from a multitude of sources, reflects, at the very least, the success of
their stated intention to demystify and deconstruct a major element of British
journalistic output.[12]

The importance and continuing relevance of their work can be seen in the
fact that, notwithstanding initial hostility, British broadcasters have come to
embrace the main theme of the GUMG's classic studies – that news *is* constructed, mediated reality, as opposed to neutral reportage, devoid of values
and subjectivities. A recent GUMG study of TV news coverage of the Israel–
Palestine conflict (Philo and Berry, 2004) contributed to a period of reflection
by the BBC, and an internal report on its Middle East coverage published in
2006 (with content analysis undertaken by Loughborough University).[13]

Developments in the critical tradition

The GUMG was criticised not only from the right of the academic and
political spectrum, but from within the critical tradition itself. A number of
media sociologists shared the Glasgow group's basic thesis that television
journalism performed an 'ideological role' in the wider process of cultural
reproduction, but argued that their conclusions were too simplistic, as they
implied a somewhat conspiratorial notion of bias. The GUMG, and the
many similar studies they inspired, were accused of class reductionism, since
they appeared to equate the content of news with what was in the interests
of the ruling class. Such an approach was denied by the group, however.
While their work sought to show that 'the ideology of one particular class is
dominant and preferred' in TV news, they also claimed 'to analyse the
inherent contradictions and varieties of permitted views and the surface
openness which exists across the range of broadcasting output' (GUMG,
1980: 415).

In 1983, Philip Schlesinger, Graham Murdock and Philip Elliot published
Televising Terrorism, which took as its case study the issue of terrorism and,

in particular, the conflict in Northern Ireland. On the basis of this study, these authors rejected:

> the commonplace radical characterisation of broadcasting as a largely uncritical conduit for official views. In opposition to these one-dimensional accounts we have drawn attention to the diverse ways in which television handles 'terrorism' and the problems this poses for liberal democracies. We have shown that some programmes are relatively 'closed' and work wholly or mainly within the terms set by the official perspective. Others, though, are more 'open' and provide spaces for alternative and oppositional views.
>
> (Schlesinger *et al.*, 1983: 166)

News programmes, they argued, were 'closed' in the main to all but the dominant official perspective on events, say in Northern Ireland. Documentaries and current affairs programmes, on the other hand, might well allow some discussion of the roots of the conflict, or the motivations of its protagonists, or even some critique of the state's position. Television had an 'uneasy, often abrasive relationship with the state, marked by struggle over the balance between autonomy and control ... these conflicts produce a symbolic field which is a good deal more open and contested than [a] one-sided stress on television's legitimising role allows for' (*ibid.*: 161). They concluded, however, by emphasising that 'the extent of this diversity should not be overstated. Although television is the site of continual struggle between competing perspectives on 'terrorism' [or, by extension, any other social phenomenon defined by the media as problematic] the contest is not an equal one. 'Open' programmes appear far less frequently than 'closed' ones and they reach smaller audiences' (*ibid.*: 166).

The key development here was to view television journalism not merely as an instrument of class domination, but as a 'space' available to be competed for by the representatives of different ideological perspectives and explanatory frameworks. As John Hartley put it, around this time: 'the dominant class may have a privileged position with respect to the available spaces, but not a monopoly' (Hartley, 1982: 55).

This approach was adopted in the author's own study of television news coverage of the defence and disarmament debate in the 1980s (McNair, 1988), which examined coverage of the concept of the Soviet military threat in the context of the publicly available evidence on such matters as Soviet military power and foreign policy objectives. It was found that news programmes tended consistently to reproduce without criticism or qualification the 'worst-case' official perspective on the Soviet threat. This position originated in the politico-military establishments of the US and UK governments, and was deployed (in its many manifestations) in the early 1980s to legitimise the huge increases in arms spending which took place in those years. However, I also observed that alternative perspectives on the threat – those not only of the Campaign for Nuclear Disarmament and peace campaigners, but of former political and military leaders – were presented from time to time on minority-audience current affairs programmes such as *Newsnight* or *Channel 4 News*. In an edition of *Newsnight* broadcast on 18 October 1983, the presenter announced that 'tonight we explore the case for regarding the Russians as perhaps less of a threat than they're sometimes made out to be'. The presenter then did what was rarely done on mainstream television news, labelling the 'Russian threat' perspective *as* a perspective, rather than objective reality, which could reasonably be set against other perspectives of potentially equal validity. Specifically, he contrasted dominant Western views of the Soviet Union as 'a very massive and threatening military power, stretching from central Europe to the extremes of Asia, poised to exploit any opportunities for expansion' with another –

> looking from the inside outwards, the view that sees the men in the Kremlin swamped by Russia's own internal problems and encircled by a whole range of external threats to their security. The Chinese in the east, the unsettled Muslims to the south, and the Afghans still unbeaten. Beyond that the Americans deploying massively in the Indian Ocean. To the west, beyond their own recalcitrant allies in eastern Europe, a whole ring of the West's nuclear and conventional systems pointing at them from Turkey around to northern Norway.
>
> (*ibid*.: 67)

In this way, the item created a rare (for the period when it was broadcast) but significant space, in which Cold War assumptions about the scale and nature of the Soviet threat could be contested, as on occasions did other minority audience news and current affairs programmes.

Is journalism biased, then? On the basis of the evidence gained by content analysts over a period of more than 40 years, we can state with some confidence that the news media of a particular society – press and broadcasting – tend to construct accounts of events that are structured and framed by the dominant values and interests of that society, and to marginalise (if not necessarily exclude) alternative accounts. In this sense, the evidence supports the materialist thesis that there is a link between the power structure of a society and its journalistic output; that journalism is part of a stratified social system – part of the apparatus by which that system is presented to its members in terms with which they can be persuaded to live.

On the other hand, as much of the work discussed in this chapter has also shown, journalism is not part of a ruling-class conspiracy. It clearly does provide spaces for alternative and oppositional views to be presented. There is growing acknowledgement from a range of scholars that these spaces are expanding, and that the media environment is being transformed from one characterised by control and dominance to one of relative chaos and competition (McNair, 2006a; Maltby and Keeble, 2007). Consequently, media sociologists have turned increasingly from the problem of proving bias to that of investigating the factors involved in the production of journalistic accounts of the world, and in particular the conditions under which openness – to accounts and interpretations of social reality which are not those of established elites – can be maximized.

Further reading

This chapter summarises ideas and arguments that can be pursued in greater depth by accessing the monographs and essays referenced. Journals such as *Journalism Studies, Media, Culture & Society* and *Journalism: Theory, Practice & Criticism publish cutting-edge research in the field.*

4 Making news – approaches to the sociology of journalism

This chapter contains an introduction to current sociological perspectives on the factors underpinning the production of news and journalism. Six approaches are presented:

- economic
- political
- professional–organisational
- technological
- culturalist
- the sociology of sources.

The economics of news and journalism

The economic approach to the sociology of journalism (also known as the *political economy* model) asserts that the output of journalistic media is principally determined by the economic structure of the organisations concerned. It is founded on the *materialist* view of society (as opposed to pluralist) elaborated by Karl Marx and Friedrich Engels in the nineteenth century.

In a capitalist society such as Britain, the media generally take the form of privately owned business enterprises which, like other forms of capitalist ownership, tend to be concentrated in the hands of a small minority of the population. The essence of the economic approach is that the journalism produced by these organisations is inflected in such a way as to serve the interests of that minority – to reproduce their ideas, values and ways of seeing the world as part of the process by which society is able to reproduce itself. It emphasises 'the centrality of economic ownership ... and the strictures and logic of the market' (Curran, 1990: 139). Ralph Miliband articulated this viewpoint when he wrote that:

> Rather obviously, those who own and control the capitalist mass media are most likely to be men whose ideological dispositions run from soundly

conservative to utterly reactionary; and in many instances, most notably in the case of newspapers, the impact of their views and prejudices is immediate and direct, in the straightforward sense that newspaper proprietors have often not only owned their newspapers but closely controlled their editorial and political lines as well, and turned them, by constant and even daily intervention, into vehicles of their personal views.

(Miliband, 1972: 205)

To assess the validity of this approach, we must examine two separate issues. First, is it *true* that ownership and control of the news media are concentrated in the hands of a relatively few corporations and individuals? And second, do owners of media organs *use* their power to influence output in ways favourable to themselves?

As we saw in Chapter 1, a few corporations control about 90 per cent of the British press; a handful control the commercial broadcasting organisations. These are demonstrable facts, but what is their sociological significance? Do owners use their economic power as an ideological weapon?

The liberal pluralist answer to this question is that they do not, for two reasons. First, it is argued, 'economic ownership of the media has become increasingly separated from managerial control due to the growing dispersal of share ownership' (Curran, 1990: 143). The argument is frequently heard in relation to the capitalist economic system as a whole, and states simply that, as a rule, no single individual or corporation holds enough shares in any particular media outlet to influence its editorial direction. Nowadays, it is argued, the majority of shares are held by pension funds, investment houses and, since the Thatcher Government introduced 'popular capitalism' and the 'share-owning democracy' to the UK, the people. The simplest reply to this argument is that, if it is true that many more people own shares than used to be the case, the small shareholder in the media, as in any other sector of business, is virtually powerless against the weight of the large holdings. There *are* some constraints on media ownership, but as the Thatcher Government showed in its dealings with Rupert Murdoch in the 1980s (when he sought to add *The Times* and the *Sunday Times* to his newspaper empire), these can often be waived if it is politically convenient to do so.

This brings us to a second objection frequently made to the economic approach. Some observers may accept that there is excessive concentration of ownership in the media today, but will argue against this that 'journalists enjoy a considerable degree of independence from supervisory control' (*ibid.*: 143). Robin Morgan points out that during the Conservative Party leadership struggle in November 1990, the *Sunday Times*, under the editorship of Andrew Neil, supported Michael Heseltine against the wishes of proprietor Rupert Murdoch. Such examples prove, he argues, 'the unpopular truth that proprietors concede a considerable amount of independence to editors and invest millions in their instincts and views with only one condition – circulation success'.[1]

There are many examples to suggest the opposite, however. Rupert Murdoch has taken a great personal interest in the running of his media properties, frequently intervening directly to impose a certain editorial line, or to prevent a story being reported. It is entirely routine for journalists to see their copy altered on grounds of stylistic inadequacy or lack of space. The interventions with which we are concerned here, however, are those that have their roots in the political or business interests of the proprietor.

In an interview before his death, Robert Maxwell boasted that his ownership of national newspapers gave him the power 'to raise issues effectively. In simple terms, it's a megaphone'.[2] Political journalist Anthony Bevins once argued straightforwardly that 'dissident reporters who do not deliver the goods suffer professional death. They are ridden by news desks and back bench executives, they have their stories spiked on a systematic basis, they face the worst form of newspaper punishment – by-line deprivation' (Bevins, 1990: 15). Murdoch's *Sunday Times* editors deliberately and without permission altered copy written by journalists on the 'death on the Rock affair' in order to cast a bad light on the programme's producers and sources. The journalists concerned subsequently felt compelled to resign from the paper.

In 1998, Rupert Murdoch personally vetoed his book publishing company's agreement to publish former Hong Kong Governor Chris Patten's memoirs. A number of 'innocent' explanations for this decision were given by company representatives, but few observers doubted that Mr Murdoch's desire, because of his business ambitions, not to upset the new governors of Hong Kong, was the most important consideration. Some commentators have further alleged, despite the denials of News International editors, that 'editorial decision-making about China was driven by the business demands of Mr Murdoch' and that, in particular, 'bad news' about China was regularly censored in *The Times* and other News International organs.[3] Recent evidence to the UK Parliament's Communication Committee by News International editors and former editors confirmed that Murdoch exercises a greater degree of proprietorial control over at least some of his newspapers, depending on his assessment of their importance within a particular political space. Andrew Neil, for example, described Murdoch as the 'editor-in-chief' of the *Sun* in the UK and the *New York Post* in the USA. The current editor of the *Sun*, Rebekah Wade, on the other hand, stated that editorial interference 'just doesn't happen'.[4] Murdoch himself, when he appeared before the Committee, characterised his proprietorial style in the UK thus:

> There is nothing I can do as far as *The Times* and *Sunday Times* are concerned, but when it comes to the *Sun* and the *News of the World* I am a traditional proprietor.[5]

Whether they wish to do so or not, the main mechanism by which proprietors can exert control over newspapers and commercial broadcast news outlets is their power to appoint key personnel, particularly senior editors, who become the proprietor's 'voice' within the newsroom, ensuring that journalistic 'independence' conforms to the preferred editorial line. These are hardly earth-shattering statements, despite the attempts of some commentators to assert the role of journalistic independence, and its continuing importance in maintaining a free press. Few modern proprietors, and certainly not Rupert Murdoch, would bother to deny that they use their media interests not just to make money, but to influence public opinion and the political environment. Robert Maxwell's views have already been quoted. Other proprietors, from Lords Northcliffe and Beaverbrook onwards (Engel, 1996), have made similar statements, and many have shown a willingness to suppress or distort material that could have affected their business interests directly. Journalists and editors may attempt to resist such intervention, as in the case of the *Observer*'s dealings with the Lonrho company over a number of years, and guarantees of editorial independence are frequently written into takeover deals (such as Rupert Murdoch's purchase of *The Times* newspapers in 1981), but the economic power wielded by the proprietor continues to be the single most important determinant of a news outlet's editorial line.

There are significant constraints on proprietorial influence, however. Privately owned media organisations, like other capitalist enterprises, are required to sell their product – news, and commentary on the news – in a marketplace of increasingly sophisticated consumers, who have access to a large and increasing number of other news sources. Proprietors must therefore pay serious attention to the demands and preferences of these consumers, including their politico-ideological preferences. How else to explain the shift in editorial allegiance of the *Sun* and *News of the World* after 1994, leading to the famous '*Sun* backs Blair' headline during the general election of 1997? Although New Labour made Murdoch's realignment easier by signalling that it would provide him with a sympathetic business environment should it win the election, he and his managers were also driven by their readers' losing patience with the Tories, and opinion poll and other evidence that they were forming a preference for New Labour. Regardless of what Murdoch himself thought of Tony Blair and his colleagues, market conditions to a large extent determined a favourable coverage of Labour in the final, crucial months leading up to their historic election victory. This, although it was expressed in a reversal of the 18-year-long pro-Tory bias of the British press, is an excellent example of economic pressure – in particular, the power of the market – influencing journalistic content.

In 2008, Murdoch let it be known that he might be inclined to look favourably on a Conservative party led by David Cameron, after ten years of loyalty to New Labour almost as complete as that once shown to the Thatcher-era Tories. US commentator Michael Wolff observes in an essay for *Vanity Fair* that 'news, as much as any other media product, must be tailored to what your competitors are doing, to the consumer's shorter and shorter attention span, and to the needs of your particular news brand'.[6]

In addition to the increased power of the news consumer, the traditional power of the press baron is waning as consumer access to news sources expands, expectations change in the face of Web 2.0 media such as *YouTube*, and commercial success depends increasingly on the qualities of the news brand rather than the content of the editorial (see below). At his speech to the Worshipful Company of Stationers and Newspaper Makers on 13 March 2006, Murdoch argued that

> power is moving away from the old elite in our industry – the editors, the chief executives and, let's face it, the proprietors.

He might not like it, but as his purchase of *MySpace* for $600 million in 2006 showed, even Rupert Murdoch cannot prevent the gradual erosion of the power of the top-down media of old, and has accepted the reality of the environment in which his newspapers must now operate.

The power of advertising

Further commercial pressure is exerted, according to some variants of the economic approach, by the constraints placed on journalistic content because of the need to attract and retain advertising revenue. Such pressures exist, no doubt. Companies do on occasion withdraw, or threaten to withdraw, advertisements from publications of which they disapprove. In the USA, for example, big advertisers like Chrysler have been known to put pressure on editors not to publish material on controversial subjects like homosexuality. As Chrysler put it in one letter to potential recipients of its advertising revenue: 'Chrysler expects to be alerted in advance about any piece of writing with a sexual, political or social content that might possibly be construed as provocative'.[7] In America, too, *Sports Illustrated* magazine reportedly lost $1 million worth of advertising revenue when it published a profile of a gay athlete.

The significance of this factor as a censorial or conservative influence on journalism should not be overstated, however, since it is also true that commercial logic requires companies to advertise in popular media outlets, regardless of their political complexion. The founding editor of the *Independent* downplays the power of this particular economic force when he points out that 'newspapers have so many individual advertisers that no single one has leverage'.[8] One can go further and say that the economic logic of cultural capitalism determines that, if there is a market for it, journalism that is critical of capital, even of capitalism, will find an outlet and thrive in the commercial market place. The success of Michael Moore's feature-length documentaries is the most obvious example of the fact that dissenting journalism sells, and that there is a substantial counter-cultural market place in which radical, anti-systemic journalism can be heard. I have argued elsewhere that this trend is one factor diving the emergence of 'cultural chaos' (McNair, 2006a). This term refers to a politico-ideological climate in which traditional paradigms and oppositions have dissolved, leaving the field of journalism more open than ever before to genuine criticism of established ideas and orders. Where there is market demand, be it for anti-globalisation polemic or pro-environmental campaigning (and there is clearly demand for both in the early twenty-first century), it will be reported, often favourably, regardless of the interests or personal views of the proprietor. Australian scholar David McKnight has observed that Rupert Murdoch's British newspapers, having once been reso- lutely opposed to the idea of man-made global warming (where they covered the environment at all) are increasingly covering the issue in depth, and not unsympathetically. Why? Because, one assumes, Murdoch and his managers and editors know that their readers, just as they moved away from Conservative and towards Labour in the mid-1990s, are now embracing the arguments of the environmental campaigners (2007).

The above points on the political economy of journalism relate only to the privately-owned media. The public service broadcasting system, as we have noted, was set up precisely to avoid the possibility that radio and TV could be abused by commercial or political interests. The BBC is 'owned' by the state, funded from public taxation, and has its political independence from the executive branch of government constitutionally guaranteed. The commercial broadcasters are allowed to make profits for their shareholders, but are tightly regulated to prevent outright political biases from surfacing in their journal- ism. The economic perspective argues that such a system will nevertheless tend to produce output which is in the basic interests of the dominant economic group. In 1972, Ralph Miliband argued persuasively that the cultural institu- tions of capitalism tend to be staffed and managed by people drawn from the same elites which control the business, political and military power centres. Coming from the same family backgrounds, going to the same public schools and universities, occupying similar places in the class structure, they tend to share the same values.

It is possible to show empirically that those who control broadcasting *do* indeed tend to conform to the pattern Miliband described some 30 years ago, as measured, for example, by the proportion of former public school and Oxbridge graduates who sat on the BBC's Board of Governors (or sit now on its successor body, the BBC Trust), or the Independent Television Commis- sion, or who are editors of newspapers. A 2006 report by the Sutton Trust found that 'leading news and current affairs journalists – those figures who are so central in shaping public opinion and national debate – are more likely than not to have been to independent schools which educate just 7% of the popu- lation. Of the top 100 journalists in 2006, 54% were independently educated [i.e., in private schools], an increase from 49% in 1986.'[9] Forty-five per cent of leading journalists surveyed that year attended Oxbridge, while only 14 per cent attended comprehensive schools (up from 8 per cent in 1986). The dom- inance of a particular socio-economic group or class in the media is far from absolute, and the links between economic and educational privilege and media power are weakening, but many believe that attendance at Oxbridge still counts for more in achieving power within the BBC and other key institutions than some other considerations, such as merit.

But does the class profile of the journalistic media's senior management mean that the organisations necessarily reflect a class bias in their output? The evidence here is contradictory. On the one hand, since the establishment of the BBC in the 1920s, British broadcasters have frequently aligned themselves to a concept of the 'national interest' defined by the establishment. As historians of British broadcasting have frequently noted, during the General Strike of 1926 the BBC refused to allow representatives of the trade union movement, or even of the official Labour Party opposition in Parliament, access to the airwaves to put the strikers' case. By 1926 the BBC had become part of the British state, 'with roles and functions delegated to it by Parliament, committed to coop-eration with government and sharing its assumptions about what constituted the "national interest"' (Scannell and Cardiff, 1991: 39). After their establish-ment in the 1950s, the commercial broadcasting organisations were subsumed into the same system, while the majority of newspapers have tended to be on the right politically. Yet there have been many examples of both the BBC and the commercial media coming into conflict with the British state, or with the government of the day. From the Munich crisis of 1938 (identified by Scannell and Cardiff as the first such instance), through the Suez crisis, the Falklands War and the conflict in Northern Ireland, to the invasion of Iraq and its aftermath in the Gilligan affair, the David Kelly suicide and the Hutton inquiry (see Chapter 7), journalists have often found themselves at loggerheads with politicians over the content of their coverage.

Politics and journalism

The economic interests of media proprietors may be expressed in the more-or-less direct support of their media organs for political parties, as in News International's support for the Conservative governments of the 1980s and early 1990s. We should remember, however, that politicians have their own motives and interests in seeking to influence news and journalism, indepen-dently of their business supporters. These motives and interests may be selfish, as when politicians seek to suppress damaging facts about their performance (many examples of attempted cover-ups, from many countries of the world, could be cited, but Watergate and Irangate in the USA, or arms-to-Iraq and cash-for-questions in Britain, are well known cases). In such cases, political intervention in the workings of the journalistic media may become a source of bad news in itself, leading to greater political damage in the long run.

Political intervention in the media may, on the other hand, have the more legitimate function of trying to maximise the effective administration and good government of society. Legal censorship of sex and violence in film and TV drama is one accepted function of government, as is the placing of restrictions on the more intrusive reporting of the press (a recurring source of political pressure on British journalism, from the excesses of the 1980s *Sun* to the much-criticised coverage of the Madeleine McCann case in 2007, subsequently the subject of court action). Another example of political influence of this type in the British news media would be the Conservative Government's 1988–94 ban on the broadcasting of statements by Sinn Féin representatives. This form of political censorship was defended by ministers on the grounds that it would deny Sinn Féin and its terroristic allies in Northern Ireland 'the oxygen of publicity'. In fact, it merely allowed members of Sinn Féin to be portrayed across the world as victims, and was eventually repealed when the 1994 IRA ceasefire was declared.

Insofar as governments have the power to impose such restrictions, and regardless of the rationale used to justify such imposition, they are clearly an important factor in the analysis of journalistic production. One observer writes of the political pressures on an organisation like the BBC that 'the BBC's future is entirely in the hands of the government of the day. There were many close shaves under the Tories, who did not like Auntie's inbuilt Liberal bias' (see Chapter 4).[10] New Labour, too, has shown a readiness to attack the BBC. From the famous 'O.J. fax' of 1995 (when Alistair Campbell sought to change the BBC's news agenda to the benefit of a Tony Blair conference speech), to well publicised attacks on individual BBC interviewers such as John Humphrys and Jeremy Paxman, culminating in the aforementioned Gilligan affair of 2003 and the subsequent Hutton inquiry into the BBC's reportage of the infamous government dossier on weapons of mass destruction, Labour has shown itself to be just as likely to interfere (or at least attempt to) with the corporation's editorial content.

Professional–organisational approaches

Professional–organisational approaches to the study of journalism reject an overly deterministic stress on the political and economic factors of journalistic production, focusing instead on the professional culture and organisational structure underpinning the process: the implementation of the objectivity ethic, as well as the limitations imposed by the news form, deadline pressures and other elements of routine journalistic practice.

Bruhn-Jensen notes that 'the news form is at least to some extent a function of the organisational structure which is needed for large-scale communication of information to the public' (Bruhn-Jensen, 1986: 46), while Paul Rock emphasises that 'news is the result of an organised response to routine bureaucratic problems' (Rock, 1973: 73), such as the need to produce material according to strict limits on space and timing. Both print and broadcast journalists must present news within certain confines of space and layout (in the case of the former) and, in television and radio, according to conventions on such matters as running order. For online journalists, the look of words and pictures on the screen, and the ease with which material on the internet can be navigated, are key to success. These constraints, argues Rock, determine 'the rough system of priorities which will be allocated to the description of events; decide the proportion that these reports will occupy in the total presentation; and limit the entire volume of events which can evoke a journalistic reaction' (*ibid*.: 75). The availability of space, according to this perspective, is a basic organisational factor which may explain, better than any presumption of bias, why a certain newsworthy item is absent from a news programme or newspaper.

Time, too, is an important organisational factor. Galtung and Ruge (1973: 63) point out that events are far more likely to make it onto the news agenda if their time frame 'fits' the rhythm of the news outlet concerned. Newspapers, for example, appear daily. They are therefore more likely to report events if they can be made sense of within a 24-hour time frame. News has to be comprehensible to the audience as an 'event' with a beginning, a middle and an end. Events that can be presented this way are more newsworthy than those that are not. Rock suggests that Western newspapers (and broadcast news outlets) are 'unable to contend with slow-moving historical cycles; they are far better equipped to accommodate rapid, unexpected change. They are generally incapable of reporting what seem to be indeterminate or fluid situations' (*ibid*.: 77). More 'fluid' and 'indeterminate' stories will be reported in the context of weekly current affairs programmes, or one-off documentaries, or perhaps in weekly print media, but will tend to be absent from regular, daily news until they 'explode' in such a way as to be unavoidable. The *process* by which famine in Africa came about and is perpetuated has largely been ignored by mainstream news outlets: only when Michael Buerk 'discovered' the refugee camps in Ethiopia in 1985, with all the picture-opportunities they presented and the individual stories that could be told, did the famine become 'news', and then only as an event, rather than a process.

Journalists, then, must construct their news 'to meet the space and time-tabling demands of [the journalistic organisation]' (*ibid*.). Not only does this help to explain why news is characteristically about events rather than processes, and effects rather than causes; it might also be thought to be part of the reason why news media tend, as content analysis shows, to favour the definitions of the powerful when constructing their accounts of events. 'Because of the demands of time and deadlines', argues Rock, 'journalists are inclined to position themselves so that they have ready access to institutions which guarantee a useful volume of reportable activity at useful intervals'.

A variant of the organisational approach explains journalistic output in relation to the codes and conventions of the profession: what are often referred to as 'routine professional practices'. As the previous chapter noted, Gaye Tuchman has argued that the practice of objectivity is best viewed as a 'strategic ritual' performed by journalists in order to command authority and legitimacy in the view of the audience (Tuchman, 1972: 661). Like academic writers, journalists must be seen to be objective in the conduct of their profession, and to this end they have developed a number of conventions which are used when constructing material.

To be 'objective', Tuchman argues, the journalist must present both sides of a story (or, in the case of a more complex debate, all credible sides); supporting evidence for any assertions made in the story must be provided; *authoritative* sources, such as politicians must be quoted (in this way the journalist is seen to distance him or herself from the views reported by establishing that they are someone else's opinions); 'fact' must be separated from 'opinion' and 'hard news' from 'editorial comment'; and the presentation of information must be structured pyramidically, with the most important bits coming first, at the 'top' of the story.

Taken together, the pursuit of these practices signifies 'objectivity' to, and thus mobilises the trust of, the audience. In a TV news political story, for example, 'objectivity' would demand that the views of a Labour source be balanced by those of an equivalently senior Conservative, and also by a Liberal Democrat; and that a recognised 'specialist' correspondent be enlisted to give an authoritative comment on the situation. The newsreader will not give his or her opinion directly, since this would break with the conventions of impartiality (see above).

Technology and journalism

The technology of newsgathering is also an important explanatory factor in the sociology of journalism, since the introduction of new information and communication technologies inevitably has an impact on the nature of the journalistic production process, and on the form and content of journalism. Some examples: the invention of lightweight video cameras has greatly increased the mobility of correspondents in the field, while the availability of laptop computers, satellite uplinks and digital editing has enhanced their 'live-ness' and ability to prepare coherent accounts of what is happening on the spot.

Such innovations increase the possibilities of newsgathering, but have also increased the pressures on journalists to deliver 'news' before anyone has had time to think about and analyse the events being reported. The result is what Nik Gowing has called, in response to the rise of CNN and other channels, and even more applicable in the era of the internet, 'real-time news' (Gowing, 1994); and Brent MacGregor 'knee-jerk grandstanding' (MacGregor, 1997) – content of such immediacy and intimacy that it may destabilise the political environment in which the news is received, and hinder rather than clarify public understanding of complex events.

New technologies have also destabilised the boundaries that used to exist between print, radio and TV journalism, and between all those and online journalism. They have driven the development of multimedia and convergence in news production (see Chapter 8). Today's journalists are increasingly expected to produce content for use in print or broadcasting *and* online for-mats (sometimes all three), including video packages for podcasts. The BBC is moving its news organisation away from TV and radio departments towards multimedia structures that assume all content can be made digitally accessible across a range of platforms. These innovations have implications for the form and content of professional journalism, as well as enabling and encouraging the increased use of what is sometimes known as 'citizen journalism' or *user-generated content*. Increasingly, what is seen on TV screens and websites, or on newspaper front pages, alongside the input of the professionals, is images and text provided by amateurs lucky (or unlucky) enough to have been on the scene of a major newsworthy event, such as the Asian tsunami of 2004 or the September 11 attacks on the World Trade Center in New York.

The culturalist approach

Professional–organisational and technological explanations of content tend to be opposed to the political and economic approaches, stressing the constraints acting on journalists rather than the ideological biases emanating from or directed at them. Both sets of approaches are not mutually exclusive, however, and a paradigm has emerged which actively seeks to integrate them. What James Curran once called the *culturalist* approach links elements of all the above approaches within a framework that retains a materialist analysis but incorporates elements of the pluralist model. It has evolved as a result of the difficulties experienced by sociologists in trying to reconcile the materialist approach with the visible evidence of dissenting journalism. Consequently, it focuses not on who owns the news media, but on how those media are positioned relative to the power elites within society. It locates the source of 'bias' in the environment external to the journalistic organisations, so that content is not simply a function of ownership, or political pressure, or of journalistic practices and rituals, but of the interaction between formally autonomous news organisations, the sources of their output, and other social institutions.

An early example of the application of this approach is contained in Hall *et al.*'s (1978) *Policing the Crisis*. This study argued, as we saw in Chapter 2, that the media tend to engineer moral panics and amplify deviance, using as evidence press coverage of the 'mugging' scare of the early 1970s. Having made this observation at the level of content analysis, the authors went on to explain how they wished to 'draw attention to the more routine structures of news production to see how the media come in fact, in the "last instance", to reproduce the definitions of the powerful, without being, in a simple sense, in their pay' (*ibid.*: 57).

They went on to map out 'structures of dominance' within which the representatives of power elites tend to enjoy privileged access to the media as sources of information and, importantly, the interpretive frameworks which journalists then use to construct their stories. These privileged sources become what Hall *et al.* called the *primary definers* of news. The journalists, who take on these primary definitions and then circulate them in their stories, become *secondary definers*.

An organisational account of this 'structured bias' towards the powerful would focus primarily on such causes as the pressures of deadlines. Hall *et al.* argue that journalists, in any case, share the *culturally consensual* assumption that these are automatically the most credible, authoritative sources of information, and have privileged access to the media almost as of right. The powerless, on the other hand, are not seen as credible sources of knowledge and explanation, and tend as a result to be marginalised in journalists' accounts. In this model, journalistic media are seen not as crude instruments of class power, but rather as neutral channels through which social power – what Schlesinger calls *definitional* power – flows. The journalists are not *necessarily* biased towards the powerful – but their routine assumptions make them willing conduits of that power. Curran explains

> the culturalist thesis assumes that authority within media organisations is devolved to relatively autonomous journalists. Their reporting is structured by cultural and ideological influences – whether inscribed in news routines, relayed through sources, mediated through market influences, or simply absorbed from the dominant climate of opinion – rather than by hierarchical supervision and control.
>
> (Curran, 1989: 120)

The sociology of sources

In the 1980s, Philip Schlesinger and others developed the culturalist framework in the direction of what came to be known as *source-centred* approaches, presenting a critique of the earlier primary definition model developed by Hall. For Schlesinger, this *hegemonic* model was too tightly bound to the concept of dominant ideology and failed to recognise that, in many instances, there is no single primary definition of an issue or an event's meaning; that structures of access to the media – through which primary definitions emerge – shift over time as the political environment changes; and that primary definitions are the product of complex processes of contestation and negotiation between competing social actors. The primary definition thesis, for Schlesinger, 'tends to understate the amount of conflict among those who principally define the political agenda in "polyarchic" political systems; it is largely atemporal; it ignores how new forces may reshape definitional space; and finally, overstates the passivity of the media' (Schlesinger, 1991: 64). The source-centred approach shifts attention away from the journalists towards the various categories of source professional now active in the public arena – public relations professionals of various types, who are paid to shape the news agenda and to persuade journalists that certain definitions of events (certain 'spins' on things) are preferable to others.

In general, such approaches are more optimistic than some of those reviewed above, as they imply that 'shifts within the power structure, and in the field of contestation in which the media are situated, can lead to space being given to definitions that are opposed to those that are dominant' (Curran, 1989: 117). The relative autonomy of journalism highlighted by the source-centred approach means that subordinate or marginalised political actors can make the news agenda and influence public debate. It suggests that a struggle takes place, outside the media organisations themselves, for *access*, shifting the critical emphasis away from journalistic bias to the skill and entrepreneurship of social actors in winning this access.

The culturalists concede, however, that access to the journalistic media is not equitable: the powerful can call on greater resources to attract the journalists' attention than poorly funded pressure groups or political parties. The Prime Minister's office has far more power to shape the news agenda than the Opposition leader. The Opposition leader, in turn, has more 'definitional power' than the leader of the Liberal Democratic Party. But the general point remains: the news media in liberal democratic capitalist societies are relatively open to oppositional and dissenting viewpoints. From this perspective, such 'openness' is the condition for the wider legitimacy of the system.

Propaganda versus gatekeeper models: the case of Chomsky and Herman

To explore further the differences between the approaches reviewed above, we can look briefly at the work of Noam Chomsky and Ed Herman, who reject the range of professional–organisational and culturalist approaches – what they call 'gatekeeper' models, because they imply that journalists and their sources, rather than proprietors and owners, are the key actors in the production of news – described above. In a 1986 essay, Ed Herman accepts that gatekeeper models, with their 'stress on the possibilities of dissent, openings and space', have contributed a great deal to the sociology of journalism, but criticises them for failing to reconcile theoretically the materialist hypothesis that the media have a reproductive social function with their apparent 'openness' to dissent. Gatekeeper models *do* tend to support the materialist view that the media are biased towards the *status quo* (explaining this with reference to external or organisational factors), but have not satisfactorily theorised the significance to this model of 'openness' and the presence of oppositional accounts of events within the news. They are, he argues, something of a ragbag.

Instead, Herman argues for a 'propaganda model' of journalistic production, so-called because it can be employed, as he puts it, 'to analyse the numerous and important cases where the mass media serve as instruments in campaigns of ideological mobilisation' (*ibid.*: 175). In using the term 'model', he signifies his intention to develop an analysis that can *predict* the way in which news and journalistic media will report particular events. Premised on a straightforward economic framework, the propaganda model asserts that the media's (assumed) power to manage and manipulate public opinion will be used by elites in the pursuit of what they define as the 'national interest'. It also asserts that cases of media dissent are exceptional, and relatively insignificant when set against the more general tendency of journalists to reproduce dominant ideology.

The empirical case for the propaganda model comprises the observation that the US media tend to apply a 'dichotomous treatment' to coverage of international events, according to the political context within which they occur. During the period of the Cold War, for example, dissidents in the Soviet Union and its satellites were covered far more intensively (if one considers the relative scale and frequency of the human rights abuses being reported) than those in 'friendly' countries such as Brazil, El Salvador and Uruguay. US coverage of the imposition of martial law in Poland vastly exceeded that of a similar clampdown that took place around the same time in Turkey, a NATO ally. As Herman puts it, 'these dichotomies have great ideological significance' (*ibid.*: 177), and are the direct consequence of decisions by elites in the economic, political and military sectors of American society, often linked to parallel elites in the media, to highlight some phenomena, marginalise others, and manage public opinion in a manner that suits the 'national interest'. For Chomsky and Herman, the American news media function as 'propaganda agencies' of the 'national security state'. They seek to demonstrate empirically

> the capacity of Western ideological institutions [principally the media] to falsify, obscure and reinterpret the facts in the interests of those who dominate the economy and political system ... and the process of brainwashing under freedom as manifested in the selection and analysis of issues by the media.
>
> (Chomsky and Herman, 1979: 71)

As one of their case studies, they take the category of 'terrorism' and argue that 'among the many symbols used to frighten and manipulate the populaces of the democratic states, few have been more important than "terror" and "terrorism"' (*ibid.*: 6). They argue, on the basis of detailed content analyses of American press and broadcasting journalism, that US journalists use these terms in ways that serve the interests of the economic, political and military establishments.

Chomsky and Herman distinguish between three categories of terror: *constructive* – 'that which positively serves important domestic interests'; *benign* – 'that which is of little direct interest to the elite but may sometimes serve the interests of a friendly client'; and *nefarious* – 'that committed by enemy states (or by bearers of hostile ideologies)'. According to these authors, examples of 'constructive' and 'benign' terror tend to be ignored or marginalised in US news coverage of foreign affairs (Herman, 1982: 146). For example, when in the 1970s tens of thousands of people were killed in Central America by regimes armed and financed by the USA, this was not defined by journalists, they argue, as 'terror', but tended to be ignored by the media. Violence by Arab groups in the Middle East, on the other hand, was highlighted by the media, labelled as 'terrorism', and condemned. Their point was not that 'terrorism' should not be covered, but that 'mass media attention to it is a function not of terror *per se* but of the relation of terror to larger national interests' (*ibid.*: 164).

Chomsky and Herman have also studied human rights coverage, observing that here, too, human rights abuses in friendly states tend to be ignored by the US media, while those that occur in enemy states are highlighted. From these and other examples, they argue that the propaganda model can be used, systematically, to explain the characteristics of particular news stories and media campaigns, such as the one that followed the shooting down of the Korean airliner in late August 1983 (Herman, 1986). In the USA, as in other NATO countries, coverage of the incident was unprecedented in quantity and quality. The Soviets were denounced by Ronald Reagan as 'terrorists', 'barbarians' and 'murderers'. It was alleged that they had known KAL 007 to be a civilian airliner when they ordered it shot down (it was later conceded by the CIA that, in fact, the Soviets had believed KAL 007 to be a military spy-plane, possibly the RC-135 which had been in the area on a top-secret mission at the same time as the Korean plane). The US media reproduced the Reagan administration's line virtually without qualification in a torrent of coverage. The resulting media image of the USSR as a 'criminal regime', and its impact on public opinion, contributed substantially to a mood in which previously contentious key Administration arms procurements, such as the MX-missile and binary gas weapons, were passed by Congress without protest. In Europe, too, the KAL affair effectively ended what had been until then mass opposition to cruise missiles and other NATO deployments.[11]

The KAL 007 affair was a tragic and distressing incident. Herman points out, however, that coverage of similar incidents in the past, such as the Israeli shooting down of a Libyan airliner in 1973, with 108 lives lost, was much less aggressive and accusatory because, Herman suggests, the Israelis were an ideological ally, a friendly state in a strategic area of the world. The Soviets, on the other hand, were the 'enemy', whose existence was at that time the main justification for the US Defense Department's $300 trillion budget. Thus it was in the interests of the American 'National Security State' to highlight the KAL 007 disaster, firmly blame the Soviets for it, and marginalise any evidence that might have suggested a genuine error on the part of the Soviet military, or even worse, implicated the US government.

Herman's essay was published in 1986. Two years later, in June 1988, an opportunity arose to test the propaganda model. That month, in the Gulf of Arabia, the US navy opened fire on an Iranian passenger jet, which had just taken off on a scheduled flight through international airspace; 279 civilians were killed. The American military, like the Soviets five years before, claimed that the Iranian Airbus had been mistaken for a hostile military aircraft, which was probably the case. While the Soviet defence of their actions in 1983 was dismissed as the cynical propaganda of cold-blooded murderers, the official US account of what had happened to the Iranian plane set the news agenda from the outset. In this comparative analysis, the propaganda model correctly predicted how the media would report the two incidents.

Chomsky and Herman are often criticised for their tendency to generalise from the American experience to those of all liberal, democratic, capitalist societies, including Britain where, clearly, the political and economic environments within which the media work are very different. However, a comparative analysis of British television news coverage of the KAL 007 and Iran Air shootdowns shows some consistency with the propaganda model. In the case of KAL 007, the TV news agenda was set, from the outset, by the Reagan administration. Ronald Reagan's view of the shootdown as 'a barbaric, terrorist, heinous act', an 'atrocity', a 'massacre', and an 'unspeakable act of inhuman brutality' quickly became the primary definition of the event.[12] Since the Soviet account – that KAL 007 had been involved in some kind of US/CIA reconnaissance mission – could not be taken seriously, elaborate theories had to be worked up to explain how a Jumbo jet, equipped with three independently functioning navigational computers and flown by one of the most experienced pilots in South Korea, could have accidentally penetrated 500 kilometres into Soviet airspace, by coincidence passing over one of the most sensitive Soviet defence establishments, just at a time when the 'new Cold War' was at its peak. The 'Marie Celeste' hypothesis was made the basis of one news item, for example, postulating that a sudden loss of cabin pressure had caused the plane's occupants to lose consciousness. Such efforts to explain the inexplicable reflect the journalists' adoption of the Reagan administration's framework for making sense of the incident – its 'primary definer' status.

This privileged status was also evident in coverage of the Airbus disaster. Here, however, the effect was to minimise media interest. On 2 September 1983, 48 hours after the KAL story broke, the BBC's *Nine O'Clock News* devoted 19 of its 25 minutes to the incident. ITN's *News at Ten* gave the story 13 minutes. At the same stage in the Airbus shooting, the story warranted only 5 minutes 40 seconds on BBC1, and 4 minutes 6 seconds on ITV. *Channel 4 News*, which has almost an hour to deal with stories 'in depth', gave it 1 minute 51 seconds of news time that day.[13] The Reagan administration's definition of the event as an 'understandable accident', for which the Iranians themselves were largely to blame, was accepted uncritically. Indeed, the Iranians were portrayed as cynically exploiting the tragedy for their own ends.

In this case, then, the propaganda model seems to fit. Two very similar incidents produced two entirely different patterns of coverage. This does not, however, mean that the propaganda model is superior to the gatekeeper model, always and everywhere. The extent to which journalism is open to alternative or oppositional accounts of controversial events is dependent upon the political and economic frameworks within which the journalism is pursued (public service or commercial, a more or less strict censorship regime, etc.); the extent to which elites are united behind one particular reading of an event; and the skill of the source-strategies employed by the protagonists competing for access to the media. It is also a reflection of the east–west, capitalist–communist divide which structured politics and ideology in the years from 1945 to 1989, during which journalists and media on both sides subscribed to rigid views of an enemy Other, and routinely produced 'images of the enemy' (McNair, 1988). In the post-Cold War years, as traditional ideological divisions have broken down to be replaced by resurgent nationalist, ethnic and religious conflicts, the propaganda model has looked increasingly creaky as a way of describing or predicting coverage of events in, say, Kosovo, Afghanistan or Iraq. While some on the left, such as journalist John Pilger, continue to adhere to it and use it to criticise the Western media for 'demonising' a figure like Saddam Hussein, others welcome the journalistic exposé of the human rights abuses of dictators such as Hussein and Slobodan Milosevic, and the fact that Western news organisations regularly provide space for public debate on such issues as the appropriate Western response to al-Quaida and the September 11 attacks.

One does not have to accept Bush administration definitions of 'the war against terror' to see that Chomsky and Herman's propaganda model, developed in the very different ideological and political environments of the 1970s and 1980s, no longer corresponds to the openness and diversity of view present in much Western (and certainly, British) journalism in the current period. Even the near-universal revulsion that greeted the September 11 attacks in New York soon gave way to expressions of dissent in the mainstream media, written by such as John Pilger, Susan Sontag and Noam Chomsky himself, as they sought to resist the rush to hasty retaliation and all-out war with those countries and organisations grouped together in George W. Bush's 'axis of evil'. On the first anniversary of the September 11 attacks, on 12 September 2002, the British current-affairs programme *Question Time* broadcast a special edition from New York. Among the panel were Sheikh Hamza, a well known Muslim scholar, and Michael Moore, best-selling author of *Stupid White Men* and fierce opponent of US foreign policy in the Middle East. On this peak-time programme, Moore frequently talked of Bush as a 'liar' and of US foreign policy as corrupt and hypocritical. Whether or not one agrees with his views, there can be no doubt that Moore and others found ample mainstream media space in which to express them, as the US built up to war with Iraq. In the UK, coverage of the war itself was frequently critical of the US and Blair governments, and far from being 'propaganda' (Tumber and Palmer, 2004).

Conclusions

The various approaches to the sociology of journalism reviewed in this chapter are not mutually exclusive. But they are premised on profound differences as to the nature of the state's functioning, of journalism's role and the concept of ideology. From one perspective, the economic base determines in various ways (economic ownership, competition for advertising revenue) the form of the cultural and ideological superstructure, of which the journalism industry comprises a major part. Economic, political and managerial control of the means of intellectual production by a dominant class ensures the percolating down through society as a whole of that class's ideology, which thus also becomes 'dominant'. Subordinate or oppositional ideas are excluded by or marginalised in the mainstream media.

Culturalist and source-centred perspectives, on the other hand, assert that the cultural institutions of advanced capitalism are sites of struggle between competing ideological positions. Some groups have privileged access to these sites, by virtue of economic or political status, and thus their ways of seeing the world may become 'hegemonic'. They are, however, frequently contested in the struggle to make sense of the events and issues thrown up by social and economic processes. In liberal pluralist societies, it is argued, the relative autonomy, objectivity and impartiality of journalistic media must be taken seriously by journalists, who will preserve spaces in which subordinate ideas and dissenting explanations can be heard, even if only on the fringes of mainstream media output. Without such openness, characterisations of the system as pluralistic or democratic would be much harder to sustain.

The professional–organisational perspective (and the technological, which may be viewed as a sub-category of the organisational), finally, tends to absolve journalists from much of the responsibility for their output by saying that the constraints and conventions imposed on their work – whether imposed by audience expectations, limitations on resources, or the demands of deadlines – are more important in understanding output than any concept of ideological class bias, no matter how 'open' one concedes it to be.

Each of these approaches has a contribution to make to the understanding of how and why journalism is produced. There clearly are proprietors who actively seek to influence the content and tone of their media, whether by the appointment of key editorial personnel, or simply by attempting to 'spike' stories they do not like. Others adopt a 'hands-off' proprietorial style, content to view their properties as cash cows, rather than instruments of ideological and political influence. Some combine both approaches, depending on the media property in question. Rupert Murdoch, by his own admission, is more likely to call the editor of the *Sun* in the middle of the night than his or her counterpart at *The Times*. While the 'megaphone' approach works for the *Sun*, and is expected of it, market forces demand the perception of greater editorial independence from *The Times*. On his appointment as editor of *The Times* in 2002, Robert Thomson declared that the title would remain 'a fact-based newspaper at the quality end of the market ... not at all ideological in its news pages and as objective as any journalism can be'.[14] And so, most observers of *The Times* would agree, it has been. In this case, as in many others, the proprietorial power is subject to significant constraints imposed by the market itself, and the place of a particular media property within it.

Likewise, it is beyond argument that journalists are limited in their work by constraints built into the production process, such as deadlines, limits on space and access to sources. All contribute to the shaping of output and the form of the final product. Any sociological account that fails to acknowledge the importance of these constraints is of minimal value in our understanding of how journalism is made. But neither can one allow journalists to refer all criticisms of their work as 'organisational factors' over which they have no control. Journalists hold beliefs and assumptions about who are the most authoritative and credible sources in the construction of a given story; about what is the most important story on a given day; and about how a story fits in with common sense or 'consensual' ways of seeing the world. These beliefs and assumptions are – inevitably – value-laden, and will tend to reflect the culture within which the journalist is working and has been – or wishes to become – professionally successful.

Thus we arrive at the culturalist position, which stresses the dynamic, conflictual nature of the processes whereby journalists (and citizens in general) form their values and beliefs. When 'dominant values' begin to fragment – as was seen in Britain after the re-election of the Major government in April 1992, or the succession of Gordon Brown to the UK premiership in June 2007 – the news media (even those traditionally most associated with those values) may move into an adversarial position *vis-à-vis* political and other elites, as they did in reporting the government's decision in the autumn of 1992 to close most of Britain's coal mines, and the succession of sex scandals that dogged John Major's second term. They may, as in the case of the Brown government following the Northern Rock debacle of 2007 and many other perceived failures of post-Blair New Labour, become a site of dissent, contributing to the breakdown of a previously hegemonic worldview and its replacement by another. When the British establishment lacks unity and coherence, the British media reflect that disunity and become more open. This openness can be further stretched and widened by effective source strategies.

Further reading

On the social construction of journalism, see McNair (1998); James Curran's (2002) recent collection of essays reviews and updates many of the debates explored in this chapter.

5 Journalism and its critics – (II) beyond the academy

This chapter contains a review of recent public debates around the content of news and journalism in the UK, organized under the following categories:

- tabloidisation and dumbing down
- feminisation
- hyper-adversarialism and journalistic cynicism
- the crisis of trust in broadcast journalism.

Having explored academic perspectives in Chapters 2 and 3, we turn now to the broader critique of news and journalism in the UK, incorporating the views of both scholars and non-scholars as they survey the media landscape and engage in public debate about the state of the British news media. Later chapters focus on trends and issues affecting the various sectors of the UK journalism industry. This chapter explores the arguments advanced about journalism by commentators in the public sphere – the *meta-discourse* of news, as it were, or journalism about journalism.

Such commentaries are commonplace since the emergence of media supplements in the broadsheet newspapers in the 1980s and 1990s. The expansion of journalism described in Chapter 1 has also contributed to a growing sense that the content of the journalistic media does matter – to the health of democratic processes, to sound social administration and good governance, and to general public well-being and the quality of life. All categories of media output are important, and all are discussed regularly in the media. The state of journalism, however, real or perceived, has the potential to bring forth particularly heated debate, often accompanied by calls for legislation and senior resignations, such as those of the BBC's Director-General and Chairman following the publication of the Hutton report in 2003. We will consider the issues raised by the Hutton inquiry in this chapter. First, though, we will address a long-standing anxiety of observers of British journalism – the extent to which it has been, and is being, degraded by commercial and competitive pressures.

Tabloidisation, infotainment and the dumbing-down debate

The now universally accepted role of the news media as key providers of public information (see Chapter 2) has fuelled concerns about the impact on journalistic quality of processes variously described as 'commodification', 'marketisation', 'tabloidisation' and 'Americanisation'. More recently, commentators have written of the 'McDonaldisation' of journalism, or 'McJournalism', referring to what they characterise as the unwelcome standardisation of content in a process analogous to that adopted by the producers of hamburgers and chicken nuggets.

These trends are argued to be replacing the normative content of news – objective information about issues of public importance, and adequately resourced investigative journalism, perceived by Nick Davies and others to be in crisis in the UK, if not terminal decline (Davies, 2008; De Burgh, 2008) – with a cultural form that is more like entertainment, which is, indeed, 'infotainment'. The rise of infotainment is argued to have major adverse consequences for the integrity of the public sphere and the management of society, insofar as it deprives citizens of the information necessary for them to make rational choices about politics and other significant matters. It trivialises serious issues, marginalises important information, and leads to mass apathy and cynicism about the world – a 'dumbing down' of the culture – which is bad for society as a whole.

For those who support the thesis, the dumbing down of journalism is a consequence principally of heightened commercial pressures and the infiltration of market principles into the previously protected (partially, at least) sphere of public information. In 2004, the UK editor of German periodical *Die Zeit* expressed the argument in clear form, arguing that 'to succeed, the media industry tries to appeal to the lower instincts of people ... to the lowest common denominator'.[1] Even where strictly commercial criteria do not apply to the manufacture of news, as in the case of the BBC, the organisational need for popularity, and for success on market terms, tends to favour the dumbing down of all programming, it is argued. News becomes less concerned with the weighty matters of party politics, economic policy and foreign affairs – 'hard news' – and more with the frivolous topics of presidential affairs (sexual rather than political), celebrity lifestyles, and other staple subjects of the red-top tabloid agenda (or 'soft' news; we recall that most of the former broadsheets have now become tabloids in format). Broadcast current affairs moves away from serious investigative reportage of such matters as corporate fraud and governmental deception towards consumer-oriented doorstepping, or real-life drama about firemen and police officers, or 'docu-soaps' about 'real' people (i.e. non-celebrities). The rise of reality TV and other popular factual genres has squeezed 'serious' current affairs out of the schedules, particularly in the peak time hours of 7–11 in the evening.

Infotainment not only trades seriousness and depth for popularity, the argument continues; it reflects and promotes within its content and style the inappropriate notion of information as a commodity, to be sold with the aid of the most sophisticated marketing techniques available. It promotes the market itself, as John Pilger suggested when he wrote of the BBC in 1998 that its news output is 'now openly ideological and uniform, replete with the assumptions and cliches of the market supercult'.[2] In his *Newszak and News Media* (a title that nicely encapsulates the critics' vision of news as a cultural narcotic), Bob Franklin sums up the argument thus: 'news media have increasingly become part of the entertainment industry instead of providing a forum for informed debate of key issues of public concern' (Franklin, 1997: 4). As a result:

> Journalism's editorial priorities have changed. Entertainment has super-seded the provision of information; human interest has supplanted the public interest; measured judgment has succumbed to sensationalism; the trivial has triumphed over the weighty; the intimate relationships of celebrities, from soap operas, the world of sport or the royal family, are judged more 'newsworthy' than the reporting of significant issues and events of international consequence. Traditional news values have been undermined by new values; 'infotainment' is rampant.

Heightened commercial criteria and the pre-eminence of the profit motive in what is undoubtedly an important and powerful sector of the capitalist culture industry are alleged to have removed the essential public service function of news, transforming journalistic culture from a source of mass enlightenment and civic empowerment to a cause of mass pacification and intellectual degeneration. 'Quality' journalistic media have been forced to go down-market (hence the term 'tabloidisation', referring to the now redundant notion of the tabloid newspaper as a form of journalism aimed at the C2DE sections of the reading public), adopting the structures of news values, marketing techniques and modes of address characteristic of the popular press since its establishment in the late nineteenth century (Engel, 1996). The *Jerry Springer Show* and its UK-produced imitators, documentaries propounding conspiracy theories about the death of Diana, interminable docu-soaps about life in hotels and on cruise ships, the explosion of reality TV formats – all are cited as evidence of a trend in British journalism away from difficult subject matter towards material which is easy to make and consume, but is lacking in social relevance and significance. The late Anthony Sampson lamented in 2005 that what he termed 'serious journalists' are 'pressed towards more entertainment and sensation, to compete with their rivals, while the distinction between quality papers and tabloids has become less clear-cut'.[3]

The dumbing-down thesis has been until recently a central plank of the critical orthodoxy in journalism studies, featuring prominently in a 'narrative of decline' shared by commentators of left- and right-wing views equally, expressed by journalists and politicians as often as academic observers in newspaper columns, television and radio talk shows, and debates in parliament. It amounts to the assertion that, as far as journalism is concerned, more means less. No-one disputes that there is more news and journalism available to the average citizen than at any time in the UK's cultural history; it is argued, however, that this quantitative growth detracts from, rather than adds to, the quality of the public sphere insofar as it distracts people from the 'important' issues and dulls the senses. For advocates of the dumbing-down thesis, the British people are positioned as the victims of a journalistic trash culture that deprives them of objective information and, ultimately, their democratic right to make informed choices. These are serious charges which, if true, would question the true meaning of all the democratic advances of the past century, and locate the media as the new 'opiate of the people'.[4]

To repeat – this cultural pessimism has been a central plank of the critical orthodoxy for most of this author's professional life as a student of journalism. Increasingly, however, a range of more optimistic views (sometimes lazily labelled 'postmodernist') reject many of the premises that underpin the tabloidisation thesis, arguing instead that, far from dumbing down, Britain is 'braining up', journalistically as in other ways.[5] Steven Johnson's (2005) provocatively titled volume of popular sociology, *Everything Bad Is Good For You*, defends the growing sophistication and complexity of capitalist culture as a whole, taking in everything from computer games to reality TV to *Desperate Housewives*, but his argument also applies to journalism in particular. In the following extract he draws attention to the elitist premises underpinning the dumbing-down thesis.

> For decades we've worked under the assumption that mass culture follows a steadily declining path towards lowest-common-denominator standards, presumably because the 'masses' want dumb, simple pleasures and big media companies want to give the masses what they want. But in fact the opposite is happening; the culture is getting more intellectually demanding, not less.
>
> (Johnson, 2005: 35)

With specific reference to TV news in the UK, Hargreaves and Thomas's study *New News, Old News* notes that 'claims that TV news has dramatically shifted its focus away from "serious" to "light-hearted" or "dumb" news are overstated' (Hargreaves and Thomas, 2002: 96). Leading BBC journalist John Humphrys, meanwhile, writing of the press (and never slow when it comes to identifying negative trends in culture), argued that British newspapers 'are probably better today than they have ever been', and that 'we [the UK population] probably have the best press in the world'.[6] At the end of 2003, former tabloid editor and commentator Roy Greenslade observed that newspapers were, on the whole, devoting more space to the normatively preferred topics of foreign affairs, politics and economics than they had been two decades before, and that domestic news coverage in the UK media had become 'infinitely more comprehensive' as a result.[7] At a more general level, he added:

> The dumbing down debate [is] underpinned by snobbery. Many critics hark back to a time when broadsheets sold only to an elite of which they

were part. They are ignoring the demographic, social and cultural changes
wrought as a result of growing affluence and greater educational attainments.

The argument against the 'dumbing down' thesis is, first and foremost,
empirical. There is, as we have noted, much more news and journalism
circulating in the public sphere than ever before in British history, a fact that,
other things remaining equal, can be considered a good thing in itself. The
public sphere, once a restricted space of journalism and commentary available
mainly to white, male, educated elites, has expanded – thanks to the enhanced
distributive capacity of new information technologies, the internet most
dramatically – to the point of genuine mass accessibility. Through universal
suffrage the masses have, in the course of the twentieth century and into the
twenty-first, for the *first* time in human history acquired political rights The
media have developed to service those rights and make them meaningful.

If this is true as a generality, it is also the case that in specific categories of
journalism, such as broadcast current affairs, the evidence also supports a
degree of optimism about the trends, albeit qualified. Research conducted by
the UK regulator Ofcom in 2006 found that there is more current affairs on
British public service broadcasting than ever before, with the number of hours
devoted to current affairs on the five terrestrial TV channels increasing by 6.5
per cent. Of this output, one-third was devoted to what Ofcom calls 'social
affairs' (including everything from the July 7 London bombings to bird flu, and
the rise in UK demand for surgery conducted overseas). Just under a third was
devoted to domestic and international politics, and the rest to economics,
business, and 'others'. Ofcom noted that over this period, all broadcasters
with a public service remit reached or exceeded their quotas for current affairs
programming (McNair, 2008a). In 2003, former broadcaster David Liddiment
defended the latest example of allegedly 'dumbed-down' current affairs TV
journalism, Martin Bashir's interview with Michael Jackson. In his view,
'indulging our guilty interest in the rich and famous can also be a perfectly
proper role for a current affairs programme'.[8]

On international current affairs – where public service broadcasting is
required to provide audiences with their 'window on the world' – a similar
picture emerges. Seymour and Barnett's report on factual TV about the developing world concludes that 'there has been a resurgence in factual international programming on UK television, following fourteen years of steady
decline. The 2005 total of 1170 hours across all free-to-air public service
channels is the highest recorded' (Seymour and Barnett, 2006: 34). In an article
for the *Guardian*, Barnett reported 'a growth of documentary and serious
factual programmes in peak time', welcoming the evidence of content analysis
conducted by himself and others that 'the Reithian high-culture approach has
been replaced by a more democratic style that is more in keeping with the age
and better exploits the medium'.[9]

The quantitative expansion of current affairs and other categories of journalism has, it is true, been accompanied by the extension of the market as a

regulatory and distributive mechanism, and one consequence of that fact has been the 'colonisation' of the public sphere by a more populist structure of news values and a more diverse mix of styles, appropriate to the diverse, fragmented, mixed-ability audiences of our time. Much of the expansion of coverage of the developing world noted by Seymour and Barnett, for example, includes popular factual genres such as reality TV shows set on tropical islands. It is not, by any means, all about wars, conflict, famine and poverty.

But what is wrong with a bit of entertainment in foreign coverage? 'Quality' journalism (and the term is problematic – who defines what 'quality' is, or 'dumb' for that matter?) thrives in the form of heavyweight newspapers and public service broadcasting, but the undoubtedly important matters of party politics, economics and foreign policy increasingly compete for attention in the contemporary public sphere with coverage of issues which are at least as, if not more, important to ordinary people in their daily lives – subjects of 'human interest', perhaps, but no less important for that (we are all human beings, are we not?). To condemn this trend, it is argued, is profoundly elitist, even reactionary.

Research conducted in the late 1990s for the ITC and the BBC by Steven Barnett and Ivor Gabor found that journalists, as opposed to dumbing down their output, are 'working harder to make difficult stories more understandable to people watching them'. For these authors, describing the situation as they found it in 1999, TV news displays 'a healthy balance of serious, light and international coverage' (Barnett *et al.*, 2000).

The late Pierre Bourdieu's polemic on the decline of French journalism typifies the anti-popular character of the dumbing-down thesis when he asserts that 'human interest stories create a political vacuum. They depoliticise and reduce what goes on in the world to the level of anecdote or scandal' (Bourdieu, 1998: 50). Apart from the fact that this is a huge generalisation, his argument ignores the possibility that for some people – most people, one might tentatively suggest – some anecdote, a little scandal, a little gossip, is part of what makes the world go round; not, hopefully, to the exclusion of 'serious' matters, but as one element of a rounded cultural life, lived in the real world by real human beings. French journalism has itself experienced this realisation, as the elitist President Chirac was replaced by the populist Nicolas Sarkozy, who came to the office with a troubled marriage. Within months of his election in 2007, Sarkozy was divorced by his wife and remarried to Italian former supermodel Carla Bruni. The President's state visit to the UK in March 2008 produced acres of positive media coverage in Britain, as journalists and audiences warmed to the young, modern (in presidential terms) couple, and undoubtedly enhanced France's reputation after the tense Chirac years (during which the red-tops talked jubilantly of the French as 'cheese-eating surrender monkeys' and worse because of Chirac's reluctance to back the invasion of Iraq). In France, however, still some years behind the UK and America in its readiness to cover and celebrate the private as well as the public lives of politicians, Sarkozy's presidential style provoked disquiet about the dumbing down of his office. Bourdieu, had he lived to see the spectacle of the president and his celebrity wife, would have been appalled.

Bourdieu and others who dismiss 'popular tastes' (*ibid.*) as if they were anthropologists observing primitive tribes assume that the rhetoric of politicians, the minutiae of policy and the in-fighting of political elites are the only subjects of legitimate journalistic interest, the only subjects about which people in general have any right to be concerned. They exclude the possibility, too, that subjects of human interest are not at the same time important in the economic and policy spheres. Bill Clinton's adventures with Monica Lewinsky were clearly in this category, as were the sex scandals of the Major years in Britain, the revelations about Mitterrand's mistresses in France, or the circumstances of Princess Diana's death in 1997. More recently, as noted, we have seen extensive coverage of the marriage(s) of French President Nicolas Sarkozy, the Governor of New York accused of participation in a prostitution ring, and many other stories in which the public and private merge. And who can say that the public should not know that their law-and-order-toting governor regularly spends thousands of dollars on prostitutes, and the criminal gangs that run them? Sarkozy's divorce from Cecilia and marriage to Carla were not merely entertaining stories, but frequently came packaged with quite challenging and sophisticated narratives about the role of women in politics, and the appropriate public style of a twenty-first century French politician – popular or elitist? The Nicolas and Carla show, whatever else it was, was a story about the changing nature of French culture and society.

From this point of view, the separation of reality into weighty or trivial, serious or flippant, is largely arbitrary; an elite–intellectual response to the democratic advances of the twentieth century, which have threatened that elite's monopoly on defining what counts as 'good taste'. There *are* serious economic pressures which threaten to undermine the quality of British journalism, as we will see below, but the dumbing-down thesis is not principally an argument about resources: rather, its opponents argue, it mythologises a past era of 'quality' journalism that never actually existed and that, if it did exist, was never available to more than a tiny proportion of the population.

John Carey points out that there is a long intellectual tradition, extending from Friedrich Nietzsche to George Bernard Shaw, of denouncing popular culture – particularly its commercial forms – as worthless trash, consumed like a drug by an ignorant mass. This tradition has included, since at least the late nineteenth century, the viewing of popular journalism as an expression of debased mass culture, and warnings about the impending 'Americanisation' of the media. Carey argues, from his analysis of critical writing of the late nineteenth century, that 'the popular newspaper presented a threat, because it created an alternative culture which bypassed the intellectual and made him redundant. By adopting sales figures as the sole criterion, [popular] journalism circumvented the traditional cultural elite' (Carey, 1992: 7). It has been accused of dumbing down (the phraseology changes, but the argument remains essentially the same) ever since. As the previous chapter showed, journalism has been criticised for many things, including ideological bias and lack of objectivity, and often with good cause, but the dumbing down/tabloidisation thesis can be argued to have more in common with that long-established, intellectual fear of the popular, identified by Carey, than with progressive critical thinking.

Attacks on 'newszak' and dumbing down can also be viewed as a response to the 'feminisation' of journalism (see below). Oft-criticised trends, such as the rise in consumer and lifestyle coverage, might just as readily be interpreted as the positive influence on journalistic agendas of the rise of feminism, bringing with it a new visibility for what were once dismissed as 'women's issues'. Mary Ann Sieghart, one of the 'post-feminist' generation of senior media managers, argues from her own experience on *The Times* that the professional advances of women in recent years have 'feminised and humanised what was hitherto a male-dominated news agenda'.[10] One observer argues that 'tabloid TV news simply means news led by the audience's interests – less pompous, less pedagogic, less male; more human, more vivacious, more demotic'.[11] The appointment of Anne Koch as head of Radio 4 News in early 1998 was viewed by many as evidence of the 'incremental feminisation' of the BBC's journalistic output,[12] a process frequently attacked by critics of the BBC.[13] To this day, the appearance of a woman with blonde hair as a presenter on a news or current affairs show – even highly talented journalists such as Kirsty Young or Emily Maitlis – generates heated debate about the dumbing down of TV.

One senior female journalist observes that, as a consequence of journalism's feminisation, 'the edges of our public and private domains have become blurred'.[14] The dumbing-down thesis condemns this blurring, while 'post-modern' commentators accept, even welcome it as one manifestation of the anti-elitist cultural democratisation of the late twentieth century.

The dumbing-down thesis is increasingly criticised for imposing a monolithic concept of 'quality' journalism on society as a whole. One of the key cultural shifts of the late twentieth century was the breaking down of the notion of a single, clearly defined public who exist as an imagined community to be served by a London-based elite. In the twenty-first century, it is clear that we inhabit a society composed of many 'publics', each with distinctive needs and demands in the cultural sphere, and with historically unprecedented access to a media system capable of satisfying those needs. This development, which could never have been foreseen by the pioneering social theorists of capitalism, has its roots in such trends as technological innovation (digital technologies and the internet, most obviously), and the emergence of ethnic, feminist and other forms of identity politics (which have then formed a market for the multiplicity of journalistic styles and agendas made possible by new technology). Journalistic culture has been commodified in the process, and not all of what is available in the media marketplace is appealing to everybody, but the fact that it *is* a marketplace, rather than a top-down cultural monopoly, means that no member of the audience is forced to watch, read or listen to anything against his or her will. Conversely, that which is not required by at least some portion of the audience will not survive the harsher competitive environment that commodification encourages. Of course, the use of marketing and adver-tising techniques can sometimes 'manufacture' demands that are not authentic, in the cultural sphere as well as in other branches of capitalistic production. But the evidence of circulation trends since the first edition of this book was published indicates that the market is a relatively efficient means of regulating journalistic style and content.

Some media, in short, are 'dumber' than others. But so are some people, and why shouldn't they all get the media they want, when there is room enough in the public sphere for every taste and preference? (I am aware that the 'dumb-ing' word is offensive, but since the proponents of dumbing down have championed its use to describe popular tastes, we are obliged to follow suit.)

None of this challenges the importance of a continuing system of public service journalism, funded by taxation and thus shielded from purely com-mercial considerations. Indeed, in a competitive, resource-squeezed system, the public service apparatus becomes even more important as an example of 'best practice', setting a standard that Sky News and other new entrants to the journalism market are obliged to match, or at least approximate to. But just as 'the public' to be served has gradually come to be viewed as a network of overlapping and interacting 'publics' rather than a homogeneous whole, public service journalism must adapt to reflect the new cultural context in which it must retain broad popularity and relevance to people's lives.

Who is right about dumbing down? My own views on the matter are probably clear to the reader by now, but they are only my views. In the end, assessments of contemporary journalistic form, content and style must always be a largely subjective matter, with individual preferences dependent on cul-tural and social background, political affiliations, interpretation of normative standards, and other determinants of taste. Apart from the identification of factual errors and their causes, the critique of journalistic content can be no more absolute than the critique of art. The only certainty of this debate is that the narrative of decline underpinning the dumbing-down thesis is only one way of accounting for the recent development of journalistic style and content – one founded, moreover, on what many argue to be rather elitist, old-fashioned, socially conservative ideas about the functions, effects and dangers of mass culture.

A note on the feminisation of British journalism

As argued above, one strand of the narrative of dumbing down is often found to be a concern that 'serious' journalism is being replaced by 'human interest' and other categories associated with the realm of the feminine. I earlier quoted the views of one scholar that 'news media are framed within an all-encompassing project of propaganda' (Boyd-Barratt, 2007: 99), with audiences positioned corresponding to the 'idealised role of the feminine in patriarchal society, whose features include passivity, trust and nurturing support for male authority'. Femininity, in general, and whether idealised or not, has tended to be regarded as antithetical to the normative values of the public sphere (a flaw in his own argument that the key theorist of the public sphere, Habermas, later acknowledged and sought to rectify). In this respect, however, journalism is no different from other cultural categories. Traditionally, British journalism has been a male-dominated craft, a stronghold of patriarchy in the cultural sphere, with women relegated to the wifely, motherhood-oriented pages of *Woman's Own* or, in the mainstream media, to 'women's issues' and problem pages. This sex-based division of journalistic labour is still evident in the British media, but as feminism has gradually reshaped society, and as women have begun to penetrate the bastions of male power and privilege, the gender make-up of the journalistic profession has changed accordingly, if not yet to the point where one could say that the battle against institutionalised sexism in the news industry is won. At the same time, the status of what used to be described in disparaging terms as 'women's issues' has risen.

A 1998 report by the Women in Journalism organisation, despite its rather pessimistic title – '*The Cheaper Sex: How Women Lose Out in Journalism*' – told a story of significant advances for women in the profession. The report revealed that journalism is still top-heavy with older, more experienced and senior, but less-educated men – a profile reflecting the recruitment and career paths of an earlier era, which bypassed university in favour of 'the university of life', and tended at the same time to discriminate against women. The higher one goes in the profession, therefore, and the older the staff, the fewer women one finds, and those women earn significantly less on average than their male counterparts. However, the broad cultural impact of four decades of feminism is now being felt in the media industry, as a new generation of women enters the profession from university and slowly makes its way up the career ladder. The Women in Journalism study found that young female journalists (up to the age of 35) appeared to be doing better than men of the same age, on a range of indicators. They tended then, for example, to earn on average 25 per cent more than their male colleagues.[15]

Does this mean there is no longer a 'glass ceiling' in the journalistic profession – a point at which women are blocked from further advancement because of deeply ingrained prejudices and presumptions? From the perspective of individual women seeking a career in journalism, the answer to that question is a resounding yes. In both print and broadcast news media, there are now many women who have risen, or are rising, to senior positions as editors, producers, chief correspondents and presenters. In 1998, Rosie Boycott became the first female editor of a daily newspaper (the *Independent*), moving quickly on to the editorship of the *Express*. Janet Street-Porter became editor of the *Independent on Sunday* in June 1999; Rebekah Wade of the *News of the World* in 2000 and then the *Sun* in January 2003 (at the comparatively young age, for a man or a woman, of 34); and Veronica Wadley of the *London Evening Standard* in 2002. These appointments (and others of women to senior positions in UK journalism) signify a genuine shift in the sexual division of labour within the British media; one which, as more and more women embark on media and journalism studies at British universities, will not be reversed. But ownership remains a male preserve, and for women media workers as a whole the same pressures and obstacles that hinder their progress in other professions – principally those associated with child-bearing and child-rearing, alongside a more generalised 'institutional' sexism – continue to be present in journalism, if to a declining extent. The Women in Journalism report found that 'if difficulties arise for women in newspapers, it is usually once they become mothers', a pattern that will be familiar to women in most walks of life. Institutional sexism survives, therefore, but appears to be in retreat, with consequences not just for the gender structure of the profession, but for the form and content of journalism.

There is still a long way to go, of course, before anything like genuine gender equality in the journalistic profession is achieved. In December 2007, the Fawcett Society reported that only two out of 17 editors of national newspapers in the UK are women, and that 100 per cent of deputy editors are men. Forty-four per cent of news presenters were women, but only six per cent of broadcast news editors. Twenty-six per cent of political journalists in the Westminster lobby were women, but only 12.5 per cent of political editors in the national press. The report concluded that, progressive trends notwithstanding, women continue to be under-represented in the UK journalism industry, even if the trend is moving in a progressive direction. The coming years will tell how far and fast those trends are able to change that situation.

Cosy conspiracy or corrosive cynicism?

Let me turn now to one of the most heated debates to have raged around news and journalism in the UK since the previous edition of this book appeared in 2003 – the issue of whether or not journalism, and political journalism in particular, has become guilty of what Steven Barnett called in a 2002 article 'corrosive cynicism'.[16] This issue was already prominent in the 1990s, recurring with some regularity whenever politicians and journalists clashed in the media. Broadcast journalists in particular, such as John Humphrys and Jeremy Paxman of the BBC, were singled out for their aggressive, confrontational interviewing styles, first by politicians in the Conservative government, and then, too, by New Labour after its election in 1997 (McNair, 2000). The issue was also raised in the United States, where journalist James Fallows accused some of his colleagues there of a tendency towards 'hyperadversarialism' (Fallows, 1996).

Then-Director-General of the BBC, John Birt, expressed some sympathy with the critics of his staff at a speech in Dublin that year. Fourth estate critical scrutiny of the political elite was desirable, indeed essential for a healthy democracy, all conceded, but the impact of commercial and competitive pressures on journalists and news organisations to be more sensational and dramatic, to entertain audiences with gladiatorial contests inspired by the question – first posed, according to legend, by Walter Cronkite and then adapted by leading BBC 'bulldog' Jeremy Paxman – 'why is that lying bastard lying to me?', had tipped the balance too far towards criticism for its own sake; what Barnett called, indeed, 'corrosive cynicism', fuelled also by the growing intensity of political public relations and 'spin' in Tony Blair's New Labour party. Birt argued that:

> Journalists naturally resent what they perceive to be a political class trying to wriggle out of proper democratic scrutiny. Most take pride in their fourth-estate duty to act as a check on government and are therefore fiercely resistant to spin. The problem with this perfectly honourable determination to assert a critical independence is that it risks being gradually transmuted into a relentlessly negative approach to both politicians and politics itself. There are now questions being asked on both sides of the Atlantic about whether a line has been crossed from detached scepticism to derision, cynicism and ridicule. There is concern that we have entered a new and destructive era in political journalism: the age of contempt.[17]

The catalyst for the resurgence of the debate in 2002 was a series of bruising encounters between journalists and New Labour ministers, leading in the case of popular Education Secretary Estelle Morris to her resignation. Here and elsewhere, journalists were accused of harrying able politicians from office, turning the public sphere into a gladiatorial arena, and generally putting people off the democratic process by their sneering cynicism. In Scotland's *Sunday Herald*, John Lloyd attacked his own profession with the observation that:

> all journalism is infected with malevolence ... Journalists hope that bad things will happen and, if they don't, make sure that what does occur is represented as bad. It's the joy of being superior; the joy of having the journalistic power to paint public figures as contemptible. Those who have not experienced the surge of joyous adrenalin that goes through newsrooms when a figure of power is under attack – or better, brought down – have no notion of how close journalism is to a blood sport.[18]

Journalists had indeed become more adversarial, and less deferential, over time, particularly in the context of the interview format. Competitive pressures and spin were partly responsible, as Barnett suggested, and so too was a changed cultural environment in which journalists saw it as their democratic duty to be as tough as possible with politicians (and other elites, such as members of the royal family and celebrities from the worlds of sport and entertainment), most of whom had been trained in media management techniques and had highly paid spin doctors such as Alistair Campbell sitting at their side, invisible to the viewer and listener, coaching them in their responses.[19]

Academics such as Barnett were diverging, clearly, from the critical stance of many journalism studies scholars (see Chapters 3 and 4) who were still working within paradigms of dominance and control, viewing journalists not as corrosive cynics but as cosy conspirators with the powerful. Adherents to the propaganda model, in particular, would not have recognised the picture painted by Barnett, which implied that journalists were less interested in reproducing dominant ideology than in gaining audiences with entertaining displays of knowing scepticism. One might speculate that the presence of New Labour in government was one factor in this shift, or that the de-ideologised post-Cold War environment, and the impact of the September 11 attacks on how scholars and journalists viewed the responsibilities of the media towards politics (Allan and Zelizer, 2002), removed much of the underpinning of pre-1989 journalism studies paradigms (as I have argued elsewhere; McNair, 2006a).

Then, as a consequence of 9/11, came the 2003 invasion of Iraq, and the fierce public debate around the merits and demerits of war with Saddam Hussein. Coverage of the war was analysed by academics, as noted above (Miller, 2004; Tumber and Palmer, 2004), who reached different conclusions about the biases or otherwise of journalists. Discussing research conducted on the content of BBC news coverage of the Iraqi conflict at Cardiff University's Centre for Journalism, Media and Cultural Studies, Justin Lewis argued that, 'far from revealing an anti-war BBC bias, our findings tend to give credence to those who criticized the BBC for being too sympathetic to the government's pro-war stance. Either way, to accuse the BBC of an anti-war bias fails to stand up to any serious or sustained analysis.'[20]

Other researchers, including Howard Tumber and Jerry Palmer (2004), identified in UK media a pronounced current of criticism of government regarding the Iraqi conflict. Both readings of the news cannot be correct, obviously, even when, as sometimes happens, they are advanced by the same commentator at different times. It is fair to say, however, that in the period since the previous edition of this book, the critics of UK journalism's anti-government bias have been more visible in public debate than those who see cosy conspiracy and pro-government propaganda everywhere. One incident in the aftermath of the invasion sparked a huge controversy around BBC journalism, and its relationship to the British political process.

On 29 May 2003, just after the previous edition of this book was published, BBC journalist Andrew Gilligan broadcast a report for the Radio 4 *Today* show about the dossier on Iraq's weapons of mass destruction. This document had been prepared by the government as part of its effort to persuade parliament and the people of the necessity of invading Iraq. The dossier was clear in its assertions that Saddam's regime possessed usable weapons of mass destruction, or weapons that could easily and quickly be assembled, posing an unacceptable threat to the Middle East, western allies in the region, and indeed the UK itself. On the basis of official sources interviewed by Gilligan but not named in the broadcast, he claimed that the dossier had been creatively edited, and that the government knew all along that its claims were exaggerated and unsubstantiated. According to the unnamed source cited by Gilligan in his interview with John Humphrys, the dossier:

was transformed in the week before it was published to make it sexier. The classic example was the claim that weapons of mass destruction were ready for use within 45 minutes. That information was not in the original draft. It was included in the dossier against our [the source and his colleagues] wishes, because it wasn't reliable.

The report went out live, early in the morning before most BBC listeners were up and about. It was not missed by the Prime Minister's Director of Communications Alistair Campbell, however, who immediately interpreted Gilligan's report as an assertion that the government and the Prime Minister had lied. This, he and others in the government later insisted, was an accusation so serious that had it been true, Tony Blair would have been obliged to resign.

The details of what happened next have been widely written about, and exhaustively analysed in the report of the Hutton Inquiry set up to investigate the affair (www.the-hutton-inquiry.org.uk), which led directly to the suicide of Gilligan's main source, government scientist David Kelly. The Hutton report cleared the government, was critical of the BBC's editorial management, and led to the resignation of Director-General Greg Dyke and the Chairman of the Board of Governors Gavyn Davies. Alistair Campbell resigned his post as Communications Director for the government not long after. The BBC's governors, meanwhile, in the wake of the Hutton findings, were reported to be 'split over the future of *Today*'.[21]

The arguments will continue for many years about who was right and wrong in the Gilligan affair – did the journalist fail to source his story adequately, as many argued (a cardinal sin for a BBC reporter, especially when the story was of such import), and put David Kelly in a position where he felt he had no choice but to commit suicide? Did the government indeed 'sex up' its dossier, and thus knowingly mislead the British people? These are questions that may never be answered conclusively to everyone's satisfaction. For observers of political journalism in the UK, however, the affair proved just how corrosive and cynical the British news media had become, that an organisation such as the BBC should think an uncorroborated accusation of prime ministerial lying defensible on a flagship news programme such as *Today*.

First, though, the BBC itself acknowledged its errors (as it had to do, politically, given that it was approaching yet another review of its funding settlement and Royal Charter – see Chapter 7). In his Cudlipp Lecture in 2005, Dyke's successor as Director-General, Michael Grade, described the Gilligan affair as 'a failure in the BBC's journalism'.[22] The government, for its part, accused BBC journalism of 'arrogance and cynicism'.

While this was understandable (if not necessarily valid) criticism from the likes of Alistair Campbell and others engaged in the agenda-setting struggle with news media, more surprising was the intervention of journalist John Lloyd, whose 2004 book *What the Media are Doing to Our Politics* was a trenchant assault on the corporation. Taking the Andrew Gilligan story as his best example – 'carelessly done', and 'a grave charge, lightly made' (Lloyd,

2004: 7) – Lloyd argued that 'if the best of journalism – the BBC – could both put out a report like that and defend it, and remain convinced that it had been fairly criticized by Hutton and traduced by government, then we have produced a media culture which is many ways contradicts the ideals to which we pay homage' (*ibid.*: 140).

A few months earlier, in a column responding to the interim findings of the Phillis Commission set up by New Labour to explore the politics–media relationship in the UK, Polly Toynbee, herself no stranger to criticism of government, wrote in an echo of Barnett's 2002 piece that 'journalism has become obsessed with the processes of government, but incurious about any complex problem that cannot be blamed upon some hapless minister'.[23] More than this:

> Journalism of left and right converges in an anarchic zone of vitriol where elected politicians are always contemptible, their policies not just wrong but their motives all self-interest. Intense circulation wars have created a vicious press pack which ultimately might make the country ungovernable.

From the specifics of the Gilligan affair, the attack widened to the general, extending to the oft-criticised hyperadversarialism of such as Jeremy Paxman, whose gladiatorial, confrontational interviewing style was described by former policy researcher and press secretary to Tony Blair as 'punk political journalism', which 'puts the journalist at centre stage. It judges itself by how many hits it can rack up against the subject. The interviewer becomes the auteur; the politician is merely part of the set'.[24] In similar vein, the late Anthony Sampson wrote that 'journalists have gained power hugely ... [and] become much more assertive, aggressive and moralizing in confronting other forms of power'.[25] This, he implied, was not a good thing. In a rare outbreak of agreement between media commentators and senior politicians, Tony Blair, in one of his final speeches as Prime Minister, spoke of political journalism in the UK as a 'feral beast, tearing people and reputations to bits'.[26] In an earlier contribution to the debate, Polly Toynbee reflected on the media's capacity (not just print, of course, although she singled out the *Daily Mail* for criticism) to drive the policy-making process with erroneous and alarmist coverage of, for example, health.

> Health coverage is in inverse proportion to real risk. What kills most people gets less coverage ... Politicians have often been forced to change policy priorities and health spending according to what the media highlights, regardless of public good.[27]

Criticism was further stoked up by high-profile cases of unethical reporting methods, such as that which saw the *News of the World*'s royal editor imprisoned for illegal phone-tapping of the royal family, and its editor Andy Coulson forced to resign (emerging shortly afterwards as Tory leader David Cameron's new spin doctor). The previous year, a Scottish jury found against the same paper in its defence of a libel action taken against it by Scottish Socialist MSP Tommy Sheridan. While an appeal and perjury investigations remained active in the latter case as this edition went to press, it was generally accepted by observers of the case that the jury's allegedly 'perverse' verdict (finding, in effect, that 16 members of his own party had conspired to lie under oath against Sheridan, in alliance with the hated Murdoch empire and the 'boss classes') was influenced in part by a perception that the *News of the World* had violated acceptable ethical standards in its lurid reportage of the scandal and needed to be taken down a peg or two.

In the face of such ethical lapses, Blair's June 2007 speech called for a revision of the regulatory framework in order to tame the beast. This suggestion was not taken up by commentators, who preferred to point to the responsibility of his own spin operation for the increasingly cynical attitude of the news media. Neither was it endorsed by the Select Committee for Culture, Media and Sport, at that very moment reviewing press regulation in the wake of the royal phone-tapping scandal, and the press harassment of Kate Middleton, girlfriend of Prince William. While the Committee's report, published in July 2007, was highly critical of the UK press on a range of grounds, it concluded that 'any move towards a statutory regulator for the press would represent a very dangerous interference with the freedom of the press'.[28] The Committee noted with approval that the Press Complaints Commission, set up by the Conservative government at the height of concern about 'yellow' and 'bonk' journalism in 1991, was doing a good job in managing the majority of complaints, if not all. In 2006, noted the Committee, of a total of some 3600 complaints received, the PCC had resolved around 800 of them by conciliation or adjudication, a figure up substantially on ten years before.

Truth, faking and the crisis of trust

Shortly after Blair's 'feral beast' speech, criticisms of an overly aggressive news media developed into a full-blown crisis of trust, culminating in the several faking scandals that descended on the BBC and other organisations in the summer of 2007. While these raised distinct and quite complex issues around the nature of journalistic truth, they were linked to the growing sense of a UK media out of control, its journalistic practitioners in breach of their duties to be objective, honest and fair.

The rise of reality TV since the late 1990s played a part in making visible the manipulation of 'reality' in reality TV. Although not easily categorised as journalism, the explosion of reality TV genres has been seen as part of the universe of factual media output by practitioners and scholars (Hill, 2005, 2007). They represent the hybridisation of journalistic conventions with those hitherto associated with the documentary, the drama and the game show. They feature 'real' people, in 'real' situations, which are scripted in various ways and then edited into drama-building packages for viewers. This, it seems fair to say, has been understood by audiences. *Big Brother* is reality TV, and its participants are not actors, but we know when watching that the producers have concocted elaborate scenarios to heighten competitiveness and drama.

Suddenly, however, in the summer of 2007, the artificiality of all factual TV output became a focus of public debate. The crisis was sparked by the revelation that a number of phone-in reality and game shows had been 'fixed'. 'Winners' of competitions turned out to be invented names; the counting of viewers' votes made on premium rate phone lines was revealed to have closed while calls were still flooding in, generating substantial illicit income for the channels concerned. A BBC Scotland children's show was found to have been guilty of this crime, and although no money was made in that case, the revelation that a public service broadcaster would do such a thing in the interests of making a programme run smoothly outraged many.

Then it was revealed that documentary-maker Alan Yentob was not always physically present in scenes where he appeared to be interviewing a subject for one of his arts documentaries, but was recorded separately asking the questions, and then edited in to give the illusion of a genuine two-way exchange.

Suddenly, the media were full of instances of such artifice, and debate about the ethics and authenticity of broadcast journalism. At the height of the debate, Channel 5 news managers announced that they would no longer use techniques such as 'noddies' in items – that is, shots in which the camera cuts to a journalist nodding in agreement with his or her interviewee, having just been filmed from behind posing the question. Such devices would no longer be tolerated by Channel 5, so concerned had producers become by the apparent crisis of viewer trust in the authenticity of TV news.

For the BBC, the nadir of the trust debate came with the revelation that a prestigious documentary series about the Queen, which followed her for a year, *cinema verité-* style, as she went about her duties in the UK and overseas, had been edited in the manner of reality TV shows everywhere to maximise the drama and suspense. More precisely, since the series had not yet been shown, a promotional film advertising the series to journalists at a press conference had been manipulated in order to make it appear that the Queen had taken the royal huff with celebrity photographer Annie Leibovitz and stormed out of a photo set. The incident, it was conceded by the independent production company responsible, had not taken place as suggested by the editing, and further prevarication by the controller of BBC1 led to his resignation shortly after. The company responsible was suspended from bidding for BBC commissions until further notice.

In July 2007, commentator Steve Hewlett observed that 'truth and reality have become negotiable concepts'.[29] Giving the MacTaggart Lecture at the 2007 Edinburgh International TV Festival, Jeremy Paxman reacted to the controversy by pointing out that 'all television involves the use of artifice. Constructed sequences and creative license should still be allowed'.[30] It was all an over-reaction, he maintained, and indeed, within a few weeks, the controversy had died down. In the process, however, the artificial, constructed nature of journalistic truth, and the basis of trust in public service broadcast journalism in particular, had been questioned as never before. As this edition went to press, the BBC had worked hard to regain audience trust, even establishing a Trust of independent overseers to replace its Board of Governors (another casualty of the Gilligan affair – see Chapter 7). Other broadcasters, too, having been fined by Ofcom and generally pilloried for their lack of trustworthiness by the press (ironically, perhaps, given the record of UK print journalism, up to and including the outrageous tone of much of the coverage of the Madeleine McCann story – see Chapter 6), had struggled to restore their reputation. The UK TV audience, however, would never again watch their news, current affairs and popular factual programming with quite the same degree of interpretive innocence.

Further reading

For recent critical writing on political journalism and conflict news, respectively, see Barnett and Gabor (2001); Maltby and Keeble (2007). Barnett *et al*.'s (2000) *From Callaghan to Kosovo* is a useful analysis of TV news content in the context of the dumbing-down debate. Nick Davies' *Flat Earth News* contains a trenchant critique of the state of journalism in the UK.

6   Print journalism in the UK

This chapter contains:

- a brief history of the British press
- a review of the economic and professional impact of new technologies on the British press, from the introduction of computerised production in the 'Wapping revolution' to the rise of the internet
- discussion of the changing editorial allegiances of the British press
- a discussion of recent press controversies such as the Madeleine McCann case and the royal phone-tapping scandal.

As this edition went to press, print journalism in the UK was grappling with a number of significant challenges to its economic well being, and to its traditional place in the British media landscape. These included a long-term, steady decline in newspaper paid-for circulation, linked to the rise of the internet and the migration of readers away from print to other platforms for news delivery; and the rise of the free-sheet sector, which by 2008 accounted for more than four million of the newspapers read in Britain every day. This chapter explores those challenges, as well as the regulatory and legal issues affecting the British press, highlighted in March 2008 by the fining of the *Express* and *Sunday Express* for their coverage of the Madeleine McCann case. Chapter 9 tells 'the regional story'. In this chapter we consider those print media of UK-wide reach.

Before and after Wapping: the changing political economy of the British press

It has been argued that Fleet Street, the historical centre, physically and figuratively, of the British newspaper industry – ceased to exist on 26 January 1986, 'the day on which Rupert Murdoch proved that it was possible to produce two mass-circulation newspapers without a single member of his existing print force, without using the railways and with roughly one-fifth of the numbers that he had been employing before'.[1] The flight of News International's newspaper production from buildings in the City of London to a custom-built, high-technology 'fortress' at Wapping in London's Docklands was, on one level, the entirely rational and, as it turned out, highly profitable act of a ruthless and hardheaded publisher. But it also, in combination with the actions of another media entrepreneur, Eddie Shah, set in motion processes that, according to one viewpoint, revitalised a moribund, loss-making industry and created the conditions for its profitable expansion in the late 1980s and 1990s and beyond. An opposing view asserts that the 'Wapping revolution' in fact did nothing to address the long-standing problems of the British press, particularly those of concentration of ownership, right-wing political bias and deteriorating editorial standards. This chapter assesses these contrasting interpretations of what has happened to the British press since 1986, and considers how the industry was affected by the Wapping revolution. Before that, however, we should perhaps answer the question, what was wrong with the British press anyway?

The British press: a brief history

The story of the British press as a genuinely mass medium begins with the emergence in the late eighteenth and early nineteenth centuries of large urban populations, descendants of the feudal peasant classes who had been displaced from their traditional rural environment by encroaching capitalist property rights and social relations, and who were forced to make their living by entering the rapidly developing factory system. To labour efficiently in a manufacturing, factory environment, the members of this new urban proletariat were required to learn skills of numeracy and literacy, which they began to acquire from the embryonic state education service. As the masses became more educated and more literate, they developed an appetite for reading material.

In the eighteenth century, newspaper readership had been limited to a relatively small elite of educated members of the bourgeoisie and upper classes, and the pro-establishment views and interests of these groups naturally predominated in the content of early newspapers. With the rise of a literate working class, likewise, a number of newspapers emerged that were targeted at the urban proletariat and that reflected their concerns. In the aftermath of the French Revolution of 1789 and in the first half of the nineteenth century, culminating in the revolutions of 1848 across Europe, these concerns were with social reform and justice. From 1815 a 'radical' press developed in Britain, which set out to shape working-class opinion and thereby influence events. By 1817, the foremost example of this press, William Cobbett's *Political Register*, was selling more than 40,000 copies a week. At the same time, trade unions were gaining in strength and reach, often using the contents of the radical press as material for political education.

For British capital, which had fought successfully for press freedom in the context of feudal authoritarianism and thus understood the power of newspapers as disseminators of radical ideas, these were threatening developments.

From 1818, libel laws began to be used more frequently to prevent radical publishers from issuing 'seditious' material, while in 1819 taxes on newspapers – stamp duties – were extended to cover the radical press. These 'taxes on knowledge' were intended, as Curran and Seaton put it in their account of British press history, 'to restrict the readership of newspapers to the well-to-do by raising cover prices; and to restrict the ownership of newspapers to the propertied class by increasing publishing costs' (Curran and Seaton, 1997: 11). These repressive measures failed, and instead the establishment embarked on a 'sophisticated strategy of social control', whereby the Stamp Laws were repealed and the radical press replaced by apolitical, commercial publications, read by the mass audience, but in the ownership and control of capital. In these authors' view, 'the common concern of most leading supporters of the campaign [to repeal newspaper taxation] was to secure the loyalty of the working class to the social order through the expansion of the capitalist press' (Curran and Seaton, 1991: 27). A later edition of this book adds that the repeal of the press tax was also viewed as 'a means of propagating the principles of free trade and competitive capitalism' (1997: 27) through the reduction of newspaper prices.

As newspapers became cheaper and the market for them expanded, capital investment and start-up and running costs increased beyond the capacity of radical publishers to keep up. Dependence on advertising revenue increased. By the end of the nineteenth century, the radical publications had either been forced out of existence, moved up market and to the right politically, become small specialist publications with dedicated readership, or become financially dependent on institutions such as the Independent Labour Party and Trades Union Congress. Replacing them in the popular newspaper market were publications controlled by a small number of 'press barons' with the capital resources to found titles and build empires. By 1910, Lords Pearson, Cadbury and Northcliffe between them controlled 67 per cent of national daily circulation, establishing a trend of concentration of ownership that has persisted in the British newspaper industry ever since, with the exception of a brief period during and after the Second World War when state intervention in the newspaper market reduced dependence on advertising and allowed left-of-centre newspapers to strengthen their positions on the basis of readership alone.

The late 1960s saw the arrival in the UK of Rupert Murdoch and News International. In 1968 he bought the *News of the World*, and followed this by taking control of the *Sun* in 1969. Both were loss-making titles when taken over by Murdoch, and he was able to acquire them at what appear, with hindsight, to be knock-down prices. In the course of the 1970s, they came to dominate the British tabloid market and moved into profit. They also moved to the right of the political spectrum editorially. In 1981, Murdoch bought *The Times* and the *Sunday Times*, and in 1987 he took control of the *Today* newspaper (which he later closed).

Murdoch was the first, and to date most successful, of a new generation of press barons: ideologically committed and politically interventionist, but also a hard-headed pragmatist, ready to change horses when he feels that the time is right. They tended to have interests in a wide variety of other media and also in non-media sectors of industry. They were also, with the exception of the late Robert Maxwell, well to the right of centre in their political views, lending their support from the late 1970s onwards to the Conservative Party and its leader, Margaret Thatcher. In return for services rendered in 1979 and subsequent general elections, several of them (and their editors) received honours from the Conservative government. The Thatcher government also assisted the building of their empires by consistently refusing to use the Monopolies and Mergers Commission (MMC) as a means of preventing excessive concentration of ownership. The most obvious beneficiary of this *laissez-faire* approach was Rupert Murdoch who, on the eve of the Wapping dispute at the end of 1985, had acquired four national titles and 33 per cent of total national circulation. In purchasing *The Times* and the *Sunday Times*, Murdoch had to overcome the rule that the owner of a newspaper with sales over 500,000 was required to have a bid for another national title referred to the MMC. This could be avoided, however, if the paper (or papers) to be bought would otherwise go out of business. Despite the fact – as Murdoch himself quickly showed – that *The Times* titles were inherently economically viable, the government accepted his argument that they were not, and allowed the purchase to go ahead without reference to the MMC. The authors of a financial biography of Murdoch argue that this bending of the rules in his favour was a reward for his tabloids' loyal support of the government – and Margaret Thatcher in particular – over the years (Belfield *et al.*, 1991: 74).

It was this overt political bias, and not merely the evidence of increasing ownership concentration, that so disturbed many observers of the British press in the 1980s. As Harold Evans put it in his published account of life as editor of *The Times*, 'the daily news in print in Britain is more brilliantly polluted by partisan judgements than the press in most other democracies and certainly by comparison with the press of the United States' (Evans, 1983: 4). Moreover, 'the arithmetic favours the Conservative Party'. The McGregor Commission on the Press stated clearly: 'there is no doubt that over most of this century the Labour movement has had less newspaper support than its right-wing opponents and that its beliefs and activities have been unfavourably reported by the majority of the press' (McGregor, 1977: 99). Left-of-centre publications such as the *News Chronicle* and *Daily Herald* were driven out of the market in the 1960s, despite relatively healthy seven-figure circulations, leaving what McGregor called 'a gap in the national press for a newspaper generally supporting left-wing parties and opinions' (*ibid*.: 109). By 1985, the political affiliations of Britain's national daily newspapers were as follows: nine fully supported the Conservative Party; one, the *Financial Times*, leant heavily in that direction; leaving only the Mirror Group titles and the *Guardian* tentatively backing 'moderate' elements in the Labour Party. The *Morning Star*, of course, backed the 'hard' left, but its circulation was so small as to be negligible in terms of political influence.

Such an overwhelming bias was recognised to be, at the very least, unrepresentative of political opinion in the UK. Tom Baistow observed in the 1980s that 'the national press has never reflected the political attitudes of a large – often a major – sector of the population in any representative degree since the rise of the Labour Party after the 1914–18 war' (Baistow, 1985: 3). Many of the right-wing tabloids were read by people who declared their political support for the opposition parties, but who nevertheless received (quite willingly, it would appear) a steady diet of anti-Labour and pro-Conservative propaganda in their newspapers. This feature of the British press, it has been argued, was profoundly undemocratic, since the output of the right-wing press swung just enough working-class voters to the Conservative Party at election time to guarantee their supremacy in the context of a first-past-the-post system for parliamentary elections.

A 1991 report by the Hansard Society stated that 'research has suggested [the right-wing bias of the press] has had a significant electoral impact, with the tabloids exerting an especially strong effect'.[2] William Miller has argued, on the basis of his study of the 1987 general election campaign, that perceptions of economic optimism – which tend to favour the Conservative Party's election prospects – are higher among those (even Labour supporters) who read the right-wing press (Miller, 1991: ch. 7). Miller's thesis received a boost following the outcome of the 1992 election when it was noted that the Conservative marginal seat of Basildon was the one that showed a particularly small swing to the Labour Party. It was also the constituency with the highest proportion of *Sun* readers in the UK.

The UK political environment has been transformed since then, of course, but as we saw in Chapter 2, the suggestion that newspapers, irrespective of their bias, have the power to influence voting behaviour, or any other type of behaviour, is problematic. If they can, why did so many *Sun* and *Star* readers support the Labour Party in the period before these titles switched their editorial allegiance to Tony Blair? Could it be that, having lost to the Conservatives in four consecutive elections, Labour Party supporters found the Tory press, with its overtly propagandistic and shamelessly distorted coverage of politics, a convenient scapegoat? After John Major's victory on 9 April 1992, left-wingers immediately attributed their defeat to the Tory-supporting tabloids, with the tabloids themselves rigorously denying any such impact. the *Sun*, for example, despite initially taking credit for Labour's defeat, subsequently took exception to the suggestion that its readers could be so malleable and stupid as to be affected by such headlines as 'Nightmare on Kinnock Street'. This uncharacteristic denial of influence was, in large part, a defensive response to growing public concerns about the bias of the British press, as much as a considered view by the *Sun*'s editors on the question of media effects. As such, it did little to undermine the belief of such as Martin Linton (then a *Guardian* journalist, later a Labour MP) that pro-Tory bias on the scale of the 1979–92 period made a Labour general election victory impossible. For Linton, the outcome of the 1992 general election confirmed his view that

Labour was suffering from an insurmountable, and profoundly undemocratic, 'press deficit'. Labour, he pointed out, 'has never won an election when it was more than 18 per cent behind the Tories in press share'.[3]

Pro-Labour bias

While the effects of political bias may be said to be unproven, the fact of its existence cannot be denied. Historically, as we have seen, the bias has been towards the right of the political spectrum in Britain – the chief beneficiary for most of the post-war period being the Conservative Party. Indeed, one of the most frequently heard justifications for the traumatic transformation of the newspaper industry which took place after 1986 was that it would give the Labour movement and the left new opportunities to enter the market and redress this bias. By the mid-1990s, however, it appeared that such redress might not be so urgent as it once was. After 1992, there was a significant, perhaps unprecedented, shift in the allegiances of the pro-Conservative press, such that the notion of a 'Tory press' had become outmoded.

'Tentative and symbolic' criticism of the Major government was to be found in the (still) Tory press as early as the autumn of 1992,[4] but was elevated to a higher plane with the appointment of Peter Stothard as editor of *The Times* in 1993. *The Times*'s criticism of the Major government has been interpreted as, at least in part, a management response to falling sales and influence in an environment where public opinion appeared to be slipping away from the Tories. More fundamentally, fiercely anti-government *Times* editorials were reported '[to] exactly reflect the proprietor's reputed contempt for the way things have gone in Britain'.[5]

With *The Times* in the lead, other formerly Tory-supporting titles joined in, and by the summer of 1993 only the Express Group of newspapers remained truly loyal to the government. A *Guardian* item of January 1994 surveyed journalists' views on the matter, and came up with the following explanations for why government–press relations 'have never been so bad': (i) the weakness of the Labour opposition (before John Smith's death), requiring the press *de facto* to take up the opposition role; (ii) the government's long period in office, leading to laziness, arrogance and press frustration; and (iii) the poor quality of the government, and Major in particular. As one former *Sun* columnist was quoted as saying: 'Everyone is agreed that John Major is a hopeless berk who must go, and that he is surrounded by a bunch of unprincipled spivs and clones'.[6]

Press hostility to the Tories continued into 1994 and Tony Blair's election as Labour leader, at which point some usually pro-Conservative newspapers began to hint at their qualified support for 'New Labour'. And once again, News International took the lead. In July 1995, to the consternation of conservatives on both left and right of the British political spectrum, Tony Blair was invited to deliver a keynote address to a conference of senior News International executives in Australia. One source interpreted Rupert Murdoch's swing to Labour as 'a combination of the group's commercial interests, a broader political assessment and a judgement on the mood of the readers'.[7] In September, Henry Porter noted the dramatic improvement in News International–Labour relations.

> The bloody fight at Wapping, the favoured status that Murdoch achieved under Thatcher's administration, the viciousness of the campaign against Neil Kinnock's leadership, the persistently bruising coverage of Labour policy – all is apparently set aside in a convivial singularity of purpose.[8]

As the Major government stumbled on, battered by a succession of sex and corruption scandals, and Tony Blair's new-model Labour party captured the imagination of the British public, market forces encouraged the hesitant shifts of the 1992–94 period. the *Sun*'s editorial staff continued to have political reservations about Labour up until the 1997 election, but followed its readers into the Labour camp nevertheless, declaring for Blair on the first day of the campaign, 18 March. This was not so traumatic a move as the 'Nightmare on Kinnock Street' headline five years earlier would have suggested, given the wooing of Murdoch undertaken by Blair and his advisers after 1994, but it was a significant break with the biases of recent history, given the *Sun*'s ten million-plus readership, and confirmation of Murdoch's 'market-led pragmatism'. Few observers doubted that Murdoch remained a right-winger at heart, but he calculated that the political environment, and public opinion with it, had shifted so far that it was in his commercial interests to favour 'new' Labour over the old and discredited Conservatives. The *Daily Star* followed suit in the popular tabloid sector, largely in competitive response to the *Sun*, leaving only the *Express*, *Mail* and *Times* titles either pro-Tory or ambivalent come election day.

In 1997, therefore, for the first time in decades, it was the Tories who suffered a 'press deficit', and Tory leader John Major who could be found complaining about his party's poor media coverage. While many may find it difficult to sympathise with the party that benefited for so long from what Jeremy Tunstall calls the 'cheerleader tendency' of the right-wing British press (Tunstall, 1996), there can be little doubt that the reversal of that tendency, and the resultant focus on negative Tory stories between 1994 and 1997 (cash for questions, sex scandals of various kinds, and in particular the affair of Piers Merchant MP, exposed by the *Sun* early in the election campaign) helped Labour to victory. A review of the election by the CARMA International public relations company concluded, not least because of the *Sun*'s contribution, that 'the press had a significant role to play in the extent of the landslide victory, particularly among key voting groups'.[9] We will never know if New Labour could have won without the support of the *Sun* and other formerly pro-Tory 'cheerleaders', nor if, had it won, the size of its majority would have been reduced.

In the run-up to the 2001 and 2005 general elections, a similar pattern of pro-Labour press coverage was apparent. Given Labour's good economic record since 1997, Tony Blair's strong line on foreign policy issues such as Iraq, and a weak Tory opposition, there appeared to be no good reasons why Labour should not get another two terms in office, and once again formerly pro-Tory titles such as the *Sun* and *The Times* backed the party, withholding support only on the question of European monetary union (New Labour adhered to a policy of 'if it's good for Britain, and when certain economic tests are met, we'll go in'). On this issue, declared a *Sun* editorial shortly before polling day in 2001, New Labour risked 'all-out war' if it called an early referendum on Euro membership. 'Our opposition wouldn't just be unprecedentedly ferocious', it thundered, 'it would be deeply, even mortally damaging to Tony [Blair], Gordon [Brown] and everybody connected with the project'. Despite these reservations from the Murdoch stable, the only UK newspapers that supported the Tories in the 2001 campaign were Conrad Black's *Telegraph* titles (McNair, 2002). In 2005, by which time Blair had led the UK into an unpopular war in Iraq, pro-Labour press bias was less unequivocal, although still overwhelming. Only with the election of David Cameron as Tory leader, and the beginnings of a Conservative revival in 2007, did editorial allegiances begin to waver. There was little doubt that by the next general election, due in 2010 at the latest, and with Blair gone, widespread press endorsement of the Tories was much more likely.

Shah, Murdoch and the newspaper revolution

The 'newspaper revolution', which began in 1983 and climaxed in the Wapping dispute of 1986, was closely related to the ascendancy of radical right-wing principles in the British government. Just as the Conservative government in 1979 had begun a sustained attack on the public services, so too had it identified the trade unions as a major obstacle to the implementation of the Thatcherite economic project. Having come to power on an anti-union ticket, exploiting popular anger caused by the 'Winter of Discontent', which saw the unions locked in bitter industrial disputes with James Callaghan's Labour government, Margaret Thatcher quickly moved to neuter the unions' power by introducing a series of employment laws. The cumulative effect of legislation introduced in 1980 and 1982 was to make it extremely difficult, if not impossible, for unions to organise meaningful industrial action against determined employers. The most important measure in this respect was the outlawing of 'secondary action' – action taken by unions in support of other unions – and the tight restrictions placed on the numbers of those allowed to picket places of work. These measures made illegal the effective expression of solidarity between different groups of workers while, of course, employers could still cooperate to defeat industrial action.

This legislation established the conditions in which employers could, if they dared, engage their employees in disputes over hitherto sacrosanct staffing levels and working practices. Within the trade union movement as a whole, few groups enjoyed terms of employment that were more advantageous than those of the print workers of Fleet Street. In the traditional manner of labour aristocracies, the print unions – primarily the National Graphical Association (NGA) and the Society of Graphical and Allied Trades (Sogat) – had secured relatively high wages for their skilled members, high levels of employment, tight closed-shop agreements, complete control over entry to the printing trade (women were excluded from the lucrative typesetting positions, for instance), and 'Spanish' working practices such as claiming payment for shifts not worked. Such terms were, of course, extremely expensive, and contributed substantially to the poor economic health of the industry identified by the McGregor Commission when it noted that in 1975 four of eight national dailies were in loss, and six of seven national Sundays. McGregor noted that labour was the main component of the newspaper industry's costs, since staffing levels were exceptionally high, as were wages (McGregor, 1977: 31).

The ability of the printers to extract such terms from their employers was a reflection of their pivotal position in the newspaper production process, combined with the short shelf-life of news as a commodity. The 'hot-metal' process, employed in Fleet Street since the nineteenth century, was heavily dependent on printers' labour which could easily be withdrawn, with damaging loss of output. In the late 1970s, the printers used this power to resist the introduction of new technologies, which could have made newspapers more profitable, but at the cost of fewer print jobs. These included the techniques of photocomposition and direct input of editorial copy by journalists into pagesetting computers.

In 1978–79, *The Times* newspapers closed for almost a year, at a cost in lost production to their owners, Thomson, of £40 million. Between 1976 and 1985 industrial action by *The Times* and the *Sunday Times* print workers led to the loss of six million copies. These losses played a key part, according to Harold Evans, in persuading the Thomson Group in 1981 to sell *The Times* and the *Sunday Times* to Rupert Murdoch (Evans, 1983). In 1984, with Rupert Murdoch now in control, the papers lost 11.4 million copies to industrial action.

For some on the left, such militancy on the part of the unions represented the wholly legitimate defence of their members' interests in the face of big business. Others, however, by no means unsympathetic to the goals of the Labour movement in general, argued that 'Luddism' on the part of the print unions would be counter-productive to the long-term survival of the industry and the jobs which it provided. As Tom Baistow noted before the Wapping dispute, 'in Fleet Street the corrupting cynicism that can come with unfettered power is not the monopoly of the press barons: the erosion of journalistic standards and ethics by self-interested proprietors and their house-trained editors ... has been paralleled down the years by an equally self-interested distortion of the economics of production by a workforce that has played its part in creating the conditions for that decline' (Baistow, 1985: 77). After Wapping, Baistow again referred to a 'Fleet Street workforce that played its part in creating the conditions of decline which paved the way to Wapping ... the whole tragic affair was much of the chapels' own making, the bitter fruits of greed and arrogance and a sectarian selfishness that betrayed the collective principles of honest trade unionism' (Baistow, 1989: 65). Former industrialist and Labour peer Lord Goodman wrote that 'there can have been no period in industrial history where a greater demonstration of reckless irresponsibility has been displayed by a section of organised labour ... the behaviour of the unions prior to the Murdoch revolution can only be described as suicidal'.[10]

The print unions, like others in the labour movement, had grown used to the status and influence bestowed upon them by the post-war social democratic consensus, and failed to recognise the extent to which Thatcherism had undermined their position. With the Employment Acts of 1980 and 1982, the legal framework was in place – backed up by political will at the highest level – to enable proprietors to begin to erode the unions' power.

The struggle began, not in Fleet Street itself, but in Warrington in the northeast of England, where from 1980 local free-sheet publisher Eddie Shah had been striving to loosen the grip of the NGA on the production of his *Stockport Messenger*. The NGA resisted Shah's attempts to introduce electronic publishing technologies and thereby reduce staffing levels, leading to a dispute that culminated in November 1983 in illegal mass picketing outside Shah's Warrington plant. Shah successfully took the NGA to court and became the first employer to 'sequestrate', that is, have a union's assets seized by the court. The dispute and its outcome were covered enthusiastically by Rupert Murdoch's *Sunday Times*, whose editor Andrew Neil correctly recognised it to be a watershed in industrial relations within the British press. Shah's success in destroying the NGA's power in Warrington thus became the catalyst for News International to attempt an analogous feat – although on a much bigger scale – in Fleet Street.

Since buying into the British newspaper industry in the 1960s, Rupert Murdoch had been forced, like other Fleet Street proprietors, to accept the print unions' reluctance to countenance new technologies and absorb the consequent losses. Shah, however, showed that with the help of Conservative employment legislation, the unions could be taken on and defeated. In March 1984, a stoppage at the News International plant in London's Bouverie Street cost Murdoch the loss of 23.5 million copies of the *Sun* and three million copies of the *News of the World*. This dispute, Sogat's General Secretary was later to concede, probably convinced Murdoch that radical measures had to be taken if his newspapers were to be made profitable in the long term. And achieving such profitability was crucial to the expansion of what was, by the mid-1980s, already a global media empire spanning Europe, the USA and Australia – an empire, moreover, in some financial difficulty.

By 1985, Murdoch's new printing plant at Wapping had been constructed. He had a plant in Glasgow intended for printing Scottish and northern editions of his titles, but this lay idle because the unions would not permit the facsimile transmission of copy from London. By February of that year, Murdoch had apparently lost patience with trying to win agreement from the printers to bring these new facilities into production, and announced to his senior managers that he was making a 'dash for freedom' (Melvern, 1988: 122).

For the rest of 1985, News International management planned and prepared for the transfer of all newspaper production from the plants at Gray's Inn Road and Bouverie Street to the new Docklands site, secretly installing an Atex computer and putting in place a system that would enable the company to dispense with thousands of print workers. Negotiations continued with the unions, but without success, each party blaming the other for its failure. In the unions' view, Murdoch had already decided on a course of action and had no intention of negotiating a compromise agreement. According to this view, his final, unproductive meeting with the unions before the move to Wapping, on 23 January 1986, was calculated to provoke a strike which, under Tory employment law, would mean that he could dismiss the print workers without being legally required to offer expensive compensation. Murdoch, for his part, insisted that he and his managers had made every effort at conciliation over a long period, but that union obstinacy prevented a negotiated solution.

On 24 January 1986, following the meeting with Murdoch, the Fleet Street printers announced strike action to close down the News International titles. That evening, journalists and support staff at the two City plants were invited to turn up for work the next day at Wapping. Failure to do so would be treated as resignation. At about 8:00 pm on Saturday 25 January, with only one day's edition of the *Sun* lost, the production lines at Wapping began to run and, as Linda Melvern puts it in her account of the dispute, 'two hundred years of Fleet Street history were over' (*ibid.*: 155).

News International's ensuing dispute with Sogat and the NGA was one of the most bitter and violent in Britain's industrial relations history, but with the full weight of the government and the state behind him, Murdoch was never in danger of losing. He used the services of the Australian haulage company Thomas Nationwide Transport (TNT) to establish a union-proof distribution network for his titles, all of which would now be printed in Wapping and Glasgow. Attempts at a settlement were made but never came to anything, and by the end of 1986 the printers had conceded defeat. Soon thereafter, other newspapers joined the exodus out of Fleet Street.

With the unions thus emasculated, Murdoch and the other proprietors could begin to transform their cost structures and increase profitability. While the treatment of the unions was presented by Murdoch as a regrettable necessity for which the workers themselves were to blame, the proponents of change held out the promise that lower labour costs and the introduction of new technologies would lead to a more diverse, pluralistic and financially sound print media. In the words of Cento Veljanovski (in a book, it might be noted, published by News International), 'improved industrial relations [*sic*] combined with advances in print technology have significantly lowered barriers to entry, enabled the introduction of new enhanced graphics and colours, and stimulated the proliferation of magazine titles and other publications' (Veljanovski, 1990: 11). If concentration of ownership and political bias were indeed valid concerns, the argument went, the Wapping revolution would ease the problem by extending access to new groups, hitherto excluded because of prohibitive start-up and running costs.

The first proprietor to attempt to take advantage of the new economic environment, after Murdoch himself, was, appropriately enough, Eddie Shah. Following his victory over the NGA in Warrington, he began to make plans for the establishment of two new national titles, *Today* and *Sunday Today*, believing that 'given the Tory union laws, a new non-union newspaper printed on greenfield sites, using colour and aimed at the middle market between the *Daily Telegraph* and the *Daily Mirror*, was now on the British agenda' (MacArthur, 1988: 35).

Shah raised £18 million of capital in the City and proceeded to establish a newspaper operation that would utilise direct input and satellite page transmission, with distribution by road rather than the more expensive and less reliable (because heavily unionised) rail. Given the labour savings made possible by the new relationship with the unions, it was estimated that *Today* could break even on a circulation of 330,000, and the paper duly launched on 4 March 1986, less than two months after News International's move to Wapping. Despite the new technologies, however, and the cowed state of the unions, *Today* and *Sunday Today* failed to give Shah the break into national newspaper publishing which he desired. Teething troubles with the computers used by journalists, and problems with the advanced colour and graphics printing equipment, led to missed production deadlines. Distribution was poor, and the printing equipment bought by Shah failed to match up to its specifications. Sales dropped quickly after the launch, and even such basic matters as revenue from newsagents proved difficult to collect. Annual running costs were estimated at £40 million, which meant that even a healthy circulation of 500,000 would be insufficient to cover the paper's costs. Four months after the launch, in June 1986, Shah sold 35 per cent of *Today* to Lonrho (owner of the *Observer* and Glasgow's the *Herald* and *Evening Times*), which quickly gained full control. *Sunday Today* ceased publication in June 1987, while *Today* continued to operate on an estimated annual loss of £28 million, before being sold to News International in July 1987, in whose hands it remained until it was closed down in October 1995 on financial grounds.

The early failure of *Today* – 'the paper that was going to revolutionise Fleet Street, put power back in the hands of journalists, and end the curse of the printers and the restrictive practices that were reducing papers to penury' (*ibid*.: 16) – is attributed by its first editor, Brian MacArthur, to weak business management, poor design, difficulties associated with the introduction of new technologies, and excessive ambition on the part of Shah. *Today*, he argues, was under-resourced to meet its production targets of one million copies daily (an output that turned out to be simply beyond the capacity of Shah's presses). But if Shah could be accused of inexperience, naivety and over-optimism in assuming that the defeat of the print unions would enable him to challenge the dominance of the Fleet Street press barons, his 'vision of the electronic newspaper' eventually bore fruit, in MacArthur's view, in the contrasting shapes of the *Independent* and *Sunday Sport* (one an aspiring 'quality' broadsheet, the other a *National Enquirer*-style soft-porn comic), while his revolutionary system of distributing newspapers by road was central to the success of Rupert Murdoch's operation at Wapping (*ibid*.: 46).

The success of the *Independent*, the idea for which was inspired by Eddie Shah's experience (Crozier, 1988), has been attributed to the care with which, in contrast to the *Today* operation, a realistic business plan was drawn up. Another important difference between the *Independent* and *Today* was the quality of the former's personnel. As MacArthur makes clear in his account of *Today*'s setting up, Eddie Shah was suspicious not merely of Fleet Street's printers, but also of its journalists, seeing no reason why he should pay the (in his view) inflated salaries that would have been required to attract a sufficient number of the top names in the journalistic profession to his title. Whether or not he was correct in believing that the quality of the established journalistic superstars' writing was not appreciably higher than that of lesser-known and lower-paid hacks, he neglected to take account of the valuable status and credibility established names could bring to a new title starting out from scratch in a fiercely competitive market. By contrast, the group of journalists, led by former *Daily Telegraph* City Editor Andreas Whittam Smith, who initiated the *Independent* intended from the outset to attract the 'best' writers in the field.

They were greatly helped in this task by the manner and timing of News International's move to Wapping, the abruptness and uncompromising nature of which drove many *Times* and *Sunday Times* editorial staff out of Murdoch's employment. Unwilling to work in 'Fortress Wapping' and under siege from disgruntled printers, such influential journalists as Peter Jenkins and Isobel Hilton left News International and ran into the waiting arms of Andreas Whittam Smith. From its launch, therefore, the editorial content of the *Independent* carried a weight and authority which *Today* never achieved. It was also exceptionally well designed, while the technological glitches suffered by *Today* never afflicted the *Independent* to the same degree. By November 1987, with a total staff of only 403 (of whom 209 were editorial), the *Independent* was well on its way to being profitable, with a circulation of over 300,000. In September 1989, the *Independent on Sunday* was launched, and both titles have since become firmly established in their respective markets, although they have not performed especially well. The sale of the *Independent* titles, first to the Mirror Group, then to the Irish media baron Tony O'Reilly, was a consequence of their steadily declining circulations and profitability over a period of years. Explanations for the *Independent* titles' difficulties have varied from editorial incompetence to the adverse effect of successive price wars on its circulation. But regardless of how one explains the failure of the *Independent* titles to remain independent, their current status as the property of a foreign media baron illustrates the limited character of the Wapping 'revolution'.

The other spectacular success of the post-Wapping era was the *Sunday Sport*. Launched by pornographic-magazine publisher David Sullivan in September 1986, the *Sunday Sport* utilised only a handful of editorial staff to produce a heady, down-market mixture of sex, crime and sport. While some have disputed that the *Sunday Sport* could legitimately be called a newspaper, since many of its stories are fictional and its content largely soft-core pornography, it differed from the other tabloids only in the degree to which these elements predominated in its pages. With its small staff and low running costs, the *Sunday Sport* was able to make a healthy profit with a circulation, in December 1986, of only 230,000 (small by tabloid standards), leading one commentator to describe it as 'the only unqualified press success of the newspaper revolution'. As S. J. Taylor remarked, the *Sunday Sport* was 'the first successful post-Wapping tabloid' (Taylor, 1991: 376). With the defeat of the print unions by Shah and Murdoch, and the introduction of labour-saving technologies which that defeat allowed, David Sullivan, like the founders of the *Independent*, was able radically to reduce what had hitherto been regarded as the minimum break-even circulation for a national tabloid newspaper.

One year after its launch, circulation had reached 500,000, selling to a readership mainly of young males and generating annual profits for Sullivan's Apollo group of £750,000. The financial success of the *Sunday Sport* enabled David Sullivan in 1987 to buy the *Morning Star*'s print works in London's Farringdon Road for an estimated £2.5 million and to seek £3 million start-up capital for a *Daily Sport*. The *Sport* launched on Wednesday 17 August 1988, was published initially on only three days a week, but by October 1991 had become a six-day newspaper, with a profitable circulation of some 350,000. Since then, circulation has declined, but both *Sport* titles remain profitable.

If the *Independent* and *Sport* titles can be viewed as the success stories (or perhaps, survivors) of the Wapping revolution, others found it more difficult to exploit the new cost structures. *Today*, as noted above, closed in 1995. Robert Maxwell's attempt in February 1987 to set up the *London Daily News* to compete with the *Evening Standard* failed at a cost to his company of some £30 million. Eddie Shah made a second attempt to break into national newspaper publishing with the *Post*, launched in November 1988, but despite receiving some favourable reviews, it quickly 'disappeared into a black hole'.[11]

And what of the hope held out by advocates of the Wapping revolution for a more diverse and representative press? In the second half of 1986, when there was still such a thing as a 'Tory press', plans were announced for the long-awaited launch of a popular newspaper with a left-wing editorial policy – the first such to be established since the *Daily Worker* in 1930. To be called *News on Sunday*, the paper would be launched with £6.5 million raised from trade unions, sympathetic local councils and business. To assist in raising this capital, the paper's founders commissioned market research by Research Surveys of Great Britain, which indicated a sizeable potential market for a left-wing Sunday tabloid of about three million people. This research appeared to confirm the long-standing conviction of the British left that an audience existed for a paper reflective of their opinions and agendas. With the transformation of cost structures promised by the introduction of new print technologies, it was estimated that the title could break even on a circulation of 800,000.

News on Sunday was launched on 26 April 1987, but failed from the outset to reach its break-even circulation target. Despite the optimistic evidence of the market research, sales of the first issue were only 500,000, not in itself a shockingly poor figure, but not enough to give *News on Sunday* the necessary kick-start which might have sustained it through the initial loss-making period experienced by every new title. Moreover, circulation declined steadily after the first issue. The final edition was published six weeks later, on 8 June.

A number of explanations have been advanced for the failure of the *News on Sunday*. Chippindale and Horrie place the blame largely on a combination of bad marketing and weak management (Chippindale and Horrie, 1988). The *News on Sunday*, as they cheekily put it, was set up by, and intended for, 'right-ons' – the anti-sexist, anti-racist 'new left'. This meant that its editorial policy and news agenda would have to be 'ideologically sound' and politically correct. For example, there would be no page three girls.

At the same time, however, the *News on Sunday* would have to be popular. To market the paper, advertising agency Bartle Bogle Hegarty was employed, on a budget of £1.3 million, to combine the necessary ingredients of political correctness and popularity within a series of advertisements which would be 'challenging, campaigning, anti-establishment and irreverent' (*ibid.*: 102). Exploiting the lack of page three girls, Bartle Bogle Hegarty designed a poster advert based on the slogan 'No Tits, But a Lot of Balls'. Another depicted Margaret Thatcher, Neil Kinnock, David Steel and David Owen, with the caption 'These are the only tits you'll see on our page three'.

The agency's market research suggested that these posters (and others in a similar vein) would be effective in attracting the audience *News on Sunday* was seeking. The management team rejected them, however, on the grounds that they were sexist. As one member of the management collective put it, 'at bottom the advertisers were looking for their mark, and their mark was a man. The campaign thus became one that addressed men rather than women' (*ibid.*: 116).

Chippindale and Horrie go on to show how marketing decisions were obfuscated and delayed as arguments went on within management – most of whom had no experience of producing newspapers – over the ideological soundness of this or that advertisement. As the arguments continued, deadlines for booking advertising space and producing copy ran out, forcing hasty last-minute decisions to be made. As one of the paper's financial backers explained after *News on Sunday* had gone under, the advertisers had designed a campaign which 'might have proved to be very effective but was found to be offensive to the staff and to the founder of the newspaper'.[12] The strictures of political correctness won over the requirements of effective marketing. For Peter Chippindale, the failure of the paper proved, not that the idea for a left-wing tabloid was a bad one, but that members of the concerned middle class, essentially ignorant of journalism, cannot just wade into the arena in the belief that the moral rectitude of their brief will bring readers flocking to them. ... With little or no experience, they awarded themselves senior management posts and plunged into their obsession with putting into practice their ideas of consensual decision-making and positive discrimination with little or no thought for the realities of the newspaper business.[13]

Ex-editor Brian Whittaker attributed the failure of *News on Sunday* first to the fact that, even with £6 million raised, it was under-capitalised from the outset. Given the much greater investment of both Eddie Shah and the *Independent* team, £6.5 million was not an especially large sum. On the question of management, he argues that 'the paper's original guiding lights were amateurs who suddenly found themselves running a public company. They were reluctant to hand over control to professionals – apparently for fear that the paper would turn into a Tory rag'.[14] In the view of Keith Sutton, another former editor, the paper suffered from the consequences of trying to apply 'a direct input system virtually untried in Britain, with a bunch of executives who had never executed anyone in their lives; seven subs; three handfuls of reporters, one staff photographer and a freelance budget that would buy Robert Maxwell lunch for a fortnight'.[15] The poor quality of management led not only to a disastrously confused marketing strategy and launch, but also to a failure to obtain cost-effective deals from the print unions. The member of management responsible for employer negotiations, Alan Hayling 'proved no match for hard-bargaining contract printers and ended up with deals that would have made a Murdoch or a Maxwell laugh'.[16] Others have argued that the *News on Sunday* was simply a weak product editorially, the failure of which, like that of Eddie Shah's *Post* a year later, proved only that 'a bad paper, badly promoted, will rapidly meet the fate it deserves'.[17]

The *Sunday Correspondent*, by contrast, was not generally perceived as a 'bad' newspaper, but failed nevertheless, largely because it launched at a time – September 1989 – when the second great recession of the Thatcher era was just beginning to bite. When advertising revenues were falling, as they did in the late 1980s and early 1990s, sales of anything less than 600,000 were insufficient to make a Sunday newspaper such as the broadsheet *Correspondent*, standing alone in the marketplace without the support of a larger parent company, financially viable. In January 1990 the *Independent* launched its Sunday sister, inevitably eating into the *Correspondent*'s market. In addition to coping with the competitive strategies of the already established Sundays (see below), the *Correspondent* now had to find and retain readership in the face of another brand-new title. In July 1990, the floundering *Correspondent* attempted to resolve its difficulties by relaunching as a 'quality tabloid', under a new editor more experienced in the business of popular journalism. This shift in strategy failed to make the paper profitable, and it closed in September 1990.

For some observers, the fact of these failures and the continuing gap in the British newspaper market for popular left-of-centre titles proved that optimistic hopes of a post-Wapping future in which publications of diverse political persuasions would flourish were utopian. James Curran argued that the basic economic environment within which newspapers must survive had not been fundamentally transformed, noting that 'production wages comprised only 21 per cent of Fleet Street's costs before new technology was introduced'.[18] The Fleet Street revolution had 'not significantly changed the character of the national press' since 'the basic rules of publishing have changed very little. Establishing mainstream national papers remains very expensive.' Twenty eight per cent of the *Sunday Correspondent*'s costs when it launched at the end of 1989 were allocated to staff (although a large proportion of these would have been accounted for by journalists, as opposed to printers). After the move out of Fleet Street, start-up costs for newspapers remained high, as did running costs, making it much easier for established proprietors and corporations to launch new titles and buy up existing ones than it was for new entrants to the business. Even with £30 million, Robert Maxwell's *London Daily News* failed. Eddie Shah's *Today* lost £22.5 million. In the late 1970s, when Wapping was still a twinkle in Rupert Murdoch's eye, Lord McGregor warned that 'even if all newspapers accomplish the change [to new technologies], competition may still result in some papers closing, since the new technology does little to alter the relative position of competing titles' (McGregor, 1977: 44).

The potential cost-saving benefits of new print technologies, such as they were, were substantially eroded in any case by the established proprietors' adoption of strategies specifically designed to increase the cost of production and discourage new entrants. From the late 1980s onwards, newspapers began to introduce Saturday supplements, glossy magazines and ever-increasing numbers of Sunday sections. At the same time, more money was spent on marketing and advertising. In the face of such developments, new, under-resourced titles simply could not compete. The late Paul Foot argued that the *News on Sunday* failed not only because of editorial and management shortcomings, but 'also because of the insurmountable difficulties of advertising, promoting and circulating a new popular paper without any real wealth behind it'.[19] The workings of the market – if in new technological conditions – meant that 'the new technology has had no diversifying effect whatsoever. Its only real effect has been to boost the profits of the mighty media corporations at the expense of the trade unions'.[20] Belfield *et al.* agree with this assessment, arguing that 'British newspapers have not been revitalised [as a result of Wapping]. What has been revitalised is Murdoch's finances' (Belfield *et al.*, 1991: 96).

As these authors point out, after Wapping the News International wage bill was cut at a stroke by £45 million per annum. As a result, pre-tax profits increased from £39.1 million in 1985 to £165 million in 1988, providing a substantial proportion of the finance for Murdoch's move into satellite television. Lord Goodman argued that 'newspapers, whose very existence was under threat, are now reaping handsome profits – something they owe largely to Rupert Murdoch – although his fellow proprietors may not enjoy acknowledging it'.[21] For Goodman, the Wapping revolution saved, among others, the *Telegraph* titles. And yet, 'today the industry is more dominated by giant companies than at any previous period. The effect, of course, is to increase the risks attaching to any modest size publication, with the giants' daily increasing wealth waiting for any opportunity to wolf a straggler from the pack' (Goodman A., 1988).

The *Independent*'s ex-political editor Anthony Bevins argued that 'multiplicity in itself, whether in terms of newspapers, television channels, or petrol stations, does not generate freedom. ... The predominant power will stay in the hands of the barons and their well-paid, underqualified hacks. That is the only 'golden promise' of Mr Murdoch's so-called information age. More of the same. To pretend otherwise is to fly in the face of the track record, it is an insult to a free and independent intelligence' (Bevins, 1990: 17).

For Britain's dwindling left, meanwhile, the lack of a newspaper representative of their views continues to represent a failure of 'press freedom'. Unfortunately for them, it is not likely to be rectified in the foreseeable future. More than two decades after the failure of the *News on Sunday*, the difficulties associated with establishing a 'left' press are more than those of editorial and managerial competence. What, and where, is the allegedly under-represented left in these post-Cold War, New Labour days, and what would a 'left' newspaper look like in the twenty-first century? As this edition goes to press, the mainstream left is in government, supported, more or less, not just by its traditional allies (*Guardian*, *Observer*, *Mirror*), but by media barons such as Murdoch (for a while longer at least), while the 'hard left' retreats even further into the margins than it ever was.

Despite much publicised efforts by the *Mirror* to present itself as once again the centre-left popular tabloid of choice (through such devices as opposing US policy on 'the war against terror'), the recent history of the British press suggests that notions of left- and right-wing newspapers, as these terms have traditionally been used in the critical literature, are increasingly redundant in the fluid, pragmatically market-driven media environment of the twenty-first century. The media market, interacting with and responding to a changing political environment since 1994, has *de facto* produced a very different balance of editorial allegiance from that which existed when earlier editions of this book were published.

In any event, the question of the viability of another left-of-centre mass-circulation newspaper has been made redundant by the emergence of the internet. This new medium for the distribution of information threatens all newspapers, not merely those of the left, whose potential readers are slowly but steadily migrating from print to online (see Chapter 8).

Newspapers and the internet – the death of print?

I am one of those who, throughout the emergence of the internet and other communication technologies as serious platforms for news consumption (from the mid- to late-1990s), have maintained a degree of optimism about the health of the newspaper industry. While many predicted the death of print, or at least its marginalisation in the face of online and other emerging technologies for the distribution of news, my view has been and remains that the unique use value and user-friendliness of newsprint guarantees its survival, at least within the lifetimes of the readers of this book. Notwithstanding the inevitable fact that before too long a viable electronic news reader will come onto the market,[22] news and journalism packaged within sheets of disposable (preferably recycled) paper and sold in newsagents remains at present the most convenient means of consuming one's daily news fix, whether on public transport going to work, over breakfast at the weekend, or accompanying a pint of beer down the local pub.[23]

That said, as we saw in Chapter 1, it is clear that the newspaper, as a commodity within the media marketplace, is in steady decline, and that some sectors of the print industry, such as the paid-for evening commuter paper, face particular challenges. In Britain, national daily and Sunday newspapers, and regional and local papers, have experienced steady decline between 1988 and 2008, of something like 3 per cent a year on average. Some, like the *Mirror* and the *Express*, have fallen by substantially more over that period.

Set against the proliferation of alternatives to print, however, it would have been surprising only if there had been no decline in newspaper sales these past two decades. In 1988, there were few real-time news channels (only CNN, which at that time was hardly viewed by the mainstream British audience), and online journalism did not exist. Free newspapers were relatively few and far between. Today, free titles such as *Metro*, *London Lite* and many others compete with paid-fors, especially in the evening market, with titles such as the London *Evening Standard* and Glasgow *Evening Times* under constant pressure to maintain their position (the UK *Metro* chain is the highest-circulation free sheet in the world). Against all that, a circulation decline of a quarter over two decades might be regarded as less than disastrous, as could the finding of research carried out in 2006 that 75 per cent of the UK public still regarded print as the most trusted news source, second only to television with 86 per cent.[24]

Globally, as we have seen, 'the figures confirm that the industry is healthy and vigorous and is successfully dealing with increasing competition from other media'.[25] As an industry body, they would say that, wouldn't they – but there are at least some reasons to be cheerful about the resilience of newspaper circulation at a time of unprecedented competition for the news consumer. Those titles in greatest decline, such as the *Express* and *Mirror* in the UK, have been the ones most beset by poor management and editorial decisions. High-quality newspapers, on the other hand, with management that know their market and invest in serving it, such as the *Financial Times* and the *Mail*, have seen their circulations grow over time.

Paradoxically, as Peter Cole observes in a recent survey of the health of the British press,[26] it is the tabloids that have declined most in recent times, contrary to the pessimistic pronouncements of those who, a few years ago, predicted a race down-market by the British newspaper industry in response to growing competitive pressures. Competition has increased, but quality still succeeds, and lack of quality is punished in whatever subsector one looks at. Moreover, since the Wapping revolution and the restructuring of the industry in the 1980s, the majority of national newspapers have remained profitable, with pre-tax profits of 15–30 per cent expected on titles of more than 100,000 circulation. There have been short-term losses produced by one-off events, such as the move from broadsheet to tabloid formats (Times Newspapers Ltd invested £12 million in 2004 on this; in February 2005 the *Telegraph*'s management announced 20 per cent job cuts to enable £150 million of investment in new technology intended to compete with *The Times*), or investment in online services, or in competitive tactics such as price-cutting and the introduction of free sheets in London by News Corp and Associated Newspapers respectively. However, across the sector as a whole, revenues have been robust. Even a declining-circulation title such as the *Express* is making money for proprietor Northern & Shell. The global financial crisis of 2007–08 threatened to cut press revenues as advertising was squeezed, but the underlying economics of most newspapers has remained healthy for much of the post-Wapping era, and is likely to continue to do so if the challenge of the internet can be met.

The technological challenge

Which may not be so easy. The technological challenge now facing the print media in the UK, as elsewhere in the advanced capitalist world, is immense. If it is the case, as noted in Chapter 1, that print circulations are rising globally, this is because of the impact on the figures of developing countries such as China and India. In Britain, the USA and comparable countries, newspaper circulations are generally in slow and steady decline, as the journalistic market fragments and users migrate to the internet and mobile telephony. Although still of minor importance as a platform for news consumption, the mobile phone will grow in market share as the technology improves. Particular types of print journalism, such as the Sunday newspaper, may come under pressure in a digitised world. Kim Fletcher has observed in relation to Sunday newspapers:

> The rolling demands of web publishing sit uneasily with journalists whose entire efforts are currently directed to publishing on only one day of the week; second, the most bullish forecasts of internet ad revenue fail to generate in one quiet day the sums required to keep a Sunday newspaper in the staff to which it has become accustomed.[27]

Even entrepreneurial pioneers such as Rupert Murdoch were slow to wake up to the scale of this challenge. Only in April 2005, in a speech to the American Society of Newspaper Editors, did the chairman of News Corporation acknowledge, in respect of the digital revolution, that 'many of us have been unaccountably complacent'.[28] Technology, and the possibilities presented by the internet in particular, is undoubtedly the key question mark over the future of the newspaper as a physical object, although the final extinction of print is some way down the road. As Kim Fletcher has argued

> in all this talk about the end of papers, no one suggests that people don't want news or information or entertainment any more. On the contrary, they seem to want more of all three. That demand will be met by an expansion rather than a retraction in journalistic output.[29]

In that context, it is entirely realistic to state that the newspaper has a future in British culture, just like the printed book (more books are sold now than ever before in human history). Print journalism will survive, for a generation or two at least, because print is a genuinely useful means of delivering journalism – cheap, portable, disposable, convenient to use, easy to read. Just like the book, however, the newspaper increasingly coexists and converges with a variety of electronic, online platforms, which are changing the way people consume information. As platforms and outlets proliferate, the market share of individual newspaper titles is falling, and may well fall a lot further. What remains unclear is the level, if indeed there is one, at which the decline of print will bottom out and stabilise.

Competent media managers no longer see this long decline as a threat to print, however, but as an opportunity for their businesses to develop, even expand into new activities and markets. As newspapers such as the *Guardian* have shown (and broadcasters such as the BBC – see Chapter 7), it is increasingly the news brand that counts in the media marketplace and guarantees the long-term survival of the business.

When Rupert Murdoch purchased *The Wall Street Journal* in August 2007, he paid $5 billion not for the rights to sell paper and ink on the streets of New York and Washington, but for the global brand which *The Wall Street Journal* represents (niche financial data, for online and mobile access to which business and other users will pay handsomely in the century ahead). It is what the title stands for in a globalised media marketplace that has value, not the carrier medium by which it has traditionally been distributed within national public spheres.

If the *Guardian*'s print sales have declined by around 25 per cent since 1988, the growth in its online use has more than compensated. Nearly three-quarters of a million people access the title's online outlet every day, compared with around 360,000 who buy the paper version. Of online users, around two-thirds are overseas, representing an unprecedented globalisation of the audience for British-made journalism. Of course, making money from these users is not straightforward, and viable business models for online news outlets continue to be elusive. But if 17 million monthly users, relatively affluent and well educated, is not the basis for stable advertising revenue going forward, then one wonders what would be?

Until early 2008, the *Guardian* was the UK's leading online journalism site, followed by the *Daily Mail/Mail On Sunday* (11.9 million users), *The Times/Sunday Times* (10.6 million), the *Sun* (encompassing a group of sites with some 9.44 million users) and the *Telegraph/Sunday Telegraph* (9 million). The *Daily Mail* has now moved ahead, as Table 1.3 shows (see Chapter 1), and the market can be expected to be quite volatile as investments made by the Telegraph and other groups begin to pay off (or not, as the case may be). Only one thing is certain. The audience for news is shifting to the internet as it becomes more used to the technology, and sites become more welcoming and user-friendly. There is no decline in the market for journalism, just a change in the way it is being packaged, distributed and consumed, which the innovative news organisation must learn to work with, rather than fear – to see as an opportunity rather than a threat.

Exploiting this opportunity means investment of the type embarked upon by companies such as Johnston Press in Scotland, to enable the integration of web-based video into news stories, and realise the possibilities for interaction and participation which news audiences appear to want. The implications of such developments for journalistic form and content are an issue for Chapter 8, and some observers see them as threatening what has been regarded as 'quality' print journalism (see, for example, criticism of the *Telegraph* management's rush into 'click-and-carry' technologies in 2006–07). But that they are a prerequisite of survival for what used to be print journalism is beyond doubt.

In 2007, the *Guardian* editor Alan Rusbridger argued (and his comments apply to the print sector in general) that:

> we've moved from being in competition with a small pool of British broadsheets to being in competition with just about everyone. We're no longer a once-a-day text medium for a predominantly domestic audience. Increasingly – around the clock – we use a combination of media in telling stories, and in commentary, to millions of users around the globe.[30]

There is a future for print media (or the brands currently associated with print), even if it lies in 'moving beyond journalism' and towards what one observer describes as 'tools that become part of the daily job for focused groups of users'.[31] Newspapers may or may not have a future in themselves, but the brands for which they are merely the packaging most certainly do, if they play to their strengths. Indeed, news brands, and the qualities of truthfulness, reliability, independence, etc. that they come to signify in the marketplace, may in the end be the only thing that survives.

Paper is just fish wrapping, as the best journalists have always known. the *Guardian* brand, on the other hand, stands for something in the journalistic marketplace for which people will always be prepared to pay (as, in their own ways, do *The Times*, *Mail*, the *Financial Times*, CNN, BBC and other brands).

Another observer, after Rupert Murdoch's successful purchase of *The Wall Street Journal* in August 2007, commented that 'in a crowded news world, rather than merely having to compete with new providers on the block, older, "trusted" brands can actually make a virtue of their age and use their brand to rise above the noise'.[32]

That there is a future for print journalism, there is no doubt – enough of a future for barons like Murdoch to continue to invest billions of dollars in it. But what kind of print journalism will dominate after a few more years of the economic and technological challenges discussed here, and how it will be produced and consumed by users in a globalised public sphere, is not clear.

Further reading

On press history, see Curran and Seaton's (1997) classic *Power Without Responsibility* and journalist Matthew Engel's (1996) biography of the tabloids, *Tickle the Public*. A more academic treatment of the same material is covered by Martin Conboy (2002) in *The Press and Popular Culture*.

7   Broadcast journalism in the UK

> This chapter reviews the history of British TV and radio journalism from their origins in the BBC of the 1920s until the present time. Specific topics covered include:
>
> - the changing political environment
> - the changing technological environment, in particular the implications of analogue switch-off and the move to digital
> - the changing economic environment
> - key legislative and regulatory changes affecting British TV and radio journalism.

From 1918–79, Britain was governed by what Nicholas Garnham calls a 'tripartite corporatist consensus', which established a system of public service broadcasting as 'one of its institutional forms of political and cultural hegemony' (Garnham, 1986: 28).

The organisation of British broadcasting in the form of a public service monopoly was the result of deliberations by two government-appointed committees: the Sykes Committee, which reported in 1923 and recommended that, given the potential social and political power of radio broadcasting in the UK, it should remain free of control by the government of the day; and the Crawford Committee, which, reporting in 1926, called for broadcasting to be free of commercial domination. It was believed not only that it was innately desirable for a potent new means of mass communication to be exempted from harsh commercial imperatives, but that wavelength scarcity would tend towards a monopoly structure for the emerging broadcasting industry. That being the case, better that such a monopoly be held in public rather than private hands.

The British Broadcasting Corporation, as it was to be called, would be funded by its audience in the form of a licence fee. It would be available throughout the country and free at the point of reception; it would play the role, consciously articulated, of promoting a sense of Britishness and national community, while educating, informing and entertaining in the manner regarded as desirable by the establishment of the time. Most importantly, public service broadcasting would enjoy constitutional independence from the politicians, standing aloof from their partisan debates and self-interested policies.

Thus broadcasting in Britain was defined from the very outset – in contrast to the USA, where development followed an uninhibitedly commercial path, or the USSR, where broadcasting was commandeered by the Bolsheviks and put to use as a part of the propaganda apparatus – as something too serious to be left to the marketplace or to the whims and manipulations of politicians. Its entertainment would be 'worthy' and enlightening, popularising and upholding the highest standards of British social and cultural life. Its journalism would be put to the service of British democracy, informing audiences about public affairs from a standpoint of political impartiality and balance. For the BBC, unlike the newspapers with their openly declared biases, there was to be no taking of sides.

Such a course was 'consensual', to repeat Garnham's phrase, because it reassured each of the major political parties to know that none of its opponents could hijack the broadcasting system while in office. The existing media proprietors, on the other hand, had no wish to see broadcasting become a competitor for scarce advertising revenue, and so they had little objection to a publicly funded system. And public service broadcasting was an institution of 'political and cultural hegemony' insofar as it could be, and was used to disseminate, throughout an increasingly enfranchised British society, values, ideas and information that contributed to its smooth and relatively conflict-free reproduction over decades.

The early British broadcasters regarded themselves as key players in the construction of a national culture – a culture that reflected, as it was bound to do, the unequal class and status structure of British capitalism, within which certain forms and means of expression were preferred over others; certain art forms regarded as legitimate but not others; and certain groups regarded as ideologically suspect, even subversive.

The public service principles laid down in the 1920s for the BBC were extended to commercial broadcasting when Independent Television (ITV) was set up in 1955. Although the ITV companies would operate on a fully commercial basis, deriving their income from the sale of advertising time, the organisation they jointly formed to produce their national and international news, Independent Television News (ITN), was subject to the same constraints in coverage as the BBC's news and current affairs service. Regional news and network current affairs, which were to be produced by the regional companies themselves, also had to be impartial. Neither advertisers, nor owners of the ITV companies, could exert pressure on ITN's editorial decision-making processes, although its survival and thus the career prospects of its personnel clearly depended on their ability to produce a service which would be popular with the viewers.

As a public service, British broadcasting was only one of a number of twentieth-century British institutions which embodied such features as 'universality of provision', 'quality of service', and the suppression of market forces. Education, health, public libraries and state welfare provision, as they developed after the Second World War, represented the application of similar principles in other key spheres of social life, made possible by the emergence of Labour as a governing party, and the subsequent 'social democratic consensus', which straddled the major political parties throughout the 1950s, 1960s and most of the 1970s. The 1980s crisis in the public services, and public service broadcasting in particular, stemmed directly from the ending of this consensus and the coming to power in 1979 of the Conservative Party headed by Margaret Thatcher.

The changing political environment

Some commentators have dissented from the idea that there ever was any such thing as a 'social democratic consensus' in Britain, but there can be no doubt that the Thatcher government made a conscious break with the past in deliberately rejecting the role that successive Labour and Conservative governments had allotted to public service institutions. It began to implement a political strategy of introducing market forces and commercial logic into arenas from which they had previously been excluded. The strategy was underpinned by monetarist economic theory and classical liberalism, which challenged the view that publicly funded bureaucracies were the most efficient providers of services. In the case of public service broadcasting, the influence of radical *laissez-faire* economic theory was complemented by the government's ideological hostility to what was seen by the Conservatives as a politically suspect cultural elite, fundamentally opposed to their radical reforming mission.

Relations between the broadcasters and the government of the day had never been without difficulties. From the General Strike onwards, Conservative and Labour governments regularly engaged in battle with the BBC over the content of its journalism. Winston Churchill, Anthony Eden and Harold Wilson were all, in their time, persuaded that the BBC was insufficiently deferential to government and should be brought to heel. None succeeded in doing so, and the broadcasters learned to live with what were, in one sense, valuable opportunities for them to demonstrate their much-vaunted independence to audiences at home and abroad. ITN, being a relatively late entrant to the system and thus free of the 'voice of the nation' status which surrounded the BBC, had largely avoided these tiffs. Politicians appeared to think, furthermore, that as it was not publicly funded, ITV could less easily be censured on political grounds.

The hostility that quickly showed itself between the broadcasters and the Thatcher government was of a qualitatively different kind, with roots in the changing social composition of the Conservative Party leadership and its most vocal supporters on the right of the political spectrum. The Conservative Party that came to power in 1979 was dominated by people who saw themselves to some extent as 'outsiders' in the British class system. Passionate believers in capitalism and the beneficent workings of the free market, they did not identify with the 'old' establishment – those such as Edward Heath, or Harold Macmillan, with whom were associated all the evils of consensus and public service. In their own private circles, and to the public, they presented themselves not as creatures of privilege, but as self-made men and women. They were not, in the main, aristocrats, nor did the majority benefit from vast inherited wealth. Margaret Thatcher's father had been the celebrated 'grocer of Grantham'. John Major, her chosen successor as party leader and prime minister, made it a central element of his political identity that he had never been to university and could barely remember how many (or how few) O levels he had obtained at school.

But if these politicians were not necessarily the products of British class privilege, they were zealous adherents of a capitalism 'red in tooth and claw'. While the old Conservative Party had espoused a humane capitalism, with itself cast as civiliser and reformer in the classic patrician sense, Margaret Thatcher's supporters demanded an end to all forms of liberal whingeing and attempts to prevent the market from doing its regulatory job. They opposed, and defeated, the consensual tradition in their own party, and on coming to power, attacked it wherever else it was found, reserving a particular venom for the cultural establishment in the universities and in the media. The BBC, as the media organisation with the greatest reach and status among the British population, and with the most impeccable establishment credentials, was a natural target. Staffed largely by ex-public schoolboys and Oxbridge graduates, some of whom were known to support the Labour Party, and committed to the intrinsically consensual concept of impartiality in its journalism, the BBC's ethos of fair play and its remit to inform the British people almost immediately clashed with the 'them-and-us' mentality of the new Conservative government.

The story of the BBC's fraught relationship with the Thatcher government has been told elsewhere in great detail.[1] Key points of conflict included the BBC's coverage of Northern Ireland (criticised by the Tories for giving the IRA the 'oxygen of publicity'), which also resulted in troubles for ITV. Although, as already noted, ITV's news and current affairs programming had tended to escape the critical attentions of politicians, it had developed a strong investigative journalistic tradition with such programmes as *World in Action* and *TV Eye*. These programmes frequently targeted the excesses of big business and the political establishment, and in 1988, following the Gibraltar shootings, Thames Television's *This Week* prepared and broadcast *Death on the Rock*, a programme that directly contradicted the official version of events[2] and hinted at a 'shoot-to-kill' policy by the SAS. Despite pressure from the Home Secretary, the programme was shown. A bitter and sustained attack on *Death on the Rock* and its makers followed, which saw members of both the government and the Tory press attempt to discredit the programme, its reporters and its witnesses. The government-commissioned Windlesham Report subsequently cleared the programme-makers of any professional misconduct (Windlesham and Rampton, 1989). In one sense, therefore, ITV won this battle to report an important issue with the full battery of investigative journalistic techniques. More than one commentator, however, has suggested that the radical restructuring of the ITV system unleashed by the 1990 Broad-casting Act (see below), in which the makers of *This Week* lost their lucrative franchise, was not entirely unconnected with the *Death on the Rock* affair.

If Northern Ireland was a recurring domestic source of tension between the broadcasters and the government in the 1980s, coverage of foreign policy also caused difficulties, particularly for the BBC. In 1982, when Margaret Thatcher was three years into her first term of office as Prime Minister, Argentina invaded the Falkland Islands (Las Malvinas) and claimed them as its own. The government's response – dispatching a naval task force to the region – com-mitted Britain to its greatest military challenge since the Suez crisis of 1956. And, as in its coverage of Suez, the BBC interpreted its journalistic role as being to represent 'the nation', rather than simply the government. When Britain was in a condition of total war, and the survival of the state threa-tened, as had been the case during the Second World War, the BBC willingly subordinated its output to the requirements of governmental propaganda and disinformation campaigns. Suez, however, had not been a matter of Britain's survival as a nation-state, and neither, it was felt, was the Falklands campaign. In both instances, domestic public and political opinion was split between those who favoured military action and those who did not, the latter arguing during the Falklands crisis for economic and diplomatic sanctions to be used against Argentina. For the BBC, the Falklands conflict was one which could legitimately be reported within the framework of impartiality. Government policy could legitimately be criticised, and opposition to it reported. To do otherwise would have been to relinquish its public service role.

At the height of the conflict, on BBC2's late-night current affairs magazine *Newsnight*, presenter Peter Snow used the phrase 'the British claim' when referring to the contradictory claims of British and Argentine military sources about the progress of the conflict. The detached tone of the expression reflec-ted the BBC's editorial commitment to impartiality in reporting the conflict, in the context of a situation in which the British government could not reason-ably claim to represent the nation as a whole. For Margaret Thatcher, it was tantamount to subversion.

Foreign coverage was again the reason for a dispute with the government when the BBC was called upon to report the bombing of the Libyan capital Tripoli by US aircraft based in Britain. By this stage in Margaret Thatcher's second term of office, Conservative concerns about the BBC had led to the establishment of a Media Monitoring Unit, under the auspices of Conservative Central Office and party chairman Norman Tebbit. Using comparative content analysis not dissimilar to the type employed by the Glasgow University Media Group in the 1970s (see Chapter 3), the Media Monitoring Unit published its report on television news coverage of the Libyan bombing in April 1987.

The 'Tebbit dossier', as it became known, began from what was acknowl-edged to be the BBC's 'constitutional commitment to balance and impartiality' and concluded that, in contrast to ITN's 'impartial editorial stance', the BBC had taken 'a number of editorial and journalistic decisions the effects of which were to enlist the sympathy of the audience for the Libyans and to antagonise them towards the Americans'.[3] There was much more in this vein, most of it rejected as absurd by the BBC. Opposition politicians interpreted it as an attempt to put political pressure on the BBC in the run-up to a general election (which took place in June 1987, and saw another Conservative Party landslide).

The changing technological environment

Ideologically-based Conservative Party hostility to the BBC, and the concept of public service broadcasting in general, would always have been unpleasant and discomforting for the broadcasters, faced as they were with the prospect of having to argue regularly with the government for an increase in the licence fee, but it was made more threatening by the fact that Margaret Thatcher's premiership coincided with important developments in the field of communications technology. The thrust of these developments was to remove the historical constraint on British broadcasting of wavelength scarcity, and thus to challenge the basis on which the public service system had operated for some 60 years. In the course of the 1980s, the fruits of the cable and satellite 'revolutions' became ripe for commercial exploitation.

In these circumstances, the government's ideological assault on public service broadcasting, for being not only politically subversive and dissident, but elitist, paternalistic and unresponsive to the demands of the audience, was able to mesh with practical options for change to the old system and the creation of what was described as 'genuine choice, consumer sovereignty' in the broadcasting sector.

Demands now came, from those with commercial interests in the new television channels, for an end to the public service duopoly and its privileges. Some of them, notably Rupert Murdoch, were strong supporters of the Conservative government. Murdoch also owned some of the most widely read and influential British newspapers. These were used to echo and elaborate on the complaints of politicians about the BBC, and to prepare the ground for a full-scale legislative attack upon it. The appointment of Michael Checkland as Director General of the BBC on 26 February 1987 signalled the corporation's intention to mount a defence of its news and current affairs output. In the face of government hostility, rapid technological change and increased competition from new entrants into the market, the BBC, as the 'cornerstone' of public service broadcasting, was identifying journalism as the cornerstone of its operations. Shortly after Checkland's appointment, the BBC announced the formation of a News and Current Affairs Directorate, bringing the management of television and radio journalism within one structure. In March that year, London Weekend Television's director of programmes, John Birt, was appointed to run the Directorate. The importance of journalism to the BBC's future was emphasised by the decision to grant Birt the additional title of Deputy Director-General.

The Birt revolution

These appointments, and the restructuring of the BBC's news and current affairs output which they began, were not only the product of the changing political, economic and technological environments surrounding the corporation as it prepared for Charter negotiations, but also reflected the management's view that BBC journalism was weak and thus vulnerable to the kinds of attack described in the previous chapter. A little over a year after becoming Chairman of the BBC, Marmaduke Hussey publicly attacked the corporation's journalism, suggesting that it had lost its reputation for 'integrity and independence'.[4]

One reason for the choice of John Birt to remedy these deficiencies was his own record as a critic of television journalism, dating back to articles he had written for *The Times* in 1975 and 1976. He, along with co-author Peter Jay, coined the phrase 'bias against understanding' to refer to what he believed was the bittiness and lack of context prevalent in most TV journalism. 'Present television news programmes', he argued then, 'cover a large number of stories, often more than twenty items in a space of about half an hour. As a result the focus of any one story is extremely narrow. Feature journalism [weekly current affairs programmes such as *World in Action* and *Panorama*] tends to concentrate on one aspect or one instance of a major problem rather than on the problem as a whole.'[5] 'Issue journalism', which was good in principle because it tended 'to go beyond the context provided by the feature journalist' suffered from being boring or excessively confrontational (since it relied heavily on the device of studio discussion), and in any case 'tended to be scheduled far less favorably than the very news and feature stories which issues journalism seeks to put into perspective'. At that time head of London Weekend Television's current affairs department, Birt prescribed the following remedy:

> We should redesign television news programmes so that they devote much more time than they presently do to the main stories of the day; and so that these stories are put in the fullest possible context in the time available. Feature programmes must be organised so that they are more aware of the need for a relevant focus. And the broadcasting organisations should ensure that there are more programmes which deal with issues than there are at the moment.

As head of the BBC's News and Current Affairs Directorate, Birt proceeded to apply this 'philosophy' of television journalism to the world's largest news organisation. The design and format of main news bulletins were changed in an effort to characterise – or 'brand' – the BBC's output as more 'serious' than ITN's, while at the same time retaining its popularity and building audience share. For Tony Hall, Birt's chosen successor at the News and Current Affairs

Directorate, the corporation had to 'nurture its role as the pre-eminent news-gatherer'.[6] The BBC would attempt to occupy and hold the 'high ground', developing its identity as an organisation that 'values the significant and the serious above the sensational and the merely curious'.

The number of items covered in an average bulletin was reduced, while the 'depth' of coverage devoted to the main stories of the day increased. Features output was sorted into strands. Increased emphasis was placed on popularity. In the interview quoted above, Birt accepted that

> current affairs is not an intrinsically popular form [but] there is a significant audience for it. It should have, and will continue to have, a significant place in the peak-time schedule, both on ITV and on BBC, and any pro-gramme that is in peak-time must strive to reach out for as wide an audience as possible. But one hopes that it is not necessary, in reaching out to a wide audience, to compromise in the sort of stories that current affairs should tell. The achievement will be to tell the stories of significance but to make them accessible to the widest possible audience.

In terms of ratings, 'Birtian' journalism certainly appeared to make a positive impact on the British viewing public. By late 1989, for example, the BBC's *Nine O'Clock News* was, on occasion, recording audiences of 12 million, as compared with six million for ITN's *News at Ten*, a pattern of dominance that was repeated across the news schedule, although not usually in such stark form. The greater popularity of BBC news programmes was particularly enhanced at moments of domestic or international crisis, such as the resignation of Margaret Thatcher as Prime Minister and Leader of the Conservative Party in November 1990.

Within the BBC itself, however, and among many of those who had worked for it in the past, the 'Birtian' approach generated intense criticism. Opinion inside the BBC was reported to be that Birt's coming had meant an excessive centralisa-tion of the news and current affairs operation, with a concomitant danger of increased management or governmental interference in its day-to-day running.

Birt rejected these criticisms, and others relating to his management style, his alleged lack of commitment to and belief in the BBC's public service role, and his ambitions to privatise the corporation. All such accusations were, he suggested, the inevitable consequence of change, in which the old guard always resented the new. And not all observers were critical. In 1991, a senior indus-try figure could observe that 'on the face of it, BBC journalism is in one of its better phases. It is well resourced, wins prizes, and acquitted itself well in the Gulf. The politicians are complaining enough to make the BBC look respectable, but not so much that it need feel threatened.'[7]

After Thatcher

By then, of course, the Thatcher era had come to a sudden and unexpected end. A new prime minister was at the helm of government, and a new political mood affected the Conservative Party. For the BBC, let off rather lightly in the broadcasting reform process, this was further good news. Unlike his predecessor, John Major was reluctant to endorse the more rabid criticisms of the BBC that emanated from some of his Conservative colleagues. It appeared that, with Major's accession to power, a halt had been called to what one commentator described as the 'undeclared Thatcherite war on the BBC'.[8]

Bi-media and the BBC

What the *Guardian*'s Georgina Henry described as 'Phase 2' of the Birt 'revolution' began in October 1991, with the BBC's announcement that its television and radio news-gathering operations were to be merged into one. The impetus behind this development was, first, technological. By the early 1990s, news-gathering technology had advanced to the point at which a much greater degree of sharing of resources between different media had become practical. The result was a move in British broadcasting towards what was termed 'bi-media', whereby journalists and their crews would gather and produce material for use in both television and radio programmes. Bi-media also carried the potential of considerable cost savings, a factor that understandably endeared its adoption to the BBC's management. Although Birt had been appointed to manage a strategic shift in BBC resources to news and current affairs, his directorate had also been required to make substantial cuts in staff and other costs. In such an environment, bi-media became even more attractive as it would lead to 'joint planning, joint hit squads on big stories, a joint strategy on foreign and domestic coverage. It means using the available technology and resources for the benefit of both media'.[9]

Bi-media meant a continuation of the trend towards slimmer, more efficient, less labour-intensive news-gathering, utilising all the technological innovations available to broadcasters. In October 1991, the BBC launched its *Aims for the Future* document, spelling out the Directorate's intentions in the run-up to 1996. These were further elaborated in a series of 15 'Task Force' reports commissioned by Michael Checkland in April 1991. Intended as internal discussion documents only, the Task Force reports were leaked by the BBC's staff union BECTU on 14 April 1992, shortly after the general election. In the report dealing with the BBC's future role as information-provider, it was recommended that a 24-hour television service for domestic consumption should be established; that a new approach to current affairs should be developed; and that BBC One and BBC Two should establish a clearer editorial focus than hitherto. The reports, although not binding on management, would form the basis of the corporation's 'blueprint for the future'. The Major government, meanwhile, having won a fourth term for the Conservatives, announced the preparation of a Green Paper on the future of the BBC, which was published on Tuesday 24 November 1992.

This document confirmed the post-Thatcherite movement in government thinking away from privatisation and deregulation as options for the BBC.

While the Green Paper announced a period of wide-ranging public consultation and discussion in which many elements of the BBC's traditional operation
would be up for grabs, the fundamental necessity for, and acceptance of,
public service broadcasting principles, particularly in the sphere of journalism,
was made clear.[10] As broadcaster Melvyn Bragg put it, 'in a mixed economy, a
public service institution has been given a massive domestic power base, the
right to alliance with media barons, the encouragement to expand globally,
and virtual carte blanche until 2007'.[11]

New Labour, new BBC?

Some time later, after the election of a Labour government in May 1997, and
further major reform of its journalistic apparatus, it could be reported that:

> [BBC] news and current affairs is getting more money this year and next
> [1997 and 1998]; it has launched, albeit to very few homes on cable, News
> 24, the BBC's answer to Sky News and CNN; it will retain a network of
> foreign bureaux built up under Birt's aegis which is among the largest in the
> world. Above all, Birt has come through the Conservative era with the BBC
> and the licence fee intact, to a government which no longer wants to review
> it constantly, and whose top people admire both the BBC and him.[12]

In an interview with the *Guardian*, New Labour's first Culture Secretary Chris
Smith declared unambiguously that he was against any 'future privatisation of
the BBC', and that, 'at present', he 'wouldn't want to propose any change to
the royal charter, public service corporation, licence-fee funded format'.[13] If
this was not an open-ended guarantee, valid for all time, it was nevertheless a
strong statement of the new government's approach to the corporation for the
foreseeable future.

There was recognised to be no room for complacency, however. After
Labour's victory, no less than before, the BBC continued to stress the need for
organisational and stylistic evolution in the face of the changing technological
and commercial environments of the coming century, reforming its internal
structures and expanding outwards into new markets.

When John Birt announced his resignation as Director General in the
summer of 1999, he left the BBC's news and current affairs output in a state of
greater health than would have been predicted by many commentators in the
preceding decade, and looking ahead to the new century with a confidence,
even cockiness. In March 1999, as ITV prepared to abandon its long-standing
News At Ten flagship bulletin (see below), BBC One's controller Peter Salmon
floated the idea that his flagship *Nine O'Clock News* was not sacrosanct
either. Amid growing ratings pressure on all the British broadcasters, and the
BBC in particular, Salmon argued that tying up the peak-time nine o'clock slot
with news was 'distinctive, but not competitive. It doesn't deliver the audiences into 21.30'.[14] In May that year, the important *Six O'Clock News* was

revamped, another in an increasingly frequent series of 'makeovers' designed to maximise the popularity with viewers of bulletins and presenters. Then, in August 2000, it was announced that the *Nine O'Clock News* would indeed become the *Ten O'Clock News*, occupying the slot abandoned by ITV some time before. The move was predictably controversial, but made competitive sense since it allowed BBC One for the first time to schedule ratings-builders such as feature films between eight and ten in the evening. The Labour government gave the BBC six months to show that the move would not damage ratings for peak-time news.

Another element of the same strategy was the removal of the BBC One flagship current affairs strand *Panorama* from a Monday to a Sunday night 10:00 pm slot. Despite the promise of increased resources for production, the number of programmes broadcast in a year was cut from 38 to 30, and the move was widely seen as a downgrading of the corporation's commitment to current affairs at peak time (the decision was later reversed – see below).

These changes were closely associated with the input of Greg Dyke, who succeeded John Birt as Director General of the BBC. Dyke's background was in commercial television, where he had acquired a reputation as a scheduling genius. As Director General, he began to cut away at the hated management culture of the Birt era (by 2002 management costs had been cut by one-third, from 24 to 17 per cent of the corporation's budget), and pulled back from some favourite Birtian notions such as bi-media and 'the mission to explain' in favour of the more direct 'make it happen'. On the other hand, he continued his predecessor's emphasis on news and current affairs as the cornerstone of the BBC's public service role, and maintained investment in the journalistic infrastructure.

Audiences for BBC news programmes began to climb. As ITV made a series of disastrous decisions on the scheduling of its own news (see below), BBC bulletins gained viewers. In January 2001, the BBC's *Ten O'Clock News* just sneaked ahead of ITV's *Nightly News* bulletin by 5.2 million viewers to 5.1 million, producing the observation that 'the rescheduling has been an overwhelming success'.[15] On 11 September 2001, the pre-eminence of the corporation's journalism saw 33 million people tuning into its coverage on BBC One. By early 2002, it could be reported that the BBC had entered a 'new golden age' and that 'BBC television news has never been better'.[16]

Chapter 8 considers the impact of online and digital media on the BBC's news and journalism. It is fair to say, however, that the corporation's capacity and reputation for journalistic output was strong as it entered the era of the internet and rolling news.

Independent Television News

The decision to set up Independent Television News as a non-profit-making organisation, owned collectively by the ITV companies to which it would provide news, was taken in large part because of what Richard Collins calls

'public disquiet' (Collins, 1976: 9) about the possibility (which would otherwise have existed) of a single corporation or individual gaining control of the
news output of an entire national television channel. (In 1955, of course, there
were only two such channels.) Collins also identifies strong pragmatic reasons
for the decision to proceed down this path, such as 'the economies of scale
accruing from centralised production' and ' 'insulation' of news production
and information flows from pressures of ownership and profit-making'.

A further consideration was the fact that most of the regional companies set
up to form ITV were strong supporters of the Conservative Party. In these
circumstances, the Independent Television Authority felt it preferable to
establish another, independent company for the supply of news to the ITV
network.

The new company was remarkably successful in competing with the older
and richer BBC, largely because of the many stylistic innovations which it
introduced to British television journalism, as Nicholas Fraser reminds us.

> Before ITN there were no newscasters. When an employee of the BBC
> appeared on screen, his or her name was not revealed. No flicker of per-
> sonality interfered with the austere business of delivering news. At the
> same time, the old news was distinguished by a grovelling posture towards
> the manifestations of British power. Official versions of almost everything
> gained willing acceptance. ITN changed all that. Suddenly, bright young
> men and women were standing in streets or sitting in studios reading the
> news or asking rude questions of politicians. ... The ITN writing style
> was terse and vivid. Stories came rooted in the popular experience of news
> without succumbing to what have become known as tabloid values.
>
> (Fraser, 1990: 18)

By 1991, ITN was conservatively valued at £60 million, with a turnover of
£110 million. Despite this success, however, the broadcasting reforms introduced by the Thatcher government fundamentally changed ITN's status as a
company, at the same time transforming the financial and regulatory basis of
the commercial television channels in such a way that the organisation faced
what would undoubtedly be the most uncertain and potentially problematic
decade in its existence. While the BBC's News and Current Affairs Directorate
expanded its influence and share of its parent's resources, ITN had to learn in
the 1990s to live in a broadcasting environment in which, for the first time, its
services would have to compete with others. 'The main issue', as one senior
executive put it, 'is our survival'.

The main consequence of the Broadcasting Act for ITN was greatly to
increase the competitive pressures on the organisation: to transform it from
the 'cost centre' it had been for 35 years into a profit-making business. Under
the terms of the Act, ITN's status as 'nominated sole provider' of news to the
ITV network would be protected for a further ten years, although its position
was subject to review in five, after which time, if its customers – the ITV

companies – were not satisfied, another news provider could be licensed. ITV would be obliged to continue to take three network news programmes per day, but could demand, from January 1993, more flexible scheduling arrangements. And ITN's contract with Channel 4 would come under competitive pressure, since that channel would become self-financing after the Act, and thus have a much greater incentive to 'shop around' for a good deal on its news.

With these changes in place, threats to the survival of ITN in the 1990s emerged from a number of directions. First, there was the renewed struggle for audience share with the BBC initiated by John Birt, which, as noted above, the latter was winning. Perhaps more threatening still, since it impinged directly upon ITN's principal market, was the strong possibility of commercial competition for the contract to produce ITV's news. The 1990 Broadcasting Act created a strong incentive for the commercial companies to obtain the maximum value for money from their news suppliers. ITN's position within ITV was protected until 1995, but thereafter was subject to review. Against this background, the oft-heard complaints of some ITV companies that ITN cost too much were ominous. So was the emergence of rival news organisations which might offer a cheaper service, such as Sky. Despite a difficult start, BSkyB's 24-hour Sky News channel had, by the late 1990s, established itself securely and become a formidable player in the UK television news marketplace, providing a unique service to a growing audience.

In November 1997, the BBC established its BBC News 24 rolling news service for domestic cable and satellite viewers, further increasing the pressure on ITN to compete in this market too. And while meeting these competitive challenges, of course, ITN would also have to make profits for its shareholders.

In June 1992, ITN signed a contract to produce *Channel 4 News* until the end of 1994.[17] In 1998, the Channel 4 news contract was won again, although this time against stiffer competition from a consortium including independent producer Mentorn Barraclough Carey and Sky News, whose unsuccessful pitch included the argument that it was 'democratically desirable' for news on the five terrestrial channels to come from more than two organisations. This was a reference to the fact that ITN had won the £6 million contract to provide news for Channel 5, which came on air in April 1997.

Presented by the photogenic Kirsty Young, and unapologetically targeted at an audience of 'younger adults', *Channel 5 News* was initially denigrated by critics as part of British broadcasting's alleged dumbing down (see Chapter 5), and Young written off as a ratings-friendly bimbo rather than a 'serious' journalist. *Channel 5 News*, for its part, aggressively advertised its innovativeness in paying more attention to positive news stories, and incorporating more human interest and lifestyle coverage into its programming. For its producers, such an approach was justified on the grounds that 'a lot of the public that are supposed to be watching the news, keeping themselves informed about those issues around the world and down their street, are just not bothering'.[18] The Head of News and Current Affairs at Channel 5 stated that 'we had to think differently, create a news programme which intersects with their lives, which co-ordinates with what they want'.[19] *Channel 5 News* was a conscious response to the view that 'television news for too long has interested itself in an issue-led, establishment-oriented diet of reports'. As such, it was a clear challenge from ITN to the proponents of dumbing down, and a reflection of 'our audience's strange blend of conscience and aspiration – a generation that wanted to feel good about feeling good. Even if public service meant little to them, there was still the opportunity to devise a sort of 'public interest broadcasting', where one identified the point of intersection between public affairs and the things that mattered in the viewer's private life'.[20]

Within a year, however, *Channel 5 News* was winning praise for its innovative style, which was acknowledged as a legitimate addition to the British TV news market rather than a trashy assault on good taste. Indeed, with average audiences of around 700,000 being recorded by November 1997, it was providing serious competition for *Channel 4 News* (the latter's average audience as of August 1997 was 736,000), also produced by ITN and featuring the more conventional presenting style of Jon Snow and his colleagues. Adding insult to injury somewhat, Channel 5 announced that its main news programme would, from January 1998, go 'head-to-head' with *Channel 4 News*, broadcasting, like the latter, at 7:00 pm, threatening its audience further and forcing a revamp of the latter's style. More than that, the success of *Channel 5 News* had, by 1998, 'caused every broadcaster to reassess not only how they present the news, but what their news agenda is'.[21] As another observer put it, 'every network is questioning the role and content of news programmes, partly because ratings are slipping'.[22]

In an effort to regain the offensive in the ratings battle with the BBC, and thus strengthen the commercial case for its remaining at the heart of the ITV peak-time schedule, in November 1992 ITN revamped the flagship *News at Ten* bulletin, introducing new stylistic features such as the American device of an 'anchorman', in the shape of senior newscaster Trevor McDonald. While critical response to the changes was mixed, *News at Ten*'s audience ratings increased significantly. By 1995 they were averaging 6.8 million, compared with 5.7 million for the BBC's *Nine O'Clock News*. For the first six months of 1998, *News at Ten* enjoyed an audience share of 30 per cent (5.9 million viewers) compared with 22 per cent for the BBC's *Nine O'Clock News* (5.3 million). Although the BBC's other main bulletins attracted more viewers, ITN's earlier revamp of *News at Ten* had clearly worked. The success of *News at Ten* in providing viewers with a meaningful choice of peak-time news provision was an important argument deployed against ITV managers' calls for the programme to be moved.

In September 1998, however, ITV announced that it would be cancelling the *News at Ten* strand, replacing it with networked bulletins at 6:30 pm and 11:00 pm. Despite the opposition of the Prime Minister, and concerns that ITV was abandoning a central component of its public service remit (to produce a peak-time alternative to BBC One's main bulletin), the Independent Television Commission approved the scheduling changes in November 1998, leading, as

ITV chief Richard Eyre admitted on *Newsnight* on 1 September, to 'the end of an era'. In a 1999 article, Eyre pointed out that 37 per cent of under-34s, and 25 per cent of the audience as a whole, were leaving ITV at 10:00 pm. In the interests of its commercial survival, he insisted, *News at Ten* had to go.

> The decision to move *News at Ten* was about the future, not the past. *News at Ten* was a product of 1967, when there was only BBC One, BBC Two and ITV. In 1999 there are two other terrestrial channels, all carrying news, plus BSkyB, cable, rolling 24-hour news stations, Ceefax, Teletext and the internet. In 1967, the audience was passive and the broadcasters were active. The audience received their news when the broadcasters gave it to them. By 1999, the audience was in charge.[23]

Unfortunately for ITV's managers, the BBC's audacious move into the 10:00 pm slot undermined this confident assertion of the need for change. Viewer confusion and the dilution of what had been a leading ITV brand threw ratings into decline. By January 1999, audiences for the 11:00 pm slot had fallen by half a million. Eighteen months later, ratings for national ITV news bulletins were down by 14 per cent on average, and lower than for BBC One across the schedule. Rather than holding onto its target of 40 per cent of the peak-time audience, ITV's share fell below that of BBC One in 2001. When, in January 2001, under mounting criticism, ITV reinstated a 10:00 pm bulletin for at least part of the week, it merely demonstrated management's lack of conviction. ITN's Stuart Purvis attacked ITV bosses for messing with a successful format. 'A channel's flagship news is also a flagship for the channel itself, embodying its values which are expressed in both the visual identity and in the content'.[24]

In November 2007, as part of his strategy to reverse the more general crisis of ITV's ratings, the channel's CEO Michael Grade announced the reinstatement of *News At Ten*, and that it would be presented by veteran anchor Trevor MacDonald. The programme came back on air in January 2008, although at the time of going to press it had not achieved the high ratings of the past.

Current affairs

A recurring anxiety among observers of British broadcast journalism since the 1990s has been that competitive and commercial imperatives would drive current affairs from peak-time TV schedules, to be replaced by yet more soaps, game shows, mini-series and, most recently, reality TV and related forms of 'popular factual' programming. For ITV and the commercial channels in particular, it was feared, ratings would be even more important to the maximising of advertising revenue than they had been in the past, and since current affairs was not the most popular category of programming, it would inevitably be sacrificed. In the words of Granada's Ray Fitzwalter at that time, 'everything points to less rather than more'. In the summer of 1992, *This Week* and *World in Action* were being openly criticised for losing valuable ratings at peak viewing times. For Central TV's Director of Programme Planning, harsh commercial logic was unstoppable: 'if you have a mass audience at 8:00 pm you don't waste it by handing it over to a less than popular current affairs programme'.[25]

An alternative argument was put by those who, while accepting the inevitability of increased commercial pressure on the companies, countered that it is not simply numbers that matter in ratings terms, but also the value of the audience as a consumer market. ITV would need to deliver to at least some of its advertisers an 'AB' audience, able to buy the expensive consumer goods they wished to sell. For this group, quality current affairs was an important programming element. As experienced BBC journalist Roger Bolton put it, 'ratings are not just about numbers. Advertisers value the different kind of audience that serious documentaries can command'.[26] Nearly two decades later, who was right in this debate?

According to the Campaign for Quality Television, ITV broadcast only 18 'serious documentaries' in 1996, compared with 34 in 1995.[27] The meaning of 'serious' in this context was not clear, but it would probably not have included the 1998 broadcast of a documentary on the death of Princess Diana, which featured prominently claims made by Mohammad al Fayed and others that she had been murdered (claims finally rejected by a public inquiry in April 2008). This production was widely ridiculed, not for its subject matter as such (the death of the princess was an entirely appropriate subject for popular television journalism), but for the credence it gave to the more outlandish conspiracy theories circulating around the tragedy, none of which was supported by anything more than anecdotal evidence. The programme, following so soon after the broadcast of a Carlton-produced 'Colombian drugs trail' investigation (*The Connection*) which turned out to have been faked, severely embarrassed ITV and gave the critics of its commitment to current affairs serious ammunition.

Against these clear examples, as some would see them, of declining standards and poor editorial judgement, it is the case that even if the agenda has changed, the quantity of current affairs programming on British television has increased since the 1990s. *Panorama* relinquished its 8:00 pm Monday evening slot for one at 9:30 pm, before transferring to a Sunday evening at 10:00 pm, but in January 2007 was restored to Monday evening (after many years of public pressure, it should be said). ITV's prime early evening current affairs slot (occupied by *World in Action* for most of the past 20 years) was moved in 1999 to the later time of 10:00 pm. However, the programme that replaced *World in Action* represented a greatly increased investment in production values and 'star power'. The new show was modelled on the American *Sixty Minutes*, fronted by a leading 'star' presenter (Trevor McDonald) with a target audience of eight million viewers per broadcast.[28] By March 2001, *Tonight with Trevor McDonald* was the UK's most-watched current affairs TV programme, with 4.7 million viewers. Moreover, and despite the pessimism of some commentators, one study found that the number of hours of documentary programming broadcast on ITV between the peak times of 10:40 and 11:40 pm increased from 18 in 1997 to 42 in 1998. In July 2001, ITV signed a £14 million documentary co-production deal with the US Public Broadcasting Service.

Chapter 5 discussed debates around the alleged 'dumbing down' of current affairs journalism in British broadcasting. Since the previous edition of this book was published, Ofcom has found a gradual increase in the number of hours devoted to current affairs on both free-to-air and subscription channels, including peak time. There has been ratings pressure on commercial channels and the BBC alike, it is true, but this has been offset to some extent by the political advantages of a broadcaster being seen to take current affairs seriously, as well as the increased urgency and salience of issues such as international terrorism, climate change and the global financial crisis. Styles of current affairs journalism have diversified as the popularity of reality TV has fed into other types of programming, and the line between current affairs, 'popular factual' and entertainment programming has become blurred in places. Over-all, however, one can say that, as with 'straight' broadcast news, and taking into account cable and satellite as well as free-to-air channels, there is more current affairs TV and radio available to the UK citizen than at any time in media history. What quantity and quality of current affairs will be provided after analogue switch-off, when ratings pressures become even more acute for the commercial free-to-air sector, remains in doubt, and will be determined in part by Ofcom's forthcoming review of public service broadcasting.

Rolling news

The late 1980s saw the coming of 24-hour, transnational television journalism transmitted by satellite from bases in the USA and western Europe. Some of these new entrants to the journalism business, like WorldNet and Cable Network News (CNN), were available outside their country of origin only to relatively small audiences, such as international business travellers and cable subscribers. In the UK, where cable had not by the early 1990s developed to the extent expected ten years before, this was particularly true. Other organisations, principally Sky News, used satellite transponders to transmit programmes made in the UK to domestic audiences. Another new entrant, World Service Television News, was from November 1991 produced by the BBC in London for an international audience. The rise of Sky News in the UK, and CNN internationally, confirmed the 1990s as a period when satellite broadcasters became more important as information sources and when 'rolling news' became an increasingly important element in the journalistic ecology of the UK.

BSB and Sky

British Satellite Broadcasting (BSB) – a consortium comprising Pearson, Virgin, Granada, Anglia and the Australian Bond Corporation – won the franchise to set up a service using one of the UK's five direct broadcasting by satellite frequencies in December 1986. BSB would run a three-channel service, employing the technologically advanced D-Mac transmission system. So sophisticated was the technology that BSB could not get on air before Rupert Murdoch launched his Sky channel in February 1989. Sky used the less advanced but more reliable PAL technology, and from the moment of coming on air effectively set the pace of satellite broadcasting development in the UK (Chippindale and Franks, 1991). When BSB finally began transmitting in April 1990, it was already lagging far behind the Murdoch operation and consuming vast financial resources in an effort to catch up. These efforts proved to be in vain, and on 3 November 1990 BSB and Sky formally merged, leaving one UK-based provider of 24-hour news, the majority share of which was owned by Rupert Murdoch's News Corporation.

For the liberal broadcasting establishment in Britain, this was the worst possible outcome of the BSB–Sky struggle, since it represented the victory of the man to whom was attributed the alleged decline in the standards and ethical values of the British press. Would Murdoch use BSkyB's news channel as he had used his newspapers – to propagate the values of populist Conservatism and denigrate its opponents? Would the news values of his tabloids be reproduced on television?

At first, it seemed that such concerns would be made irrelevant by the economic pressures working on BSkyB. In January 1990 the *Guardian* had estimated Sky TV's losses at £10 million, an 'intolerable cash drain on News International'[29] which was financing the venture, mainly from the profits made by the Wapping newspapers (in an era when News Corporation can spend $5 billion on *The Wall Street Journal*, we should remind ourselves that £10 million was a lot of money in 1990). As late as June 1991, Sky News was estimated to be costing £30 million a year to run, making it, in the view of City commentators, vulnerable to closure.[30] By February 1992, however, BSkyB as a whole was able to announce that, for the first time since its establishment, it was making a running profit, with 2.8 million households by then having been persuaded to invest in Astra satellite receiving equipment. While Sky News continued to be a substantial drain on the overall BSkyB operation, Murdoch's News Corporation's profits of £105 million in the six months to June 1991 enabled the channel's survival.

And with an improved financial position, Sky News was also, by 1992, acquiring an increased, if rather begrudged, respectability as a journalistic organisation. The worst fears of 'tabloid television' had not been realised. Although a substantial proportion of the channel's output comprised relatively inexpensive buy-ins of variable quality, the immediacy, distinctive style and general standard of the 24-hour service had won many admirers. As Liz Howell, then Sky News's managing editor, explained to *Broadcast* magazine, the organisation had a distinctive and valid 'brand', consisting of the absence of a rigid schedule, and no division in programming between news and current affairs.[31] Sky News, said Howell, explicitly rejected the Birtian 'mission to explain' as 'trite', on the grounds that 'a clear news report inevitably explains'.

Sky News also resisted the BBC's movement towards more specialist correspondents, and unashamedly subordinated editorial decisions on coverage to financial constraints. For Sky News senior management, the organisation's different approach to news values and agendas was something to be welcomed in a multi-channel system. For John O'Loan, the head of news in 1992, when Sky still had to defend itself against detractors anxious about anything which involved Rupert Murdoch in the UK media landscape:

> there's nothing wrong with providing news in a different way to a different audience. the *Sun* provides a service to people who might otherwise not read a newspaper. If they didn't read a newspaper they'd know less about what was happening. The fact that the *Sun* is the way it is, and not *The Times*, doesn't necessarily mean that everything has to be like *The Times*, or like the BBC used to be, or like *Panorama*. I think the greater the diversity of news dissemination the better. Just because it's presented differently doesn't mean it's wrong. We present a different style of news from the others. We are a little more relaxed. I think we take ourselves less seriously than the others do. I think that by taking yourself too seriously you can set up a barrier between yourself and the audience to the extent that instead of informing people you can be on the verge of preaching to them. What we tend to do is put the audience first, and think about what the audience would expect, what the audience is most likely to get out of what we're doing, rather than sitting in a television station and saying what the audience will get. What we've done is to show people who were expecting downmarket tabloid television that we're not, and to people who were expecting an upmarket broadsheet that we're not, that we have quite a definite place in the TV news industry.
>
> (from an interview with the author) [32]

Resistance to Sky News remained in some quarters, however. The Royal Television Society's 1992 awards for journalism conspicuously lacked any mention of Sky News personnel. In the *Guardian*, Liz Howell asked if, given the organisation's growing reputation in the aftermath of the Gulf War, it was

> forever to be ritually punished for being set up by Rupert Murdoch? I [am] well aware that Sky News' strengths were not those of *Panorama* or *This Week*. But ... Sky News is the first and the only [until the launch of BBC News 24 in 1997] British 24-hour news channel. Many people would agree that it has changed the way that British journalists behave. It has forced to the forefront the issue of how to react to breaking news.[33]

As the 1990s progressed, the status of Sky News as a unique and valuable addition to the British news market was consolidated. Its political editor, Adam Boulton, emerged as one of the five or six leading pundits – or 'contextualising voices', as the Prime Minister's Press Secretary Alistair Campbell once put it – of broadcast political journalism. While Sky News audiences remained too small to be measured by conventional means, its importance as the first UK-produced rolling news network was generally acknowledged, and its example was followed with the launch of the BBC's own News 24 channel. In 2001, Sky News won the Royal Television Society's news broadcaster of the year award. That the channel should have achieved such success (critical, if not yet commercial) was due principally to Rupert Murdoch's decision, previously noted, not to treat the service like one of his newspapers, but to extend to it a degree of editorial independence comparable to that enjoyed by the more established BBC and ITN. The audience's perception of a broadcaster's independence and impartiality, he correctly understood, was the key to survival and success in the British news market. Sky News now commands around 90 per cent of the BBC equivalent's average seven-day audience, with an annual budget of only £35 million in 2006.

Cable Network News

Cable Network News (CNN) was launched from Atlanta, Georgia on 1 June 1980, the brainchild of media and entertainment entrepreneur Ted Turner. As Hank Whittemore's account of the first ten years of CNN's existence describes, Turner's idea of a 24-hour cable news channel, distributed by satellite across the USA, was the beginning of a 'second age' of television in which, utilising technological innovation, the nature of news and information broadcasting would be fundamentally transformed (Whittemore, 1990). With the established US networks committed to opulent, expensive flagship news bulletins, CNN came on air with a cheap, untried, day-long service which broke all the economic and technical rules of TV news. The uniqueness of the product ensured its survival, however. As the years, and the crises, came and went, the advantages of a news channel on the air 24 hours a day, live, were clear, and audiences quickly grew. With each key event – the TWA hijacking in 1985, the *Challenger* disaster of 1986, the US bombing of Libya and, of course, the Gulf War – CNN achieved an immediacy of coverage which no other organisation could match. As *Time* magazine put it, when commemorating Ted Turner's selection as 'Man of the Year', CNN had changed the definition of news from being 'something that has happened to something that is happening at the very moment you are hearing of it'.[34]

As CNN proved the worth – and the profit potential – of its product in the early 1980s, the big US networks made several attempts to break into the 24-hour news market. None was able to repeat CNN's feat of transforming the cost structure of television news, leaving Ted Turner with the field to himself by the end of 1983. That year, CNN announced its first annual profit of $20 million.

Having conquered America, Turner then shifted his attentions to the rest of the world, and Europe in particular, where there was a lucrative market for 24-hour news in the expensive hotels used by business travellers. Penetration of domestic television markets abroad was initially dependent upon the degree to which a country was cabled. In the UK, where cable had failed to reach anything like the degree of household penetration Turner could tap into in America, CNN remained a minuscule player in the television news business. In April 1992, however, CNN acquired a transponder on the Astra satellite, giving it for the first time the opportunity to reach a mass audience in the UK. In the years since, cable and satellite viewing have expanded hugely in the UK, and CNN is widely available. It seems unlikely, nevertheless, that CNN's US-dominated news agenda can achieve significant commercial success in the UK. Even at times of major international crisis, such as the September 11 attacks on New York, CNN remains an essentially American broadcaster, albeit with regional subdivisions such as CNN Europe.

BBC News

We have seen how the BBC entered the twenty-first century with a broadly expansionary posture, confident of its ability to retain a distinctive role in a rapidly changing broadcasting market. A major part of that expansion has involved the development of a global television service paralleling the established radio service. In 1986, John Tusa, as the newly appointed head of the World Service, declared his intention 'to pursue our audience by every technical means available, from short wave to medium wave, from satellite to landline, from television to cassette'.[35] After CNN was founded and became established, the BBC began to make plans to enter the transnational TV market. Director General Michael Checkland stated to the Home Affairs Committee of the House of Commons in January 1988 that the BBC wished to produce programmes for a world audience, using the editorial staff of the External Services and the resource base of the News and Current Affairs Directorate, thus exploiting the strengths of both. As with radio, the television service would be in English, but comprise 'international news, internationally ordered'.[36]

In keeping with the entrepreneurial spirit of the late 1980s, the proposed 'World Service Television News' (WSTV) would be run on a commercial basis, as part of the BBC Enterprises company. This was welcomed by the Home Affairs Committee, although its final report stressed that 'commercial finance should not be allowed to cast doubt on the integrity of the news service'.[37]

The producers of WSTV argued that the distinctive features of the World Service approach to radio journalism (see below) would grant it a competitive advantage over CNN, WorldNet and others. In *Conversations with the World*, John Tusa pointed out that WorldNet, although 'the first substantial effort in transnational television', had failed to win significant audiences because its 'main drive is to tell the world about America' (Tusa, 1990: 16). It was, in short, too parochial and propagandistic of a particular culture, ideology and way of life. In relation to CNN, Tusa told the author that 'we'll give much more of a world picture in news. I don't think they give a very consistent or reliable world picture ... they're terribly American-oriented. If in doubt they go back to very localised American feature stuff. It can get very small towney indeed.' WSTV, by contrast, would operate within a news agenda which would be 'recognisable in most places of the world'. WSTV would also seek to exploit its resource advantage over the American global broadcasters. By developing bi-media in the World Service, TV and radio operations would be able to share news-gathering resources and material with each other, and with the BBC's domestic news and current affairs production.

In a speech to the Royal Television Society, John Tusa expressed the BBC's motivation in launching WSTV thus: 'who could be content to leave the domination of this immensely powerful sector of the global information market – international network news – to one company and one nation, the United States? Now there are two players in this market, BBC World Service and CNN, and there is plenty of room for both of us'.[38]

WSTV began transmitting in November 1991, using Asiasat to reach a potential audience of 38 million homes in Southeast Asia. Shortly thereafter it became available in Europe, and preparations were under way for the service to reach Australia, Japan and Africa. By the end of 1992, WSTV was fully independent of the BBC's financial structure. Today, as BBC Worldwide, the corporation runs two global TV channels, one of which – BBC World – is dedicated to news and current affairs.

In 1992, plans were announced to make a 24-hour news channel based on WSTV available to British viewers as an encrypted service on the Astra satellite. At a conference in London, Michael Checkland argued that 'it would be ironic if our viewers had to be in Baghdad or Vienna or Oman to receive 24-hour news from the BBC but could not receive it at home.[39] News 24 was the outcome of that view, and now transmits a rolling news service to subscribers of cable and satellite television in the UK. In May 2002, for the first time, News 24 recorded more viewers than Sky News, with 3.8 million per week to the latter's 3.7 million. In April 2008 the channel was renamed BBC News as part of a wide-ranging rebranding of the corporation's news and journalism.

The subsequent progress of the two providers' rivalry has been shaped by such factors as the take-up by British viewers of digital cable, satellite and terrestrial TV, and the course of events. The September 11 terrorist attacks in New York brought News 24 onto the main BBC One schedule for a time, where it attracted 33 million viewers. Then, as in past crises (and future ones, one presumes), the authority of the BBC provides its rolling news with a competitive advantage which Sky News lacks. On the other hand, as the terrestrial broadcasting system continues to erode in the coming years, every broadcaster will have to fight harder to win the loyalty of viewers, and Sky News will have every opportunity to prove itself. Sky's ratings increased by 300 per cent during the fuel crisis of September 2000, demonstrating that there is everything to play for in its future competition with the BBC.

ITN News Channel

ITN News Channel, launched in August 2000, and in 2002 renamed ITV News Channel in an effort to bolster its brand image, was the third UK-based entrant into the rolling news market. It was the product of ITN's and ITV's desire not to be left behind in the emerging environment of 24-hour coverage. Resources were minimal, however, compared with those available at BBC News 24 and Sky News, and audiences were barely measurable (given that the three rolling news services together commanded only 1.5 per cent of the TV audience as of mid-2002). In 2005 the service was closed down.

The failure of the channel fuelled ITN management's arguments that they were in an unfair position *vis-à-vis* the BBC, which could offset the risks of involvement in rolling news and other activities with the cushion of the licence fee. Stuart Purvis explained the problem well when he argued that

> ITN is diversifying across all of these platforms (24-hour news, the Internet, data services to mobile phones, etc. But maintaining your 'news voice' across exponentially expanding and diversifying platforms is an expensive and risky business. The problem is that when ITN launches a new business – rolling news channel, news content for websites and DSL, interactive news on cable television – we bump up against one of these publicly-funded BBC tanks. How are we expected to compete when the BBC supplies a publicly-funded alternative to the consumers of what are essentially commercial services?[40]

The competitive position of the BBC in a rapidly changing media environment continues to be an issue of contention in the UK, driven now by the role of the internet (see Chapter 8).

Radio journalism in the UK

Radio has traditionally been viewed, by producers and audiences alike, as the 'Cinderella medium' – television's poor relation. In an era of rapidly proliferating television channels, radio's presumed inferiority has frequently given rise to the view that its future is problematic, and in the 1990s something akin to a siege mentality developed on the part of those who worked in the medium. Fortunately, as seen by the ratings figures presented in Chapter 1, reports of radio's death have been shown to be exaggerated. Since breakfast television services began in the UK, despite the belief of many that early morning radio audiences would decline, they have in fact increased consistently. The past two decades have been ones in which the number of radio channels, like television, have expanded, fuelled by persistently healthy ratings and market research evidence that popular demand for radio services remains high. Radio, it would appear, retains its distinctive appeal as a form of communication which can be consumed while mobile and engaged in a variety of other pursuits, with a mode of functioning quite different from that of the visual media.

Within radio as a whole, journalism and speech services remain prominent. Question marks have been raised, however, over the extent to which a quantitative expansion of radio will lead in the end to a qualitative diminution of journalistic standards, particularly in the commercial sector.

A little history: the Green Paper and radio reform

The publication of the Conservative Party's Green Paper on reform of the radio system in February 1987[41] was greeted with initial hostility by those who feared the deleterious effects of deregulation on the existing system. As with the debate on the future of public service television, the government's opponents argued that the expansion of commercial radio, combined with a new 'light touch' system of regulation – the main thrust of the Green Paper's proposals – would reduce output to a 'lowest common denominator' of chat and middle-of-the-road pop music, while 'quality' services such as journalism would be squeezed off the airwaves.

In the context of what was known about the Conservatives' attitude to public services, such fears were not unreasonable. They were, however, founded on the (as it turns out, erroneous) assumption that the marketplace would be unable to sustain 'quality' radio. On the contrary, a Broadcasting Research Unit survey reported in June 1988 that audience demand for 'speech' radio was as high as that for music programming.[42]

Reinforcing this commercial logic was the widespread perception among communication companies that the provision of news is a necessary component of any broadcasting service that aspires to be seen as 'quality'. To win respectability in the UK broadcasting market, one had at least to pay lip service to the provision of journalism. Consequently, although the 1990 Broadcasting Act did not require the new national commercial networks which would shortly come into existence to provide journalism as a part of their programming, it seemed likely that all would choose to do so, and this has indeed been the case.

In addition to legislating for the introduction of commercial network radio in the UK, the government's reforms sanctioned the creation of a large number of regional and local radio stations, for which the provision of news and journalism was from the outset an important programming element.

Taken together, the proliferation of commercial radio outlets at national, regional and local level in the late 1980s and into the 1990s meant a rapidly expanding market for companies equipped to supply radio news. The leading players in the commercial radio news market are today Independent Radio News, National Network News and Sky Radio News.

Although the 1990 Broadcasting Act specified that one of the new commercial channels should be speech-based, there were no serious bids for the franchise during the economic recession of the early to mid-1990s. As was noted earlier in this chapter, speech-based services in the USA have flourished since deregulation, but the advertising market there, and radio's share of that market, are both much larger than in the UK. In 1997, however, Talk Radio (now talkSport) was established as a commercial, 24-hour speech channel, competing with Radio Five Live. By 2000 it was attracting 2.1 million listeners compared with Five Live's 5.4 million.

The BBC

For the same reason that the BBC took a strategic decision to prioritise its news and current affairs television output in the run-up to Charter renewal in 1996, the corporation's radio journalism also entered an expansionary phase in the 1990s. In June 1990, the BBC's head of regional broadcasting stated his view that local radio was 'the grassroots of the BBC's journalistic network', and that he would be striving to ensure 'every station made high quality speech and journalism the bedrock of its schedule'.[43]

In September 1991, the newly appointed regional controller Mark Byford vigorously rejected the suggestion – then being made by some on the right of the Conservative Party – that BBC radio should retreat from local journalism. 'A key activity of the BBC is to provide news and current affairs', he insisted. 'Local radio is at the very core of that news and current affairs effort at a local level. It is distinctive because it is speech-driven and based around journalism. And the market is not doing that'.[44]

As commercial radio came under increasing financial pressure, the BBC was demonstrating its intention to consolidate and strengthen its historical dominance in this area of broadcasting. In 1991, Ron Neil, at that time head of the BBC's Regional Directorate, insisted that 'it's the single most important activity we have outside London. If we produce a local radio service that sounds like everybody else's, it'll get a big audience, but there'll be no justification for subsidising the licence fee. ... Our justification to be on the wavelength at all is that we work at trying to produce a high-quality speech-information service.'

Network radio journalism was also growing. In early 1992, the Task Force report on the future of radio recommended that the Radio 4 network be split, to make space for a 24-hour rolling news service of the type provided during the Gulf War. To finance the new service, known after its launch as Radio 5 Live, the BBC would further develop its bi-media strategy, allowing economies of scale to be made by combining the news-gathering resources of radio and TV.

The World Service

BBC radio journalism has never been simply about the domestic audience. The BBC's World Service, with a budget of £246 million in 2007, has since its foundation as the Empire Service in 1926 been providing news, current affairs and feature journalism to a global audience. Funded (and with its output monitored) by the Foreign Office, the World Service has traditionally performed the function of 'cultural diplomacy', promoting British values as well as reporting on international events.

As for other elements of the BBC's operation, the 1980s and 1990s were a period of uncertainty for the World Service, as it faced up to the Thatcherite onslaught of free-market principles at home and, on the broader international stage, the end of the Cold War and the East–West divide. The first of these challenges raised uncomfortable questions for the World Service about its long-term financial viability as a public service, while the latter raised the issue of its continuing cultural role.

An important rationale for the funding of the World Service in the post-Second World War period was the need perceived by successive British governments to provide the populations of the Soviet Union, China and other closed societies around the world with an alternative source of information to that available from their own governments. As Soviet power and that of its allies collapsed in the late 1980s and early 1990s, such a need became less pressing, and the World Service's position as the pre-eminent global broadcaster could no longer be taken for granted.

A further threat to the organisation came from the emergence of transnational television broadcasters such as CNN. In such an environment, would the World Service be able to retain its relevance? In *Conversations with the World*, Tusa quotes approvingly the view of a past Director General of the BBC, William Haley, that 'the British conception of news as something coldly impersonal and objective, and which has as its only touchstone accuracy, impartiality and truth, is one of our great services to a civilisation in which speed of communication gives news an overwhelming importance it never had before' (Tusa, 1990: 71).

Such assertions illustrate the extent to which the World Service has been perceived by its staff as 'idealistic' rather than 'ideological'. Unlike, for example, the Voice of America, it has always retained editorial independence from the government which allocates its resources, so that it has not in general been seen in the wider world as a mere mouthpiece for a particular political standpoint. Voice of America must carry daily editorials written for it by the US Information Agency. The World Service, while routinely broadcasting government messages for British citizens abroad, has not been required to reflect the government's view of a given international situation.

If the 'civilising message' includes the transmission of dominant British cultural values, the World Service has retained a reputation for impartiality, balance and reliability which is the basis of its long-standing legitimacy as an information source. In situations such as the Chernobyl disaster of 1986 and the coup of August 1991 in Moscow, it was the World Service to which the Russian people, including an imprisoned Mikhail Gorbachev himself, turned. Consequently, in a post-Cold War world, the World Service has no need, its managers would argue, to change its approach to journalism.

For John Tusa, one of its most determined defenders, the World Service has never been 'propaganda', but a journalism equally relevant to populations all over the world, regardless of the information environment in their respective societies. So, he argues, in the post-Cold War world, 'our broadcasting hasn't changed. It hasn't had to change'. The World Service, in the view of its managers, does not construct its journalism within a British-dominated framework. While its main competitors, such as the Voice of America, broadcast a country-specific agenda, the World Service aspires to a genuinely international, global news agenda, of equal relevance to the constituent parts of a multinational audience. John Tusa insists that

> we provide something which the others don't provide: international news, the global picture of the world. And there's a demand for that even in the United States. Audiences for our programmes on American public radio increased by a factor of three during the Gulf crisis. The US is an open society, with more broadcasting, more radio stations, than anywhere else in the world. But they're so fragmented, so tiny, so tied to local communities, so driven towards particular niches of the market, that they're incapable of giving the entire world picture. That's why I think there is a continuing need, even in open societies, for this kind of service.

Elsewhere, Tusa has argued that 'our broadcasting about Britain gains in credibility because it does not give special treatment to British activities. The more narrowly you interpret the instruction to broadcast about your home country, the less appealing you are to your audience. (*ibid.*: 15) [45]

Winning the arguments

For a government deeply suspicious of public service broadcasting, as was the Thatcher government of the 1980s, the World Service was clearly a potential target, absorbing substantial resources to produce output which was listened to by relatively few of the British people (approximately 1.5 million in 1991). In an era of unquestioning belief by government in commercial logic and the benign workings of the free market, the World Service might well have seemed an expensive luxury which the taxpayer could readily do without. However, management, led at that time by John Tusa, succeeded in advocating the notion that 'cultural diplomacy' was an inherently worthwhile activity for the British public service broadcaster to pursue, and demonstrating that the cultural diplomacy provided by the World Service was exceptionally good value for money. A considerable role in this lobbying process was played by the Foreign Office, which in the period under discussion tended to be less Thatcherite than the government as a whole, but the sound financial common sense of the World Service's pitch was crucial. In *Conversations with the World* John Tusa pointed out that

> we have 120 million regular listeners to our broadcasts. There are many millions more who listen to local relays of our broadcasts. At an all-up cost of £120 million in 1988 – capital and current – we deliver our message at a cost of two pence per listener per week, every week, every year. Not since

the days of Rowland Hill and the Penny Post has Britain had such good value for money in the field of communication. No other medium can talk to a mass world audience so fast, so credibly, so effectively, or anywhere near so cheaply.

(*ibid*.: 66)

As long as the principle of cultural diplomacy was accepted, such sentiments were difficult to resist and the Conservative government had by the early 1990s abandoned any attempt to do so, awarding the World Service a substantial increase in its budget for the period 1991–93. The BBC had played its part by 'proving that our resource house was in order', as a senior manager put it.[46] But, in the view of the same source, 'there's an acknowledgement now, even at the highest levels of government, that Britain is well served by having its international service possessing such a high reputation. It's a projection, if you like, of the quality of life on these islands, a listing of the values that the people on these islands hold dear.' Fortunately for the supporters of the World Service, the new Labour government elected in May 1997 agreed with this view, bolstering the organisation with a larger-than-inflation rise in subsidy and an assurance of governmental support in the longer term.

The rationale for this policy received a huge boost with the September 11 attacks and the onset of the global 'war on terror' or 'clash of civilisations'. If the end of the cold war had led some to question the need for an institution such as the World Service, the rise of Islamic fundamentalist terror around the world reinforced its value as an agent of 'soft power', a vehicle for the dissemination of the UK's global perspective.

The rise of transnational TV, on the other hand, became the rationale for the movement of the World Service into TV (and later online) platforms, with channels in Arabic, Farsi and other geostrategically important languages.

In the years and decades to come, global TV will become increasingly important for the BBC, but radio will continue to occupy a major part of the organisation's resources. As Bob Jobbins puts it, 'I can't see radio going away. It has tremendous advantages: particularly, the fact that you can do other things while you're listening. In addition, transnational radio broadcasting is much freer from interference than television, and it is still going to be the lynchpin'. In line with this view, World Service funding was increased by £44 million over the three years 1999–2002, 'to strengthen', as director Mark Byford put it, 'the World Service's position as the world's leading international broadcaster in a rapidly changing media environment'.[47] Following the events of September 11, BBC managers allocated further extra funds to support World Service activity in the Arab and Muslim world.

Further reading

For another view of British radio see Crisell (1994); on the career of Greg Dyke see Horrie and Clarke (2001).

8 Online journalism in the UK

This chapter contains:

- an account of the development of British online journalism
- an assessment of its impact on established news media
- speculation on how online journalism can be expected to develop, and its likely further impact on print and broadcast journalism in the UK.

When the first edition of *News and Journalism in the UK* was published in early 1994, the internet as we know it today was in its infancy. Netscape's Mosaic browser had not yet been launched, and use of the internet was still largely the preserve of scientists, academics and other specialists with a clear use for the possibilities it offered of shared information, distributed on networked computers. Although the various technological advances necessary to construct the basic infrastructure of the network had been emerging since the 1950s,[1] it was in those not-so-distant days far from being a mass medium, or a medium used routinely by journalists. Neither was it foreseen how important the internet would, within a few short years, become to cultural life in general, and to journalists and their audiences in particular. Consequently, that first edition of this publication, which went to the publisher in 1993, contained no reference to the internet, for the simple reason that at that point it played no discernible part in either the production or consumption of news. Journalism in the early 1990s was about print and broadcasting.

Subsequent editions of *N&JUK* gradually began to reflect the spread of the worldwide web and the growth of the internet as a journalistic medium (2003 marked the point at which over 50 per cent of UK households had access to the internet, an increase of 500 per cent since 1999, when only 10 per cent had access) – a reference here, a brief section there. That process of incremental revision was increasingly unsatisfactory, as it became clear that the impact of the internet could not be discussed adequately merely by updating a book conceived and written in the pre-internet era. In the past 15 years – and especially since the publication of the fourth edition in 2003 – the internet has not only emerged as another means of distributing news and journalism – it has fundamentally transformed the structure of the news media, in the UK as elsewhere. It has also transformed the nature of journalistic work and, as citizen journalists and bloggers have proliferated, problematised the very meaning of the term 'journalism'. The pace of change has been unprecedented and difficult to keep up with, not least for academics who, by the time a book or scholarly article has been researched, written and published, may find that the subject of their inquiries – the media – have moved on to another set of issues entirely. In this edition, therefore, this chapter devoted to the subject has been added, as well as net-led revisions to and rewritings of existing chapters on print and broadcast news.

Online journalism in the UK – history and milestones

As already noted in Chapter 1, the internet has expanded globally to the point at which it has subverted all established models of how media work, how they relate to their audiences, and what people use their media for (Deuze, 2007). As it has grown in speed, depth and reach, the internet has presented challenges and opportunities to the established print and broadcast journalistic organisations and enabled the launch of many new entrants to the journalism marketplace. I have explored the broader, sociological context of global online development elsewhere (McNair, 1998, 2006a). This book, and this chapter in particular, explores the process and its impact on the specific sphere of news and journalism in the UK.

In a book completed in 1997, I noted that there were only some 700 online journalism providers in the USA and a few dozen in the UK. Electronic newspapers, I observed then, 'are still at the experimental stage in their development, unsure of what they should be doing, who they are for and how they are to be used' (McNair, 1998b: 138). There were a handful of online news publications available, such as *Slate* and *Salon*, and a few early, and from this distance very rudimentary, online experiments from the established media. Expansion in the number of online news sites accelerated in the late 1990s, and was then halted by the bursting of the dotcom bubble in 1999. By the early 2000s, the economics of internet expansion had stabilised again, and news sites were growing alongside new applications such as social networking, RSS and search tools of rapidly growing sophistication. Nguyen *et al.* (2005) counted nearly 13,500 online news sites worldwide by 2002, and there are many more in existence now (precisely how many is not known, given the speed of evolution of the online environment; an online directory of the websites of British newspapers and broadcasters is available at www.wrx.zen.co.uk/britnews. htm). The blogosphere had also been established, to the point that in 2002 journalist and blogging pioneer Andrew Sullivan could observe in *Wired* magazine the emergence of 'a revolution in how journalism functions in our culture'.[2]

In the course of a decade the design and operation of online news goods and services have improved hugely, as established print and broadcast organisations have embarked on a steep learning curve. Early pioneers, such as the *Guardian* in the UK (the *guardian.co.uk* site launched in 1999) and the *New York Times* in the USA, now look amusingly quaint and primitive, not surprisingly as these were essentially electronic versions of print titles. They were revolutionary for their time, of course. A decade on and online news sites have become much more than just electronic versions of newspapers, but information hubs, or portals, combining the news function with a proliferating range of interactive, participatory features.

As we have seen in previous chapters, the advent of online journalism has presented both challenges and opportunities for the traditional print and broadcast providers of news. The new medium's impact on news gathering, production and distribution can be viewed as both positive and negative. This chapter considers both sides of the online coin from the particular perspective of the UK.

Beginnings

As has been the case with previous innovations in communication technology, the driving force towards mass acceptance and usage of online journalism has been events. Commentators will differ in their assessments of which events, precisely, have been the key turning points and landmarks in the history of the internet's emergence as a news medium, but we can identify a few which all agree to have been important. The 1994 San Francisco earthquake, for example, was the first story to be broken by online media before the print and broadcast news organisations could get to it. Stuart Allan's history of online news identifies the 1995 Oklahoma bombing, carried out by Timothy McVeigh and shadowy right-wing forces in the USA, as a milestone because of the use in coverage of newsgroups, chat rooms and other online tools. Grainy video footage and photographs were posted on early sites operated by *Time* magazine and the *San Jose Mercury* (Allan, 2006).

In 1997, the *Dallas Morning News* became the first major newspaper anywhere in the world to publish an exclusive – the confession of Oklahoma bomber Timothy McVeigh – on its website before its print edition. In the UK, the *Guardian* took this step for the first time in 2006, announcing the move as 'a significant departure from the established routine of newspaper publishing where stories are held for once-a-day publishing'. It is now routine for UK newspaper websites to publish breaking news stories before they appear in the next day's print edition, as well as volumes of material that is available only online.

One of the most dramatic landmarks in the evolution of online journalism is that of the Clinton–Lewinsky scandal of 1998, significant here because it was broken not by the *Newsweek* journalist who investigated the story only to see it spiked by his editors, but by the online *Drudge Report*. Matt Drudge was one of the early online 'aggregators' of news, meaning that his site did not gather and research news in the traditional manner, but merely reported the news of other organisations, or provided links to those organisations, taking no responsibility for the accuracy or honesty of the information highlighted for the growing community of internet users. The Lewinsky story turned out to be accurate, and its huge political impact in the USA made the *Drudge Report* into a household name and a global leader in online news provision; but other of his stories were false, and he remains an exemplary case illustrating the pros and cons of online journalism. (Is it, in fact, appropriate to speak of this second-hand information as journalism? See below for a discussion of the downsides of the online journalism revolution.) Most importantly, in that case, Drudge was prepared to publish where *Newsweek* would not. In a very obvious and embarrassing manner for the US media establishment, online journalism had triumphed over print and set the US political agenda for several years thereafter.

In early 2000 a South Korean named Oh Yeon-Yo founded *OhmyNews*, a website intended to provide a space for voices which he regarded as not properly represented in the mainstream media of his country. By early 2008, *OhmyNews* was functioning as a portal for the user-generated content of an estimated 55,000 of that country's citizens, and was ranked among the top ten most influential publications in South Korea. An English-language version was launched in 2004.[3] *OhmyNews* was not the first online site devoted to 'citizen journalism' (Sutton, 2006), but its scale and sense of purpose seemed to herald a new era of bottom-up news-making which has since spread across the globe. All over the world, news organisations today advertise their eagerness to receive the contributions of 'citizen journalists', and are investing resources in managing those contributions within their overall output. UK-based organisations such as the BBC and Sky News are at the forefront of these efforts, providing potential contributors with online guides and manuals on the basics of 'citizen reporting'.

A key event in the history of online news is the terrorist attack on the USA of September 11, 2001. There is little to be added here to the wealth of analysis and commentary surrounding that event and its aftermath (Allan and Zelizer, 2002; Pudlowski, 2007; Hoskins and O'Loughlin, 2008). We note only that with this era-defining event, as with no other before it, the internet provided a uniquely immediate, decentralised, interconnected channel for the communication of images, words, thoughts and feelings about its significance and meaning, contributing to its impact on publics and policy-makers. Real-time news channels followed the collapse of the towers; bloggers, citizen journalists and online news sites recorded the experiences and emotions of people on the streets of Manhattan, and posted their photographs and video footage. Then, as the dust settled at Ground Zero, the blogosphere found its killer application, as millions of people all over the world sought to participate in debate around emerging concepts such as 'the war on terror' and 'the clash of civilisations'.

The aftermath of 9/11 – the invasions of Afghanistan and Iraq (especially the latter in March 2003) – further propelled the use of online news into the mainstream of journalistic culture. For Stuart Allan and other commentators, 'the US-led attack on Iraq represented the 'coming of age' of the internet as a news medium' (Allan, 2006: 103). In Iraq, despite (or perhaps because of) the tightly managed nature of military communication, which saw careful shepherding and 'embedding' of accredited correspondents, the immediacy, interactivity and relative difficulty in censoring online sources came into their own as valuable properties. As Allan puts it, referring to the Iraqi invasion in particular, and the news environment more generally, the experience demonstrated that:

> Online journalism, at its best, brings to bear alternative perspectives, context and ideological diversity to its reporting, providing users with the means to hear voices from around the globe. News accounts that are overly reliant upon official truth-claims are likely to be revealed as such when compared and contrasted with reports from elsewhere available online, posing acute difficulties for those engaged in information management.
>
> (*ibid.*: 105)

In Britain, a good example of this phenomenon was provided by 'Salam Pax', the Baghdad Blogger, whose on-the-spot posts crossed over into the print version of the *Guardian* and were later collected for a book (Pax, 2003). Initially a web diary, the blog posts of this 29-year-old architect provided the world beyond Baghdad and Iraq with an intimate account of the situation on the ground after invasion began. The Baghdad Blog was about the politics of Iraq, but also the personal dimension of how it felt to be in a city and a country under attack. It was the distinctiveness of this perspective, in an environment otherwise dominated by Coalition media rules and practices such as the 'embedding' of correspondents and strict management of military information, that gave the Baghdad Blogger his value to a global news audience.

The relationship between Iraq and internet news in 2003 was, in a broader sense, comparable with that between Iraq and real-time TV news in the first Gulf War of 1991. The conflict provided an incentive for the potential of an emerging delivery system for news and journalism to be recognised and used, not just by the early adopters and hard-core professionals but by the mainstream audience, many of whom were, by this time, equipped with broadband internet access at home, and a growing familiarity with the possibilities of online journalism. In the UK, round-the-clock coverage of the invasion of Iraq was provided by all three domestic 24-hour news channels, but as in the USA and other countries, unprecedented numbers of people supplemented this (and their use of print and broadcast bulletins) with regular online updates, including those of non-Coalition supporters such as aljazeera.net.

It is worth noting that, during Operation Iraqi Freedom, use of all news media increased, as it had done on September 11 and other moments of perceived international crisis. By 2003, the internet had joined the mix of news media as a core element, and benefited accordingly from this surge in usage. A significant milestone in this process was September 2002, the month when users of nytimes.com exceeded daily sales of *The New York Times* for the first time, by 1.28 million to 1.2 million. In the UK, by that time, 10.6 million people were estimated to be using online news sites every month, the majority using established news brands such as the BBC, the *Guardian* and the *Financial Times* (Hargreaves and Thomas, 2002). That said, as late as 2002 the internet was the main source of news for only 2 per cent of the population.

At the end of 2004, the news-making potential of one element in the online revolution, 'citizen journalism', was demonstrated to the global mass audience in the tragic circumstances of the tsunami that struck Indonesia and other Southeast Asian countries on 26 December. Having noted the initial prevalence of what he terms 'helicopter coverage' – professional correspondents flying over scenes of devastation, reporting in grave tones on the privations of hordes of anonymous victims – Stuart Allan notes 'the extraordinary contribution made by ordinary citizens offering their first-hand reports, digital photographs, camcorder video footage, mobile telephone snapshots or audio clips' (Allan, 2006: 7). Mainstream news media took this material and built it into the heart of their coverage of the unfolding disaster. Bloggers all over the world made it the basis of their commentaries and discussion. The fact of its existence, and its impact on global public opinion and policy-makers, became a major element of the tsunami story in itself.

The Asian tsunami was a global news story. In Britain, stories of particular significance in the history of UK online journalism include the death of Diana in 1997, the chemical fire that engulfed the Buncefield oil depot in south-east England in December 2005; the July 2005 terror attacks on the London Underground;[4] the floods (England again) of July 2007; and the attempted attack on Glasgow airport by al-Qaida terrorists in June of that year. In each of these stories, material provided by 'citizens', or non-professional journalists, made significant contributions to how the stories were told in the news media. Coverage of the July 7 bombings in London was characterised by grainy images from inside railway carriages captured on mobile phones. In Glasgow, two years later, the fact that the attack was timed (in order to cause maximum casualties) for a Saturday afternoon, when hundreds of holiday-makers were queueing to check in for flights, meant that there were hundreds of cameras on hand to record the unfolding drama. One aspect of the incident in particular – baggage handler John Smeaton's attempt to neutralise one of the terrorists with a robust physical challenge – became a global phenomenon through the internet, footage of the 'have-a-go-hero' being made available to hundreds of millions of people through YouTube and other social networking and file-sharing sites.

These and other events have fuelled a steady migration of consumers of news away from print and broadcast outlets towards the internet, although as yet it remains for the majority of the British population a subordinate source of news and journalism. A report commissioned by Channel 4 in early 2008 noted that TV remains the most popular source of news across the British public as a whole. By then, however, 51 per cent of the 25–34 age group were using online journalism regularly, and the trend was clear – further fragmentation of the journalism market, further migration of audiences from print and broadcast to online, with young media users moving furthest and fastest.[5]

For the future, and if trends in the last few years can be taken as a guide, the speed of change is unpredictable (although on the post-1994 evidence change could be very fast indeed, relative to the time scales on which we have traditionally viewed technological shifts of this kind), but the direction is unmistakable. Also beyond dispute is that, within a few short years, the internet has risen to challenge, as a source of news, 'the traditional authority of newspapers and broadcasts'.[6] As this source notes, it was a blog – holymoly.co.uk – which first revealed the significant fact (for media watchers) that Director General of the BBC Mark Thompson had once bit a colleague. In 2006, the *Guardian* reported that bloggers 'are increasingly dominating public conversation and creating business trends'.[7] By then, too, the supremacy as information sources of the established media of record in the USA – the *New York Times*, CBS, the *New Republic* – had been undermined by internet-led or -initiated stories about Jayson Blair, Dan Rather and Stephen Glass, respectively. As depicted in the film *Shattered Glass* (directed by Billy Ray, 2003), the internet had by the early 2000s emerged as a key critical scrutineer of the established fourth estate, alert to its errors and merciless in exposing them to the online world.

By 2008, reported the UK House of Lords Select Committee on Communication, it was possible to distinguish the online news and journalism sector into three subsectors:

- websites operated by established providers of print and broadcast journalism (the *Guardian*, the *Telegraph*, BBC, Channel 4)
- online news aggregators (Google, Yahoo!, AOL, MSN)
- individual websites run by bloggers (professional or amateur).

The most successful of the UK-based sites include guardian.co.uk, thesun.co.uk, telegraph.co.uk and dailymail.co.uk. Just before this edition of *N&JUK* went to press, in June 2008, Audit Bureau of Circulation figures showed that the *Daily Mail* had overtaken the *Guardian* as the UK's most used newspaper website. That month the *Daily Mail* recorded just more than 18.7 million unique monthly users, an increase of 100 per cent on the preceding year.

These figures notwithstanding, users of print and traditional broadcast news still exceed online users, the majority of whom were, as of late 2007, overseas. At that time (and the figures shift constantly), of UK print titles only the *Guardian*'s daily circulation (363,562 in July 2007) was surpassed by its daily web audience (771,242). This led one analyst to conclude that 'the hype about the growth of the internet has concealed the fact that UK web audiences are generally significantly smaller than for the parent print brand' and that 'the launch pad for a stable and authoritative news website' remains in the print sector.[8] That was then. Little more than a year later, unique monthly user rates have grown quickly, and that assertion may not look so sound. Such is the speed of the online journalism revolution.

Responding to the online challenge

13 April 2005 was the day, according to the *Economist*, 'when the stodgy newspaper business officially woke up to the new realities of the digital age'[9] – the day when Rupert Murdoch, radical pioneer of the print era, at last conceded that the press industry would have to address the implications of the internet revolution.

The tardiness of Murdoch's recognition was not unusual among the media industry establishment. Nonetheless, the fact that even the world's leading media mogul, who made his reputation and his fortune on being ahead of the pack, had not until a few short years ago fully grasped the significance of the internet shows just how rapid and unexpected the 'revolution' has been. If, by 2005, most major providers of news and journalism had set up websites as part of their operation, most of those remained appendages to the print version of the title, bolted on to meet the perceived expectations of an increasingly digitised culture. Digital journalism still suffered from low status, and from the presumed superiority of print and the broadcast media 'of record'. Murdoch's 2005 speech is important if only because it made clear that no-one, not even the most powerful media proprietor on the planet, could ignore the impact of the internet any longer, not least for their financial well being.

In describing the response of the British news media to this dawning realisation, we may as well begin with Murdoch's News Corporation, responsible as we have seen for 33 per cent of UK national newspaper circulation, and majority owner of BSkyB and its 24-hour news service, Sky News. All these services have focused more resources on their web presence in recent times, building in elements of interactivity and participation. While Murdoch's corporation has bought MySpace and *The Wall Street Journal* in recent years, both central to News Corporation's internet plans, his existing UK media properties have substantially upgraded their online presence, and seen the benefits. The Audit Bureau of Circulations (ABC)'s unique monthly user rating gave the *Sun* just under 15 million as of June 2008 (nearly double the figure for June 2007). *The Times/Sunday Times* online site achieved ratings of just under 16 million in June 2008 (again, nearly double that of the year before).

Elsewhere in the UK print sector, the *Guardian* has been a leader in the transition to online, continually improving and refining its site since launch in 1999. I remember, as a media studies lecturer at that time, the impact *guardian.co.uk* had with its seemingly magical capacity to link and hyperlink stories, providing the user with layers of researchable information far beyond the capability of print. Now, of course, it looks primitive and crude. the *Guardian* was pioneering an entirely new platform for the delivery of news, however, alongside one or two others, such as the *Telegraph*. They had to start somewhere, with very little experience to go on, and quickly grew in sophistication. In *guardian.co.uk*, features such as 'Comment is free' drove it to the top of the online ratings, at least until May 2008, when for the first time the *Daily Mail*'s site took the lead in monthly unique users. On websites such as *guardian.co.uk*, the huge capacity of the internet has permitted a vast expansion of the space available for readers' commentary. In print, the venerable institution of the letters page is at the heart of a title's articulation of its public voice: here is where its readers speak, to each other, to the editors, to the broader public sphere. But letters in print could only ever occupy a page or so of a newspaper's available column inches. A site such as the *Guardian*'s Comment is free, by contrast, offers practically unlimited space for readers' comments. Some of it is transferred to the print version of the *Guardian*, but the online site is extensively used as a space for amateur writers to voice their opinions, in the expectation that they will never be published in the newspaper itself. *Guardian* staffers and paid contributors also use the section.

In broadcast journalism, the BBC launched its online news service in November 1997, and it has since become, as part of bbc.co.uk, one of the world's most-used websites, with news and journalism at its core (more than 50 million unique users in June 2008). Here, as elsewhere in its operations, the BBC benefits from its huge resource base and its extensive network of correspondents. That it should lead the online news sector in the UK is not surprising. But Sky News has also sought to set the pace. At a conference in Leeds in early 2008, head of Sky News Simon Bucks described his organisation's efforts to integrate user-generated content (UGC) through the promotion of such techniques as 'crowd sourcing', or soliciting audience contributions on potential stories, and linking with 'micro-blogging' services such as Twitter. The potential value of such UGC was illustrated, for Bucks, in the example of the John Darwin story. This was the 2007 case of a mysterious 'death' and disappearance, in which insurance fraud was suspected. The location of the (supposedly) deceased John Darwin in Panama City was revealed not by a professional journalist after hours of investigation and research, but by someone who found it in an otherwise unrelated routine search, and was presented with a photograph of the man and his wife posing at an estate agent's office. The image and link were then forwarded to the *Sun*, Sky News and others. This is an exceptional and somewhat bizarre example, but demonstrates a general point about the value of UGC to the mainstream or professional media – journalists cannot be everywhere, at all times. Their accounts of reality are, of necessity, sampled and fragmentary, from the selection of a story to report as 'news', to the account of the story that emerges from the sources utilised. In this context, UGC provides access to information about events at which professionals are absent, but in which the news audience can be expected to have an interest. The Asian tsunami of 26 December 2004 is the paradigm case, showing how the mass availability of digital cameras and mobile phones could generate footage of the disaster, which could then be integrated into a professionally produced news bulletin.

For Simon Bucks and Sky, as well as other news organisations such as the BBC, harnessing this potential has become a key goal of the internet revolution. UGC on Sky News and elsewhere will tend to be identified as such, and thus distinguished discursively from the output of the professional journalist. One illuminates and adds to the other. An assistant editor at BBC Radio Five Live describes the corporation's approach thus:

> We don't just put any rubbish on air just because a listener tells us its news. We take our listeners' or readers' stories and apply the same journalistic rigour to them as any other story. We use our skills as journalists to examine stories, looking at patterns in correspondence, and national trends. We examine a listener's background, their interests and any possible bias they bring to a story as we would any politician or pressure group. The key is applying the same journalistic rigour to UGC as any press release or diary story.[10]

An audience editor monitors texts, calls and emails, establishing relationships with potential sources. Organisations such as the Scottish-based Scoopt have emerged to act as what it calls 'aggregators and distributors of photographs and videos captured by eyewitnesses who have an accidental front row seat to a headline-making moment' (scoopt.com). Scoopt pays for contributions and splits revenues with the contributors.

Integrating editorial with the provision of online goods and service

Democratising the structure of access to (what used to be called) newspapers and broadcast news outlets is a good thing in itself – although one concern that has been raised about the implications of the internet revolution for journalism is the potential decline in professional standards caused by the increasing use of UGC (see below). It does not make money for media organisations, however, since both contributing to and consuming material on sites such as 'Comment is free' is, indeed, free. It does not therefore address the problem of how to 'monetise' the internet and compensate for the loss in traditional revenue streams (sales and advertising revenue for newspapers; advertising for commercial TV and radio). What media organisations have increasingly done, therefore, is to find goods and services that can be sold online – competitions, classified advertisements, specialist services such as 'ancestor sites'. Such services – books and CD delivery at discounted prices, holidays, etc. – have long been offered by newspapers and TV companies, as well as being advertised through them, but the interactive nature of online media is recognised to provide new modes of attracting and selling to customers, not least by its potential for micro-marketing to ever-more specialist and niche-oriented groups of consumers.

Finding new business models

As a consequence of these strategies, for one observer, 'the modern newspaper website [and indeed the TV or radio website] is now a many-headed beast and can include everything from bingo games to almost full-blown TV reporting'.[11] As we have seen above, neither newspapers nor traditional linear broadcast news bulletins are dead – far from it, but they must now learn to exist as elements of a more extensive information- and service-delivery structure which is interconnected, interactive, globalised and technologically convergent. The foundation of this multimedia structure is the news brand, no longer the paper object which used to be synonymous with the press, or the flagship news bulletin on terrestrial, free-to-air, 'appointment-to-view' TV. Paper retains its user-friendliness and thus its exchange value, if to a declining extent, but the news brand necessarily now extends across a range of media. News Corporation's purchase of *The Wall Street Journal* exemplifies this transformation, and highlights the conversion of Rupert Murdoch to a future in which news and journalism are sold on a variety of platforms according to their reputation for quality.

The challenge as yet, for all news organisations, is to find a business model that will generate online income streams sufficient to compensate for the slow decline of print and traditional analogue broadcasting (and the advertising revenue that comes with it). Newspapers have tried to charge for online content, for example, and some, like FT.com, do still charge for niche market data. But as the online revolution has proceeded, it has become clear that the great majority of content – of all kinds – will be made available to users free of charge, with income being generated on the back of that usage. As bands such as Radiohead make their music available free online, and as more and more content providers adapt to the realisation that, in the digital era, open access is increasingly the market standard, journalistic organisations cannot buck the trend. Instead, by developing successful websites and attracting a high quantity (and quality, in marketing terms) of users, the aim is to generate sufficient advertising revenue to support the free content. On top of that, as noted above, the aim is to use the interactive properties of the internet to sell online goods and services.

That this broad approach is now bearing fruit is clear. As of 2008, Google was making more advertising income in the UK market than the commercial TV giant ITV. More broadly, the share of advertising revenue had shifted significantly from print and broadcasting to the internet, a trend that was bound to continue. Against that background, the basic strategies by which online journalism will become financially viable in the long term are now clear. Achieving profitability remains elusive for the great majority of news organisations, however.

From bi-media to tri-media

The previous chapter described how the BBC adopted a strategy of 'bi-media' in the 1990s, seeking to integrate news-gathering and production resources of both TV and radio within one, more efficient structure. Today, the aim for the BBC and other major news providers is more likely to be 'tri-media'; the establishment of news-making divisions that break down the traditional barriers existing between print, broadcasting (TV, radio) and the internet. Seamless 'news hubs' are emerging within the headquarters of big broadcast and print media, where journalists are increasingly expected to produce content suitable for distribution by TV and radio, as well as online, over a website such as bbc.co.uk. In 2007, the Head of News at BBC Scotland, Atholl Duncan, stated his goal as 'surviving the internet'[12] by integrating TV, radio and online divisions. News Corporation's purchase of *The Wall Street Journal* in 2007 was followed by a similar restructuring, as Murdoch's managers sought to extend and develop the *WSJ* brand into the digital era. The BBC's investment of hundreds of millions of pounds into facilities such as the Pacific Quay headquarters of BBC Scotland in Glasgow was accompanied by the dissolution of long-established structures and divisions – no longer TV and radio news, just news (see Chapter 9 for a discussion of how the internet is facilitating localisation of news throughout the UK). At a speech given at the Leeds Institute of Communication on 9 January 2008, Peter Horrocks, Head of News at the BBC, described the changes:

> Previously BBC News was organised around four main departments: Firstly, our newsgathering team that organises our correspondents, crews and bureaux in Britain and the world. Newsgathering largely supported the two broadcast output departments – TV News and radio News. And lastly there was a separate News Interactive department which ran our web and interactive services, but which did not have the full power to be able to call on content from our largely broadcast-focused operations. Now newsgathering delivers for all platforms. We have abolished the three output departments, replacing them with two new multimedia departments – a multimedia newsroom that is responsible for the core of the BBC News website, our daily TV News operation (BBC One bulletins, BBC News 24, BBC World, BBC Breakfast) and our radio news summaries and bulletins. Alongside that is a multimedia programmes department with responsibility for interviews, investigation and analysis in our current affairs programming – through Radio 5 Live, *Newsnight*, the *Today* programme, *Panorama* and so on.[13]

At regional press level (see Chapter 9), companies such as Johnston Press have been integrating web video, podcasting and other tools into their operations, and rolling them out across their hundreds of titles.

Resisting the online revolution

The drive towards integration and structural reform has been unpopular among some news professionals, especially when they mean job losses on the scale announced by Mark Thompson, BBC Director General in 2007 (1800 redundancies across the UK, 10 per cent cut in commissioning, savings of £500 million over time, most of it in the area of news and current affairs).[14] Thompson argued that these cuts were needed to allow investment in interactive online technology, and that 'we want to build a compelling multimedia, multiplatform offer'.

Popular or not with workers and unions, the integrative trend is now unstoppable, increasingly recognised as an inevitable consequence of the challenges (and possibilities) provided by the internet. This means that journalists everywhere are becoming, of necessity, more flexible, trained to produce a podcast as well as a print version of an article, or a video package for uploading onto their own blog, or their organisation's web page. Some argue that this will stretch journalists too thinly, as expectations constantly rise about how much they produce, and in what form. Others are embracing the emerging environment, and the journalist's new status as 'information architect'. In an *Ariel* special issue devoted to the corporation's restructuring plans, Mark Thompson wrote:

> Instead of largely separate TV, radio and web operations, we plan an integrated multimedia newsroom ... we can significantly reduce duplication in newsgathering and production without our most important flagships like *Today* and *Newsnight* losing their distinctiveness and character.[15]

Many disagreed, of course. Throughout the news media there was resistance to the multimedia vision. A good example of the tensions that arise from this process is that of the *Daily Telegraph*. In 2005, the titles' managers announced the beginning of a major effort to cut costs and adapt their newsroom for the online era. In February that year, 20 per cent job cuts were announced, enabling £150 million of investment in equipment and technology. As restructuring got under way, with journalists resigning and leaking to other newspapers about allegedly dire conditions inside the *Telegraph* offices, and loyal readers questioning the editorial direction of the paper, a former editor warned of the perils of moving too quickly towards convergence and technological integration: 'If it [the *Telegraph*'s old print newsroom] is dismantled and spread too quickly and thinly between podcast, television show and afternoon 'click-and-carry' service, there is a danger of transforming a great newspaper into little more than a wire service with a handful of strident columnists attached'.[16] In Scotland, cost-cutting and restructuring by Newsquest at its *Herald* titles in Glasgow provoked strike action in June 2007 on the grounds that, as the NUJ's Scottish organiser put it, 'they've undermined the ability of people to produce the goods'.[17] Other newspapers and broadcast news outlets were following the same strategy, however, on the basis that the web, far from being a threat to their businesses and cultural role, was 'looking more and more like a potential saviour if they can drop their pretensions and yoke its communal aspects to their powerful brands'.[18] In the *Observer*, Peter Preston observed that:

> The thought of a news collection and distribution organisation without print or paper raises the prospect of a quite different future for journalists: one where few of the old skills and new convergences are particularly relevant, one where a start-up news gathering operation on the net would train and hire web people, not converts from print with ink on their hands.[19]

Online journalism in the UK: issues and debates

If, on the basis of the trends described above, few will now dispute that the future of news and journalism in the UK, as in comparable countries, is online, it would nonetheless be premature to overstate the extent to which the internet has replaced traditional print and broadcast sources of news. While advertising revenue has now shifted decisively away from newspapers and TV to the internet, and will continue to do so, the former remain the most used sources of journalistic information. For that reason, voices have been raised against a herd-like rush online that would degrade or damage established news-gathering and production standards. From this perspective, the online revolution is blamed for starving the traditional news media of resources.

Linked to this argument is the view that, while the migration to online is clearly under way, the quality of online journalism is significantly lower than that of traditional print and broadcast sources, if only because online news sites do not, in the main, originate their own stories, but reuse and distribute other people's. It is all the more urgent, therefore, that the professional practices and standards of traditional print and broadcast journalism are not allowed to decline because of inadequate resourcing.

In June 2008, the House of Lords Select Committee on Communication published a substantial report, based on extensive research and interviews with leading media executives in the UK, which set out both of these arguments. Among the report's findings was that, despite the explosion of online news sites described above, there was no case for the relaxation of media ownership rules, as has been argued by Rupert Murdoch and others in recent years. Their argument, not new but given added urgency by the expansion of the internet, has been that changing technologies make redundant the UK's established rules governing media ownership and the protection of plurality. The Lords' report disagreed with this view, on the basis that while online journalism was growing in importance as a source of information, TV, print and radio remained the main sources, at least for the time being and the medium-term future. For that reason, preserving plurality of ownership of these sources was a valid goal of government regulation. As the committee put it:

> Much of the news available on the internet and on the new television channels is not new. It is repackaged from elsewhere. The proliferation of

news sources has not been matched by a corresponding expansion in professional and investigative journalism. It is still possible for one voice to become too powerful to be acceptable in a healthy democracy. Owners can and do influence the news in a variety of ways. They are in a position to have significant political impact.[20]

A further finding of the committee, worth reproducing here at some length, concerned the impact of the internet on the quality of the news provided by the traditional platforms.

> Both here and abroad the newspaper industry is facing severe problems as readership levels fall; young people turn to other sources of news; and advertising moves to the internet. The newspaper industry is responding to these challenges in a variety of ways including establishing a high profile web presence. However, even when newspapers run successful internet sites the value of the advertising they sell on these sites does not make up for the value lost. The result of these pressures is that newspaper companies are having to make savings and this is having a particular impact on investment in news gathering and investigative journalism. The number of foreign news bureaux is decreasing, and there is an increasing reliance on news agency feed and information derived from the public relations industry. Inside the United Kingdom the regional and local press is under particular pressure.
>
> In television news the same trends are evident. Most news programmes have smaller audiences than they had ten years ago; younger people in particular are watching less television news; commercial television channels are losing advertising revenue to the internet.[21]

As expressed here, the fear is that these pressures may encourage cost-cutting by those new media that have traditionally maintained normative professional standards. This is, by common consent, a legitimate anxiety. On the other hand, as I have suggested above, the future survival of news brands such as the BBC, the *Guardian*, the *Financial Times* or *The Times* depends not least on the preservation and promotion of the reputation of the product – journalism – in a market of many providers. Quality journalism in this market is not merely a liberal aspiration to which all pay lip service, but is a commercial necessity, attracting the educated, upmarket users who will then go on to attract the desired advertising revenues and spend their disposable income on goods and services.

Let me note here one counter-example to the argument that online journalism tends to degrade quality by comparison with print and broadcast media. It is frequently said, and with justification, that the media in the UK have progressively devoted fewer and fewer resources to the pursuit of investigative journalism (De Burgh, 2008; Davies, 2008). As we have seen above, there is a debate to be had about what constitutes quality or 'serious' investigative journalism in the UK and elsewhere, but few dispute the general trend away from resource-intensive investigations such as those associated with ITV's *World in Action*, the *Sunday Times* 'Insight' team at its peak, or BBC's *Panorama*, and their replacement with more celebrity- and consumer-oriented journalism. Could it be that the internet, with its 'crowd-sourcing' character-istics and its ability to connect the diverse efforts of many investigators, could provide an alternative source of investigative journalism?

Such potential for improving journalistic quality is shown (if not yet proven) by the US-based *ProPublica* site. Funded by a US billionaire and dedicated to preserving 'the skills and values of investigative reporting',[22] *ProPublica* is a response to the decline of investigative journalism. With its resources of $10 million per annum devoted entirely to investigation (where only 10 per cent of such resources are allocated to that cause in the average newspaper), *Pro-Publica* is modelled as a 'largely web-based product which will seek both to promote the traditional skills and responsibilities of investigative journalism – encouraging it whenever it is found – and to conduct its own investigations in areas of significant public interest'.[23] In this case, the information-retrieval and distribution properties of the internet are being harnessed to the traditional standards and ethics of journalism, in order to overcome a perceived problem in the traditional industry (caused, not least, by the online revolution). If this example is a useful guide, we can predict that the internet will present new ways of doing traditional but still necessary things, journalistically speaking, such as investigation.

Quality and standards

In addition to the potentially adverse impact of online on the production of traditional journalism, another set of concerns addresses the issue of journal-istic standards and ethics. Put simply – the democratisation of the public sphere by way of online forms such as citizen journalism and UGC is a good thing, most will agree; but what if it also means the dilution of professional journalistic standards built up over an extended period? The internet has led to a proliferation of news-based websites, many of them circulating information which can fairly be characterised as rumour and gossip rather than fact. The internet did not invent such information, which has been circulating in print media since the black propaganda and witch-burning headlines of the sixteenth century, but it has accelerated the flow, and amplified the negative impacts which rumour and gossip masquerading as journalism may be expected to have.

In the UK there have been many examples of this phenomenon. In October 2003, the internet was awash with sexually scandalous stories involving Charles, Prince of Wales. British newspapers would not print the stories, which were without foundation and libellous. Overseas online sites could, and did, allowing the story to spread by nods and winks, even by those who knew it was not true. In the *Sunday Times*, former prime minister John Major asked 'are we now in a world in which peephole journalism will print anything – true or false, that is said by anyone – sick or otherwise, on the grounds that the subject is a public figure and therefore the public has a "right to know"? What sort of "right" is this?'[24] As Natasha Berger put it in *The American Prospect*, 'Blogs, with their soundbite commentary, round-the-clock updates, and open door policy to posters – make an ideal breeding ground for character assassins ... a couple of choice links and an axe to grind are all that is required to spread innuendo around the web with lightning speed'.[25] Writing in the *Los Angeles Times*, Alex Jones asserted that:

> Bloggers, with few exceptions, don't add reporting to the personal views they post online, and they see journalism as bound by norms and standards that they reject. That encourages these common attributes of the blogosphere: vulgarity, scorching insults, bitter denunciations, one-sided arguments, erroneous assertions and the array of qualities that might be expected from a blustering know all in a bar.[26]

Howard Kurtz in the *Washington Post* characterised blogs as 'idiosyncratic, passionate, and often profane, with the sort of intimacy and attitude that are all but impossible in newspapers and on television'.[27] And even if they are accurate, are they a good thing? Observing internet-led coverage of the scandalous sex life of Deputy Prime Minister John Prescott in 2006 – 'the first big British political story to be driven by bloggers' – John Barkham asked if the growing influence of the blogosphere was 'a boon for democracy' or 'a reckless deskilling of journalism where rumours are published and reputations besmirched without any supporting evidence?'[28]

Citizen journalism and UGC

Above and beyond the issue of whether online journalism is more or less accurate and honest than the print and broadcast media have been in the past, is the question of whether it – that element of it which is new, the bottom-up postings and comments of the bloggers – can be considered journalism at all. Writing for the *Sunday Times* supplement *Ecosse*, Allan Brown describes the blogosphere as 'the background radiation of the intellectual realm, the white noise of the collective unconscious, scrolling out their narratives whether anyone wishes to read them or not'.[29]

In the era of cultural chaos, as I have characterised it (McNair, 2003, 2006), boundaries are dissolving and walls are coming down. One of these dissolving boundaries is that between the professional journalist and the amateur blogger or 'citizen journalist'. Stuart Allan observes that 'what counts as journalism in the connected, always-on society is open to negotiation, with fluidly changing points of convergence and divergence between its practice in the mainstream and in the margins' (Allan, 2006: 179). Tim Gardam, former broadcast news executive, notes that 'in the digital cacophony of 24-hour services and online

news, where the barrier between writer and reader breaks down in the infinitely connected world of blogging, what were once clear certainties about the
boundaries and purposes of journalism have become far more contentious'.[30]
As we have seen, much of what we today call UGC has the status of snapshots
taken by bystanders at, or participants in, the events that later become news.
Such material, welcome though it often is to the mainstream news media, is
not always produced according to the professional ethics and standards governing staffers on, say, *The Times* and the *Guardian*. Bloggers, on the other
hand, who fill the internet with their opinions, are, in the main, members of
the public who would find it very difficult to obtain a paid-for commission
from a newspaper. Democratic, diverse and decentralised these forms of online
journalistic discourse may be, but are they of any value? And insofar as they
blur and obscure the professional/amateur distinction, might they actually do
harm to the public sphere?

The online periodical *Amateur Computerist Newsletter* devoted an issue to
the debate around the threat posed by citizen journalism and UGC to the
standards of journalism.[31] Asking if the expansion of UGC would 'dethrone
the professional news media', the journal noted that 'there is a challenge to the
authority and centrality of mainstream media. That challenge is coming from
efforts at non-commercial or at least non-profit and other forms of citizen
journalism where staff and citizen reporters contribute as part of their roles as
citizens of their societies or citizens of the net, netizens'.[32] This challenge
inevitably causes anxiety among journalists raised in the pre-internet era, and
among those commentators who worry about the erosion of centuries-old
professional standards in journalism, and what this might mean for the quality
and integrity of the public sphere on which democracy depends. These are
justified anxieties, and in response to them many news organisations, including
the BBC, the *Guardian* and others, now include on their websites online guides
and 'rule books' to aid in the practice of citizen journalism. Gate-keeping and
screening procedures are being refined all the time (Heinrich, 2008), so that
erroneous reports, malicious rumours, downright lies and offensive rants are
identified and blocked before they get to the public domain. These are useful
correctives to the otherwise welcome democratising potential of the internet,
and a necessary qualification of its unprecedented capacity to permit popular
access to the production of journalism.

The emergence of the blogosphere and the new commentariat

A rather different concern is expressed about the growth of the blogosphere,
and the rise of what has been called in the UK context a 'new commentariat'.[33]
As I and others have noted in recent years, long before the internet became an
issue the British media had seen the substantial expansion of opinion journalism – columns, commentaries, special correspondents – into territory hitherto
reserved for so-called 'hard news' (Duff, 2008; McNair, 2000, 2008c). For some
observers, this was a negative trend, since it crowded out 'serious' news to

make room for the babble of the commentators. From that perspective, the problem of 'opinion overload' in the public sphere has been exacerbated by the rise of the internet and the blogosphere, which is, it is generally accepted, (almost) nothing but commentary.

In November 2005, the *Guardian*'s Oliver Burkeman identified 'a new wave of political bloggers' in the UK, a 'new commentariat' threatening Britain's 'old media pundits, a fully fledged alternative wing of the opinion industry, challenging the primacy of newspaper commentators'.[34] A British example of this phenomenon in practice would be norm.blog, the site of former Marxist academic Norman Geras, who in 2005 attracted mainstream media coverage for his online opinions about the legitimacy of the invasion of Iraq. Within a section of the ideological spectrum where the consensus was anti-war, Geras supported the intervention on humanitarian, human rights grounds. His views were subsequently picked up by newspapers such as the *Sunday Times* in the UK, and by pro-war elements in the USA (for their own reasons, of course). According to Glenn Reynolds, founder of the Instapundit blog, '[Geras] writes well, and what he writes makes sense. Unlike too many on the left these days, his moral sense hasn't been obliterated by hostility towards the West in general and America in particular.'[35] Former Tory leader Iain Duncan Smith welcomed the fact that the blogosphere 'will become a force in Britain', since it could 'ignite many new forces of conservatism'.[36]

For many observers, from a variety of ideological perspectives, the internet was a driving force behind making the public sphere more open and diverse. For voices such as Smith, the blogosphere broke the dominance of what they perceived as a liberal media elite. For others, the break was with the traditional dominance of mainstream, established voices in general, irrespective of their ideological bias.

Supporters of the positive, democratising power of the blogosphere, such as *Sunday Times* columnist and blogger Andrew Sullivan, have characterised it as 'a publishing revolution more profound than anything since the printing press',[37] because it has undermined the top-down, elitist nature of mainstream journalism. Bloggers in their millions, independent and in the main unaffiliated to established media organisations have, in Sullivan's words, 'seized the means of production ... This is democratic journalism at its best'. They have 'quickly become a huge presence in opinion journalism'. For Dave Winer, one of the pioneers of blogging, it presents 'a revolution in journalism' and reveals 'the unedited voices of millions around the world'.[38]

For others, this democratisation is not necessarily good news. US observer Oliver Kamm concedes that the blogosphere is a 'democratic medium, allowing anyone to participate in political debate without an intermediary, at little or no cost. But it is a direct and not deliberative form of democracy. You need no competence to join in.'[39] And if bloggers often lack competence, 'blogs are providers not of news but of comment. This would be a good thing if blogs extended the range of available opinion in the public sphere. But they do not; paradoxically, they narrow it. This happens because blogs typically do not add to the available stock of commentary; they are purely parasitic on the stories and opinions that traditional media provide. In its paucity of coverage and predictability of conclusion, the blogosphere provides a parody of democratic deliberation'.

This, it should be noted, is precisely the kind of criticism regularly directed at the print pundits in recent years, and may well be valid in many cases. The issue, for Kamm, is that the blogosphere expands and multiplies the scope for those 'nattering nabobs of negativism'. All other things remaining equal, however, it may be judged a kind of progress if access to the realm of media commentary is extended beyond the ranks of the elites who have traditionally dominated it.

Online futures

As this and previous chapters have shown, the internet has not killed journalism, nor, as yet, has it killed any particular journalistic medium. On the contrary, it has contributed to a huge increase in the quantity of news and journalism available to the public – an increasingly globalised, connected and participatory public at that, with access to an unprecedented diversity of sources of journalistic information. The internet has, however, changed the way journalism is produced and consumed, sometimes for the worse, but often for the better. In Britain, online journalism has steadily advanced in the calculations of established media organisations since the first edition of this book appeared in the mid-1990s, until we are now, by this fifth edition, well on the way to an environment dominated by digital, interactive, participatory platforms in which the traditional demarcation lines separating amateur from professional, print from broadcast, TV from radio, all of those from online, are disappearing.

No-one knows for how many years yet the newspaper will remain a key element of our cultural life, nor the traditional broadcast news bulletin with its linear narratives delivered at regular and predictable times every day, an 'appointment to view (or listen)' of the analogue media era. Surveys show that print and broadcast media remain the main source of news, by far, for the large majority of people, and they will continue to do so for a while yet, albeit embedded within a globalised public sphere comprising online news sites and real-time news channels. Established print and broadcast news organisations can, as they currently do, ride this wave and emerge intact, even strengthened, if they learn to harness the democratising potential of the internet, as well as preserving the normative standards and ethics with which journalism has traditionally been associated, and on which their brands have been built over decades and sometimes centuries. News and journalism can be distributed on paper, broadcast on analogue airwaves, or bounced off satellites and sent down fibre-optic cables. The survival of particular news brands in the twenty-first century will not be dependent on the physical form of their technological infrastructure, but successful promotion of their reputation for the old-fashioned qualities of accuracy, objectivity and reliability. The journalism of opinion will continue to flourish, and not all of it will be worth taking seriously – which is why the journalism of trusted fact and reliable reportage will continue to be so important.

Further reading

Stuart Allan's *Online News* (2006) is a readable account of the development of journalism on the internet in the decade from 1995 to 2005, focused on the USA. For a less scholarly *Brief History of the Future: The Origins of the Internet*, see John Naughton's 1999 book, and the series of interviews with net pioneers published in the July 2008 edition of *Vanity Fair* magazine.

9 The regional story

This chapter covers:

- the development of regional news and current affairs broadcasting
- the impact of devolution, digitisation and the internet on the production and consumption of journalism in Scotland, Wales, Northern Ireland and the English regions
- recent trends in the regional press
- attempts by the national UK press to establish a presence in the regions
- the rise of the free sheets and the *Metro* movement.

Previous chapters have been largely about the challenges faced by the 'national' journalistic media, by which I mean those produced mainly in London and distributed throughout the geographical territory of the UK: the broadcast network news of the BBC and ITN, and the UK's 22 London-based daily and Sunday newspapers (see Chapter 1). But the UK is not a nation so much as a collection of nations, which are in turn divided into myriad regions and communities, each with its own distinctive characteristics. England, Northern Ireland, Scotland and Wales all possess particular cultural identities, in addition to being 'British'. In England, the North is perceived very differently from the South, while in Scotland, Glasgow, Edinburgh and the surrounding conurbations have as much to separate as to bind them together culturally.

Throughout the UK, these differences are reflected in local media, so that while the country as a whole shares a common culture of 'national' news and journalism, the greatest proportion of it produced in London, many of its constituent parts, from the nations of Scotland and Wales down to the remote island or rural community have their own media covering their own issues and agendas. This chapter focuses on those media – their recent history, current challenges and future prospects, against the backdrop of four trends.

The first, to which we have already referred in other contexts above, is technological. The online revolution has had an impact on the local newspaper sector as much as, if not more than, the national press, reducing circulation and advertising revenue as readers slowly but steadily migrate to the web. In local broadcast journalism, meanwhile, analogue switch-off, and the onset of complete digitisation of TV in the UK by 2012, has generated a serious crisis for the commercial producers of regional news such as STV in Scotland, as the old business model that governed commercial TV for 50 years and more fades into history. As a result, the future quantity and quality of local commercial TV news throughout the UK has never been in such doubt.

Second, these technology-led trends have added to the competitive pressures caused by an expanding 'free-sheet' sector. Free newspapers, distributed to commuters on trains and buses, have grown substantially in number and readership since the first edition of this book appeared in the early 1990s, to the point where, in the view of some observers, they threaten the very viability of the paid-for regional press and the quality of the journalism it produces.

Third, London-based editions of national titles such as the *Sun* have intensified their competitive strategies in the regions, particularly in Scotland, with major consequences for the circulations of indigenous titles such as the *Daily Record*.

Fourth, hanging over all this is a constitutional question, which has now reached a pivotal point in the UK. How should the BBC's journalists, for example, adapt to the changing needs of a devolved Scotland, Wales and Northern Ireland, as well as those of the English regions, at a time when UK cultural identity is on the agenda as never before in living memory?

2008 was a key year in the debate around these questions, with reports from Ofcom on the future of public service broadcasting; from the BBC Trust on the failures of BBC·news and current affairs to serve the regions adequately; and from the Scottish Broadcasting Commission (SBC), set up by the Scottish National Party government after its election in 2007 to review the future of broadcasting in Scotland. While a number of key decisions remained to be taken by the regulators and broadcasters as this edition went to press, the main lines of debate had emerged and are summarised in this chapter.

Broadcasting in the nations and regions

Previous editions of this book observed that one of the more unexpected outcomes of the changes taking place in British broadcasting in recent years was the boost they had given to regional television journalism. From the early 1990s, the BBC and the commercial TV channels devoted more of their resources to regional news and current affairs than ever before, as they came to believe that the key to their survival lay largely in the extent to which they could meet the demands of viewers at regional and local levels. Local news production has always been a legal requirement of the main public service broadcasters, but in the 1990s it came to be viewed as desirable, even essential, for pragmatic, competitive reasons.

Audience demand for more regional broadcast journalism was identified by market research carried out for companies such as Scottish Television and

Grampian in the early 1990s, and is in itself perhaps unsurprising. Information about one's own locality, whether in printed or broadcast form, performs a number of important social functions, from the banality of knowing which roads are open to such matters as local crime and factory closures. National news suppliers, by definition, are ill-equipped to cover local news, except when it has national repercussions, and no one has ever expected them to do so as a matter of routine. As a result, the ITV companies have always maintained the facilities to produce their own local journalism, which has traditionally been broadcast in the early evening with shorter bulletins at other times of the day, usually following ITN's national news. As for the BBC, its Regional Directorate, set up in 1987 and now renamed as Nations and Regions, maintains six regional news and current affairs centres, and 13 offices, all with substantial budgets. BBC spending on regional news and current affairs has increased over time, and further investment is planned, partly in response to growing concerns about the quantity and quality of the corporation's local news production (see below). In June 2008, the BBC launched a consultation on plans to invest £68 million in a network of 60 local, online video news centres across the UK, part of its engagement with digitisation (in November 2008 following opposition from local commercial media, the BBC Trust announced it would not be proceeding with this plan).[1]

The coming crisis of commercial TV news in the regions

The BBC has vast resources to draw on, of course, and its Royal Charter demands that it take local news seriously. For the commercial public service broadcasters, on the other hand, the onset of digitisation has complicated the financial calculations, and made local TV news on commercial free-to-air channels look more vulnerable than at any time since the establishment of the ITV network. In the view of the 2008 House of Lords report on media ownership,[2] regulatory intervention will be required to ensure its survival beyond analogue switch off. Survival is necessary, in turn, to ensure the preservation of plurality in the provision of local TV news. So what is the problem for the commercial broadcasters, given that there is audience demand for local news?

While regional news and current affairs has tended to be seen as a less-glamorous poor relation in the television journalism industry, the developments in broadcasting examined in previous chapters highlighted its potential contribution to the financial health and long-term survival of the commercial organisations that produce it. The emergence of cable and satellite television in the 1990s meant a significant addition to the number of hours of broadcast journalism available to the British viewer, as we have seen. More choice for the viewer (disregarding, for the moment, the quality of what is on offer) meant more competition for the audiences on which, for the commercial companies especially, income depends. And the providers of rolling news had some important advantages in the ratings war: notably, their ability to stay on air 24 hours a day and to be there, live, as the cruise missiles flew through downtown Kabul or Baghdad (or wherever the newsworthy event of the day may have been). Cornford and Robins argued nearly two decades ago that 'if the policy agenda of the 1980s was about "public service versus the market" this is being overlaid with – or perhaps even supplanted by – a new geographical agenda concerned with the scales of broadcasting, with the relation between the global, local and national services' (Cornford and Robins 1990: 5).

The regional companies, on the other hand, had little but their 'regionalness' on which to sell their product. A regional director of the Independent Television Commission (the commercial TV regulator before the establishment of Ofcom) argued in the early 1990s, in an interview with the author,[3] that 'in future there will be many more sources of national and international news than there are at present, and I think that the way for local regional companies to build up a reputation for themselves, to interest their viewers, to get their viewers and to keep them, is to provide a good local or regional news service'. This source believed that 'news and current affairs has an extremely large part in the commercial companies' future plans. Whether it will draw huge audiences is another matter, but it will give credibility to a station, and once you've got the credibility, the people will tend to watch you more.'

As already noted, the ITV companies' own market research convinced them that regional journalism could and would draw audiences, and was thus justified on commercial as well as 'quality' criteria.[4] As one ITV manager put it then:

> the reality is that for any local station the main point of contact with the viewer is the main evening news programme. Some years ago we took the view that with the proliferation of satellite, cable, C5 at some point, the thing we should concentrate on is the one thing those channels couldn't give them – local news. You don't get real local news on cable, because they don't have the resources, nor will they in the foreseeable future. So we've invested a lot of money in news by way of increasing staff, more cameras on the road, more editing equipment, more bulletins, and so on.

This essentially commercial logic connected with a profound cultural shift towards greater decentralisation of economic and political decision-making, and of cultural production. The trend was global – or 'glocal' – and underpinned one of the Conservative Party's main arguments for opening up the UK television system to the market in the 1990s. Audiences, it was argued, are fragmenting into ever-more heterogeneous groups, separated by class, lifestyle, region and, in the case of Britain, nation. The era of London-centred UK media was recognised to be coming to an end.

Stuart Prebble, who played a key role in the debate about the future of regional TV journalism, identified trends, pulling in two different directions. On the one hand, news coverage was becoming more global in nature, so that

> it's not unusual for us to see *News at Ten* being presented from the middle of the Sahara Desert, and we're quite relaxed about the idea of

seeing the newscaster standing in Riyadh and introducing reports from South Carolina where the Americans are getting ready to go to the Gulf, and flipping over to Tel Aviv where they're expecting the missiles to come in – only a few years ago that would have been unthinkable, but now it's routine.

Satellite newsgathering and transmission, in this sense, endowed TV news with an increasingly international 'footprint'. For Prebble, however, and those who agreed with him, this merely enhanced the need for news which is more parochial, in the best sense of the term, making it incumbent on those with a local focus to consolidate that strength and give viewers a picture of the world seen from where they live. Said Prebble, 'I think that will become the key to ITV's position as the competition [from Sky, the BBC, CNN, etc.] gets stronger.' Research conducted by Ofcom in 2004 found that regional TV news was a priority of public service broadcasting for 83 per cent of the audience, and that 72 per cent wanted to see such news on both BBC and commercial channels.

From this point of view, the regional companies' news production was no longer, if it ever had been, just a legal obligation, but potentially was their most popular local output, providing a distinctive service which the large national and international broadcasters could not match, thus attracting audiences and advertising revenue. The ITV companies' ability to address local audiences with a local news agenda became, in this analysis, their unique selling proposition. In short, it was precisely what some commentators termed the 'globalisation' of television culture occasioned by the advent of satellite broadcasting which thrust onto regional journalism a heightened role.[5] In making their 1991 licence applications, accordingly, each company's bid placed great emphasis on the continuing importance of regional television journalism and made a clear commitment to provide it in the 1990s. Scottish Television, for example, one of the few companies for whom there was no competition in the bidding process that year, pledged itself to increase local news provision from its then level of 200 hours per annum to 370.[6] Similar commitments were made when licences were renewed ten years later.

Despite these commitments, however, ITV's regional news provision was severely criticised by the ITC in March 2000. Ratings had fallen by 22 per cent for some ITV regional bulletins, attributable in large part to audience confusion around the scheduling changes discussed in Chapter 5. Since 2000, ratings have recovered somewhat, but continue to lag behind those of the BBC's regional bulletins.

The digital challenge

Ratings rise and fall, and on their own, declining or low figures for the ITV companies have been manageable until recently. A much more fundamental threat to local, commercial TV news comes from the end of the analogue system of broadcasting and its substitution by multi-channel digital. The end of analogue broadcasting means the end of spectrum scarcity, and a sharply reduced monetary value for the wavelengths on which ITV programmes have been transmitted for half a century. In the analogue era, ITV was able to make profits from selling shares in this scare resource to advertisers. This was the business model which allowed a commercial company to generate the surpluses from which public service commitments could be met. It assumed few or no competitors for advertising revenue, at least in the broadcast sector (newspapers of course relied on advertising long before TV was invented). Where the BBC had the luxury of tax-payers' money to fund its public service broadcast requirements, ITV did so in return for its component companies' access to scarce analogue spectrum and the profits this permitted from the sale of advertising, especially at peak time. Without these profits, ITV would never have been able to make minority audience investigative journalism of the type exemplified by the famous *World in Action*, or important public service material such as children's programmes. Even with analogue subsidy, ITV was transmitting fewer and fewer of these types of programme as time went on.

With the coming of digital TV comes the end of 'analogue subsidy' entirely, and the business model that depended on it. Analysts estimated that the value of the subsidy – estimated at around £180 million in 2008 – would fall to near zero following analogue switch-off, creating a large financial shortfall. As a result, ITV would no longer be able to afford public service programming, including regional news, which did not earn its keep in advertising terms. Under the leadership of Michael Grade, ITV baldly stated in 2008 that it might have to 'resile' from its public service obligations – to relinquish public service status, in other words, and the privileges which it had traditionally conferred, but which were now disappearing along with analogue technology. In the area of regional TV news, ITV estimated that it cost around £40 million per annum to provide services throughout the UK.

For most observers, the potential disappearance of local news on ITV was perceived as a major threat to the quality of the British public sphere, and to democracy itself. For the House of Lords Select Committee on Communications, plurality of broadcast news provision was just as important at local as it was at national level. 'We emphatically believe that public service broadcasting cannot be left to the BBC alone. A continuing plurality of public service broadcasters should be an aim of public policy. This is particularly crucial for news and current affairs'.[7]

As it prepared for its quintennial review of public service broadcasting in 2008, the regulator Ofcom recognised ITV's difficulties, and as this edition went to press was considering a range of options, including the 'top-slicing' of the licence fee to support ITV's public service activities. Channel 4, for its part, partly in the effort to bolster its claim for public funding post-analogue switch-off, signalled a readiness to enter the regional TV news business. In part this was an expression of self-interest, because the flagship *Channel 4 News* bulletin, supplied by ITN, has always relied on the resources of ITV regional companies for its own regional coverage. Should ITV withdraw from regional news, Channel 4 would have to find an alternative means of gathering and producing regional stories. The channel's managers indicated that, in this event, regional news would appear on its digital More4 channel and online, rather than on Channel 4 itself.

Some observers were sceptical, however. In the *Guardian*, Steve Hewlett pointed out that 'C4 has no background in regional or local news, and none of the infrastructure, people, or critically, the money needed to provide it'.[8] Realistic or not, Channel 4's proposal was indicative of the scale of the funding problem facing commercial local TV news in 2008, a problem that remained unresolved as this edition went to press (continuing into 2009).[9]

The BBC

In early 1991, the BBC placed advertisements in the press for a battery of new appointments, part of an investment of £3 million in its regional journalism (a substantial sum in those days). This was one clear signal that, as for the ITV companies, regional journalism was going to play an important role in the BBC's future. As Ron Neil, then Head of the Regional Directorate:

> we are choosing to make journalism our number one priority in regional broadcasting. I'm putting my share of the savings we made from Funding the Future into journalism and creating more jobs, because I think it's the single most important activity we have outside London. I think the licence payers should be able to expect decent local and regional information from the BBC.

The strategy reflected the perception, articulated by Ron Neil, that 'all our lives are becoming more regional. The policy centre is shifting to Brussels, and I think the regionalisation of society will be reflected in broadcasting.'

At that time, the commercial companies dominated regional television journalism in the UK. As we have seen, the ITV companies, in the process of winning their franchises, reasserted the importance of journalism to their operations and committed themselves to appropriate levels of investment. The ITV network had 21 news centres run by 12 regional companies, compared with the BBC's six regions (including the 'national' regions of Scotland, Wales and Northern Ireland), divided into 12 news-making centres.

Rather than attempt to match the ITV network's greater number of regional splits, the BBC's Regional Directorate adopted a strategy which attempted to maximise the advantages to be gained from having substantial television and radio departments in the regions. A senior BBC Scotland manager pointed out, that one of the differences between the regional journalism of the ITV companies and that of his own organisation is that 'they invest more in camera power, in order to get more [and more local] stories on screen. We will increasingly invest more into the quality and expertise end, so that you may find your local ITV station offering 23 stories in 28 minutes, while we offer seven or eight.'

Local BBC journalism, in short, like national and international coverage, would increasingly be produced by informed, specialist correspondents, capable of finding stories and breaking them, rather than merely reacting to them. For the BBC's senior management, branding their regional journalism as 'authoritative' was the key to competing with what they saw as the ITV companies' 'smash-and-grab' approach. As one regional controller put it, 'what we're about is being the authoritative voice, a high-quality dependable service which also has to be popular.'

Devolution and local broadcast journalism

That was then. Debates around the future of local broadcasting (as, indeed, of the local press – see below) were given added impetus, and pushed in new directions, by the election of a Labour government in May 1997 and that government's manifesto pledge, quickly honoured, to establish constituent assemblies in Scotland and Wales (an assembly was also established in Northern Ireland as part of the 1998 Good Friday Peace Agreement). While the constitutional powers and remits of these assemblies varied, the turn towards devolution which they signalled was a major political development for the UK, and one that would thrust new roles and responsibilities onto the local broadcasters.[10] In Scotland and Wales, for example, the setting up of devolved assemblies brought into being a whole new tier of government activity, requiring local news coverage to match. In Scotland, as a result, both the BBC and STV announced – even before the results of the September 1997 devolution referendum were known – that they were working on ways to give Scottish public affairs enhanced priority in their schedules.[11]

Following the 'Yes' vote for devolution in November 1997, both BBC Scotland and STV (which in 1997 had taken over the Grampian company, serving the north of Scotland) began to make plans to upgrade their newsgathering facilities in preparation for the new assemblies, brushing aside objections from London that Scottish broadcasters lacked the resources to compete with the UK-level providers. Once again, it was argued that new technologies would transform the resource issue. As one observer put it, 'digital services will make it easier to lift English or foreign reports, and the creation of more than 200 digital channels will see a BBC Scotland television channel. Viewers will eventually be able to opt for the Scottish-based *Six O'Clock News* or the version based in London'.[12] This did not happen at that time, but in June 2008, partly in response to a BBC Trust-commissioned report[13] that was critical of the Corporation's coverage of the UK's nations and regions, it was being speculated that such a channel would indeed come into being, with the support of First Minister Alex Salmond.

The report in question was based on research carried out by the Cardiff University School of Journalism, Media and Culture, complemented by an analysis of BBC news by political scientist Anthony King.[14] King's study, and his reading of the Cardiff findings on BBC network news content, found 'over-frequent lapses on the part of the [BBC] in its coverage of devolved and partially devolved matters'. Network news coverage, for example, often failed to distinguish between Westminster legislation which applied only to England (on the National Health Service, for example), and that which applied to the UK as a whole. Coverage of devolved matters in network news was inadequate both in quantitative and qualitative terms, King argued, and tended to marginalise the politics of Scotland, Wales and Northern Ireland within political coverage as a whole.

Having commissioned the King and Cardiff studies, the BBC Trust and management more or less fully endorsed their findings. The Trust recognised that ten years after the introduction of devolution, 'transformational change' was taking place within the UK, and that BBC and current affairs news coverage had not yet adapted to the growing 'complexity' of the emerging political environment. The Trust (and most commentators on the report) welcomed the apparent fact (as indicated in survey evidence) that a majority of people in the UK still valued high-quality local journalism, and that they valued adequate coverage of other parts of the UK beyond their own locality. The Trust also took some comfort in the fact that a majority of those surveyed for the study regarded the BBC's coverage of the nations and regions as broadly accurate and fair, as well as 'consistently superior' to that available on ITV. However, it was accepted by the BBC's key oversight body that the Corporation's political coverage was too Westminster-focused, that there was a bias towards English stories (above and beyond what might be expected from the fact that England is, after all, ten times larger in population than Scotland, and five times larger than Scotland, Wales and Northern Ireland put together), and that significant regional stories were too frequently missed or minimised in coverage. And this was not just a problem in relation to the smaller nations of the UK: 'the BBC also faces editorial challenges in reflecting the English regions on the networks, particularly the north of England'.

In responding to these criticisms, BBC management accepted that 'it is essential that accurate information about political developments in the four nations is reflected in network news and current affairs so that the authority of the BBC is maintained, and the audience has confidence in that voice'. More broadly:

> The BBC must remain in step with the changing face of the UK and ... our UK-wide journalism must deliver a range of perspectives and richness of coverage that reflects the diversity of the nations and regions of the UK.

News managers at the BBC undertook to improve their performance in this area by improved monitoring of output, more cooperation between producers in London and those in the nations and regions, more out-of-London career development (to address the London-centricity of BBC career structures and networking), less 'parachuting' of big-name, London-based correspondents into regional stories, and more coverage of evolving political and cultural trends in the UK, such as devolution.

In the aftermath of the report, it was possible to detect on the BBC's network news output a new emphasis on the national–regional dimension of particular stories, with more care being taken, for example, to highlight the fact that a particular piece of Westminster legislation was applicable only to England; or to give more attention to political developments in Scotland, which in the summer and autumn of 2008 was a volatile and unsettled environment. The resignation of Scottish Labour leader Wendy Alexander in June, and a by-election in the Glasgow East Westminster constituency, were reported as stories with UK relevance, and not merely Scottish ones.

Beyond these attempts to address a particular problem, the BBC's longer-term plans to further localise its TV and radio journalism using online channels – a proposed £68 million of investment in 60 MyLocal centres throughout the UK, for example – were condemned by private-sector media, angry at what they argued was the corporation's further abuse of its privileged financial position to distort markets on which commercial media relied. As one report put it in 2006, 'commercial companies complain that relentless BBC expansion is hurting private sector enterprise in areas from parish-pump television to magazines, the internet and classical music publishing'.[15] In November 2008 the BBC Trust bowed to pressure and cancelled its plans for local centres. The BBC was unlikely to withdraw from its localisation–digitisation strategy, however, especially in the face of the criticisms of its London-centrism. The findings of the King and Cardiff studies, and their endorsement by the Trust, gave the BBC added justification for its broader strategy of exploiting new technologies in finding better ways of providing local broadcast journalism, and to provide TV viewers throughout the UK 'with the same range of choice that is now available to radio listeners'.

> It will be possible to continue to transmit all of the BBC's UK-wide television news bulletins and current affairs programmes as now, but in parallel with one or more national programmes, drawing on material available to the whole of the BBC but compiled and edited to meet the tastes and need of those devolved nations' diverse audiences.

The Scottish Broadcasting Commission

The BBC Trust report was published after the establishment, but before the final report stage, of the SBC, and was therefore connected in public debate to the rising tide of nationalist sentiment in Scotland particularly (also seen in Wales, although calls for independence were more marginal in that country). The SBC had been set up by the First Minister of Scotland, Alex Salmond, shortly after the election of his SNP government at the Scottish parliamentary elections of 2007. Blair Jenkins, former head of news and current affairs at BBC Scotland, was appointed chairman. Although elected on a minority of the popular vote, and of MSPs (McNair, 2008c), the arrival of the SNP in government was a historic moment, with a referendum on independence at the heart of the party's manifesto. One element of the SNP's wider strategy of dividing the UK was to suggest that the BBC was in reality the 'English Broadcasting Corporation', and that its London-centric structure and culture discriminated against Scottish creativity and output. Many observers (including this author[16]) rejected this analysis as inaccurate and simplistic, while acknowledging the structural and other limitations of the broadcasting *status quo*, which had led or contributed to a declining share of Scottish production within the network schedules.

Notwithstanding devolution, both the ITV companies and the BBC regions are part of a greater whole. For both organisations, relationships with those who run the network in London have long been issues of great concern. In the case of ITV, as we have seen, there have been concerns about the integration of national, international and local news, and the desire of the regional companies to acquire more freedom in how they package ITN's material. For the BBC, too, recurring calls since the late 1990s for a 'Scottish Six' challenged the perceived dominance of a London-based news agenda, and lobbied for a peak-time news bulletin that would view the UK and the world through a Scottish editorial prism.

A different problem exists for those BBC regions and ITV companies whose managements complain of the difficulties they experience in gaining access to the network for their own regionally produced programmes. With the exception of the largest companies, notably Granada and Central, regional current affairs has traditionally been excluded from the network (one notable exception being Grampian's *Rescue* series, which followed the activities of a North Sea rescue team and included the rescue operations that accompanied the Piper Alpha oil rig disaster). STV's former head (and now Lord) Gus MacDonald described how he felt on coming to Scotland, having been head of ITV's factual programming, 'to suddenly be locked out of the network'.

> There's no way for Scottish Television's current affairs and documentaries to get onto ITV. It's blocked off by the old majors which still have a *de facto* guarantee on these slots. There's a big job to be performed in getting Scotland onto the UK commercial network. I think it's very unhealthy that inside a union of these countries only 1 per cent of what the English see on their screens at peak-time comes from Scotland, and it's the same for Ireland and Wales. Given that 75 per cent of what we see comes from England, Australia and America, I think that the English should make much more effort to encourage Scottish programming. There's nothing more marginalising than the idea that the Scots only contribute to the UK network something 'Scottish', which means that 'Britishness' is monopolised by the English companies. 'Britishness' is ceded to the English companies, and we're marginalised by our own sense of identity. The Irish and the Welsh suffer from the same thing, and it's got to be fought against.

The problem of marginalisation has also been one for the BBC regions, which, like the ITV companies, may have more than adequate resources to produce quality regional journalism, but have been under-represented in the BBC net-work when it comes to current affairs. In 1991, BBC Scotland made approxi-mately 3 per cent of networked BBC programmes, with 75–80 per cent made in London and the south-east. There were virtually no networked current affairs television programmes made outside London. Kenneth Cargill, when head of BBC Scotland's TV news and current affairs operation, argued that while recent investments had been a welcome sign of the BBC's commitment to regional TV journalism,

> what hasn't been satisfactorily addressed yet is how we can get regional journalism across to the metropolitan audience. Those of us working in the regions are very concerned about the provincialism of London. We want to get some more of our perspectives on important stories across to the London audience, and we believe that significant numbers of current affairs programmes currently made in London should be devolved to the regions. We think that there should be a greater decentralisation of pro-gramme making, because it's just as valid to make programmes outside London as inside it, and it's also cheaper.

There have always been occasional regional contributions to networked cur-rent affairs strands, but the demand here was for a more systematic and sub-stantial regional input, to balance what Cargill called 'the metropolitan bias'.

By 2008 the problem of regional under-representation remained. BBC Scot-land's share of BBC network production in 2007 was still only 3 per cent or so; STV's share of ITV network production was comparably small. Both Mark Thompson for the BBC and Michael Grade for ITV rejected the assertion that there was a systematic bias against Scottish production (or that of other nations and regions), arguing instead that under-representation reflected a relative dearth of networkable ideas.

The SBC was broadly welcomed, then, as an overdue opportunity to review the challenges and opportunities facing Scottish broadcasting as a key creative industry. With or without a nationalist spin on the situation, few doubted that Scottish broadcasting was underperforming by 2007, and that some new thinking was required. The commission duly invited contributions in the areas of economy, culture and democracy, and was due to publish its final report in September 2008.

The press

In the hierarchy of print journalism, the press outside London has traditionally been regarded as low-status and second class by those who work on the major nationals. Regional journalists are relatively low-paid, on average; their work is by definition parochial (as it has to be to serve the local market); and it is generally assumed that the more successful among them will automatically graduate to the big London titles. To some extent this is a correct assumption, if only because provincial publishers are often unable or unwilling to pay the larger salaries common on national newspapers.

The regional press, however, occupies a distinctive and important role in British journalism, supplying local communities with news and information in a way that no other medium can. One observer defined the role thus:

> It's a good pub landlord. It should make people feel that they belong, that they are valued and their lives have some significance. People need to feel, from the paper, that their community is being noted and celebrated.[17]

Regional titles have the inherent advantage of being first and arguably best in their reportage of local stories. They can also boast a high degree of reader loyalty, as would-be new entrants to the market such as the *Sunday Scot* in 1991 have found to their cost. The value of the services they provide – local news and information – has (until the onset of the internet, at least) guaranteed readers and attracted advertisers. Indeed, it is often the information contained in classified advertisements on theatre openings, second-hand cars for sale, and so on that has given the local newspaper its competitive advantage over national titles, and enabled regional publishers to maintain relatively healthy circulations amidst the general decline in newspaper circulation noted in earlier chapters. As observed in Chapter 1, some 84 per cent of the British public read one of the hundreds of local newspapers published daily or weekly, and the business has been, as Bob Franklin put it not so long ago, 'in boisterous health' (Franklin, 2006: xvii). Northern Ireland, with a population of 1.6 million people, supports 18 daily papers, while Scotland has more than 80.

However, like other sectors of the journalism industry, the regional press is vulnerable to booms and slumps in the wider economy – in the 1960s and 1970s, for instance, regional newspapers were generally profitable, while in the recessionary 1980s and 1990s times were more difficult. Recent times have been good again, with proprietors and shareholders expecting annual returns of 20 per cent and more on their capital. In 2008, however, as the impact of the subprime mortgage-induced global financial crisis and associated 'credit crunch' began to be felt across the economies of the advanced capitalist societies, advertising revenues were falling in the UK print sector at both national and regional levels. In July 2008 one of the biggest regional newspaper companies, Johnston Press, saw its shares fall by 45 per cent in the first months of that year. In December 2008 Newsquest invited nearly all of its 250 staff to Glasgow to 'reapply' for some 210 posts in a restructured operation.

Not only were regional newspapers suffering from the adverse effects of broader economic trends, by 2008 they were caught in what one commentator called 'the double whammy of online competition and a falling market'.[18] If, as suggested above, the demand for regional and local news is essentially healthy, because local news is genuinely useful, there are nevertheless a number of ways – and media – through which local information can be delivered to the audience. Two of these channels – free newspapers and online news sites – have emerged as a growing threat to paid-for regional newspapers, especially at a time of general economic slowdown.

The rise of the free sheets

By far the dominant medium of local news has been the 'paid-for' newspaper, published daily or weekly, and deriving its income from sales and advertising revenue. Since the 1960s, however, the 'paid-fors' have been joined in the market by 'free sheets', distributed free to all households within a particular geographical area and entirely dependent on advertising revenue. The 'frees' have grown steadily in number and in the share of the regional advertising market which they attract.

Since the mid-1990s, the UK has also been introduced to the *Metro* – a free newspaper distributed on a daily basis to commuters on buses and trains. Originally a Swedish innovation (the original *Metro* was founded in Stockholm in 1995), there are now 16 *Metro* titles in circulation, published in cities such as London, Manchester and Glasgow. This is an international phenomenon, with 59 editions of *Metro* being published in 83 cities worldwide as of late 2005, working to a 'strict editorial formula and standardized editorial design' and targeting 'high commuter traffic zones'.[19]

In 1970, free newspapers received a mere 1.4 per cent of all advertising revenue in the regional press. By 1990, the figure had risen to 35 per cent, more than the 19.5 per cent share claimed by the paid-for weeklies. What these figures clearly show is the rapid growth of a new subsector within the print medium, which has risen to threaten the traditional place of the paid-fors in local communities, particularly the paid-for weeklies (since the vast majority of frees are not published daily). Their success has been based on the belief of advertisers that they can reach consumers more effectively by this means than by others. The free sheet, it is argued by its proponents, will have an almost 100 per cent penetration of households in the locality to which it is distributed, since it is pushed through the door whether one wants it or not. *Metros* are picked up in their millions daily by commuters going to work, who find them a cheap (indeed, free) way of passing their journey.

There is some doubt as to whether free newspapers are actually read, and with what level of attentiveness. Are those that drop uninvited through letter boxes binned along with the rest of the junk mail? Advertisers are satisfied that they are read, at least by enough people to make them effective promotional media. In the view of one advertiser, 'free papers are almost three times more cost-efficient than the average paid-for weekly'.[20] The editor of the *Birmingham Daily News*, Britain's first 'metro morning', describes them as 'a new genre of newspaper which combines editorial excellence with all the advantages of precision targeting in a mass market'. They give advertisers 'massive penetration of households in a major metropolitan area over an extremely short time span'.[21]

In this sense, the rise of the free sheet is a reflection of the extent to which newspapers are increasingly viewed as 'product', the main use-value of which is to deliver audiences to advertisers. Free newspapers have the advantage in this respect of 'micro-marketing' – the ability to deliver advertising messages to very precise demographic groups, as opposed to the more diffuse spread of TV, radio and national press advertising. In addition, many free newspapers are part of a chain, allowing advertisers to 'micro-market' on a country-wide scale.

The majority of the early frees were set up by independent publishers, such as Eddie Shah in Warrington, and initially provoked a hostile response from the regional publishing establishment. Early examples of the genre were filled mainly with press releases, public relations material and advertisements. Since their main function, and only means of survival, was 'to provide a service for advertisers ... effectively to deliver an advertiser's message at a lower cost than competing media',[22] the quality of the journalism they provided was not necessarily their first priority. For this reason, journalists working in the paid-for sector were frequently dismissive of their rivals on the frees. The editor of the paid-for *Birmingham Post* typified this position when he warned that:

> free publications will be unable to maintain the best traditions of com-
> munity newspapers, partly because there is now only one customer, the
> advertiser, but mainly because of the inevitable trimming of editorial
> resource if times get tough. ... More companies will find it easier and
> cheaper to produce entertaining local magazines than to reflect every
> aspect of a community.[23]

This was undoubtedly true, but has not stopped the rise of the free sheets and the concomitant decline of the paid-for weeklies. In response, the regional newspapers adopted a policy that might be best summarised as 'if you can't beat 'em, buy 'em'. In the late 1980s, Thomson Regional Newspapers (TRN), Reed Regional Newspapers (RRN) and others began to buy into the free sector and to establish new free titles of their own. This produced a shift from the view of free sheets as low-quality imposters in the regional journalism business to one that saw them as 'an integral part of the product mix'. Free sheets came to be seen as complementary, rather than threatening, to paid-for titles. Companies began to strive towards a situation where they published both types of title in a given locality. Free sheets could be used to trail a paid-for's news features and give a taste of what the latter might offer.

In keeping with this shift in thinking, TRN increased the number of its frees from 13 in 1983 to 100 in 1989, claiming a total distribution of five million copies. To achieve this, TRN purchased the *Herald* and *Post* chains owned by independent publishers, merging the titles to create a new chain of *Herald & Post* free sheets. Packaged with and around its paid-for titles, TRN announced its ambition eventually to have 17 million *Herald & Posts* delivered weekly to every household in the UK, combining localisation and micro-marketing with a corporate TRN identity. RRN, then the largest regional publisher, had by 1989 more frees than paid-fors in its product mix. By late 1986 it could be reported that 'every old-established regional press publisher now operates in both the paid and free sectors of the business'.[24]

For regional publishers, the economic benefits accruing from merging the two sectors were clear. The late 1980s were generally a period of gradual decline in the circulation of paid-for newspapers, a trend at least partly associated with the rise of the free sheets. By swallowing the predators whole, the companies could afford to be more relaxed about the relative position of the paid-for and free titles. As long as they controlled both, one could boost and reinforce the readership of the other. As a result, in the late 1980s, the regional press as a whole, incorporating both paid-fors and frees, increased its advertising revenue in absolute terms and its share of total advertising revenue as against TV, radio and the national press. There were casualties of the integration process, with both paid-for and free titles going under, but by exploiting economies of scale and the introduction of new print technologies, by the beginning of 1990 the regional press had successfully incorporated the free-sheet phenomenon without appreciable damage to the paid-for sector. In 1989, 2.6 billion regional papers were sold and two billion free weeklies distributed, attracting a total classified advertising revenue of £2.25 billion.[25]

With the increasing revenues and investment which came with incorporation and integration into the big chains, the frees were able to improve their editorial content and to become more like 'real' newspapers, with substantial news-gathering resources, prestigious columnists and award-winning designs. The success of the regional proprietors in combining paid-for and free-sheet publishing prompted Roy Greenslade to observe in 1994 that 'there has been a quiet, sustained revitalisation of the provincial press in recent years'.[26]

Not all commentators were or are so sanguine, however. For critics of the trend, the rise of the free sheet has contributed further to the pressures on paid-for print titles, sounding ever more loudly the 'death-knell of quality journalism'.[27] Free sheets, it is argued by their detractors, are reluctant to invest in editorial resources, and more likely to produce the kind of 'standard content' that Bob Franklin and others have called 'McJournalism'. Assessing the implications of the rise of the free sheet at the time of the launch of *thelondonpaper* and *London Lite* (by News Corporation and Associated Newspapers, respectively), Patrick Barkham observed that:

> Investigative journalism takes time and money. Scrutinising government and town halls may not produce the sexy copy the free papers crave. Some believe that councils can get away with almost anything in areas only served by poorly resourced free papers. The fourth estate's powers of scrutiny and accountability are diminished: local and national democracy is weakened.[28]

On the other hand, the rise of the free sheets (with 5.5 million being distributed daily in Europe as of 2007) can be argued to have forced paid-for newspapers to raise their game. As one observer notes:

if the [paid-fors]' fight back focuses on quality, the cohabitation is both possible and desirable. Free sheets encourage a newspaper habit amongst the young and encourage them to trade up to high quality, paid-for newspapers.[29]

Time will tell if this optimistic scenario is realistic, or if, as more and more media content is made available free of charge, the paid-for regional newspaper is now an endangered species.

Enter the nationals

By 1989, TRN chairman Bill Heeps could state that 'the enemy [of the regional press] is no longer the predatory free newspaper but increasingly competitors for the advertising pound – local TV, local radio, local editions of national newspapers, and new electronic media'.[30] Competition for finite advertising revenue has always existed, of course, but in the late 1980s changes in the national press produced new challenges to the regionals. Chapter 6 described how, after the Wapping revolution, the proprietors of national newspapers quickly introduced new printing technologies into their production process. This not only enabled them to cut costs and increase profitability, but also made it much easier for them to 'editionise' their production – to produce multiple editions of a national title, tailored to the particular characteristics of populations in different parts of the country. From his plant in Glasgow, Rupert Murdoch adopted an aggressive strategy of editionising the *Sunday Times* and the *Sun* in a bid to break into the Scottish market. The practical results of the policy were seen when, in the period before the 1992 general election, the *Sun*'s Scottish edition ran with the headline 'Rise and be a Nation Again', in distinct contrast to the pro-unionist, pro-Conservative editorial line adopted by News International titles in England. And it was successful, doubling the *Sun*'s Scottish circulation over a seven-year period. In late 1994, the *Daily Mail* and *Daily Express* followed News International in launching Scottish editions.

The circulation battle between the *Sun* and the *Daily Record* continued over the next decade, as the former gradually but steadily encroached on traditional *Record* territory (Reid, 2006). By May 2006, the *Sun* had increased its ABC figures to within 24,000 of the *Daily Record*. In July of that year, the News Corporation title finally overtook the *Daily Record*, with 394,000 daily sales as against 384,000 for the latter. Explanations for this trend include price-cutting by the well heeled Murdoch empire (for much of this time the *Sun* was selling for 10 pence).

Price competition has played a factor, undoubtedly, as has the changing nature of the market in the west of Scotland, where both newspapers draw the bulk of their readership. Glasgow has traditionally been a Labour stronghold within Scotland, the heartland of the industrial proletariat who worked in the city's shipyards and heavy industries until recession and Thatcherism sent UK manufacturing industry as a whole into decline. The *Daily Record* (and its sister title the *Sunday Mail*) played to this market successfully for decades. After Thatcher and the Tories, however, as Glasgow regenerated and 'yuppi-fied', this pro-Labour hegemony began to weaken. Glasgow, like other UK cities, went through a social and cultural transformation, as people bought their council homes, invested in shares and embraced consumerism (McNair, 2008c). The rise of the SNP and calamitous decline of Scottish Labour in 2007–08 further weakened the *Daily Record*'s hold on the Scottish market. These trends, it can be argued, had the effect of 'de-ideologising' Scottish newspaper readers, allowing the *Sun* to encroach on the *Daily Record*'s once loyal base. the *Sun* also benefited from serious investment in the quality of its product. What had worked in England, where the *Sun* had been the unquestioned tabloid leader for decades, also worked in Scotland, it seemed, where the *Daily Record* looked increasingly complacent and tired.

Beyond the particular battle between the two big red-top tabloids in Scot-land, in response to the nationals' challenge, regional newspapers have adop-ted a number of competitive strategies. First, like the nationals, they have turned the new technologies to their advantage. Regional publishers were in the vanguard of 'the newspaper revolution' and were thus well placed to reap its benefits at the end of the 1980s and into the 1990s. By late 1987, for instance, TRN had almost completed the process of introducing direct input technology into its ten provincial printing centres. In 1988, the company announced a further £75 million programme of investment and acquisitions. In Glasgow, Tiny Rowland's Lonrho invested heavily in new colour presses for its *Herald* and *Evening Times* titles, before selling them to a management-led consortium in 1992.

Such investment enabled the regionals to improve their design and colour printing techniques. It also enabled them to editionise within their own terri-tories to a greater extent than had been possible before (editionising has long been conventional practice for local evening papers). By 1990 virtually all the UK's larger evening regionals were editionising 'to provide a distinct editorial and advertising service for the various communities into which their massive circulation areas have been subdivided'.[31] The Glasgow *Evening Times*, for example, would produce three editions between early afternoon and evening. In the early 1990s, Aberdeen's *The Press and Journal* had nine editions in cir-culation, each targeted at specific geographical areas in northern Scotland, such as the Highlands, Shetland, Kincardine and Deeside, and Aberdeen city. As a TRN editor puts it, 'the nationals have had a go at editionising, but it's not at the same level as the regional press. National newspapers will never be able to produce that number of editions.'

Because of new technologies, a greater share of resources could be invested in editorial quality (journalism). By paying higher salaries, regional news-papers could retain more and better journalists, thus slowing down the brain drain to London (a process assisted by the high cost of property in southern England in recent years). Traditionally, Fleet Street journalists earned, on average, double the salaries of their colleagues in the provinces, leading inevitably to a one-way flow of talent heading south. A 1988 report by the Henley Centre for Economic Forecasting, commissioned by the Newspaper Society (the major association of regional proprietors), urged regional papers not to respond to the nationals' challenge by chasing them down-market, but to 'adopt a serious tabloid format to provide readers with local news, information and lifestyle features which they are unlikely to get from the national press or television'.[32] To achieve this required money spent on journalism.

Regional titles have also moved online, with companies such as Johnston Press employing economies of scale to maximise the use of templates and styles for online design across their hundreds of titles across the UK.

By increasing the number of editions, improving design and presentation (including online, crucially), and strengthening 'editorial resource', the regionals took on the nationals' challenge, recognising that the new technologies that threatened them (by making the nationals more attractive in regional markets) could also work for them. For this reason, the concentration of regional ownership that has occurred in recent years may be viewed as a necessary evil.[33] Large chains with extensive resources, it is argued, can respond more effectively, and invest more heavily, than small, isolated and impoverished independents. In any case, as the late Alistair Hetherington observed in his study of regional news, 'regional and local newspapers are less subject to political pressure than the nationals. ... Nor does there appear to be much political direction from proprietors' (Hetherington, 1989: 6). If it is true that more and more regional titles are being incorporated into fewer and fewer companies, it also appears to be the case that they retain a much greater degree of editorial independence than the majority of London-based titles.

Marketing the regionals

Another element of the regionals' defensive strategy in the face of competitive challenges has addressed a traditional weakness in the marketing of their product – the failure to provide advertisers with sufficiently accurate data on readership. As we saw above, the paid-for regionals' share of advertising has tended to decline, partly due to the fact that, until 1989, the regional press did not employ particularly efficient audience measurement techniques and lost advertising revenue to those media that did. By 1989, however, in conjunction with advertisers, they had established the Joint Industry Committee for Regional Press Readership (JICReg), a database designed to provide extremely accurate information about who reads what in precisely defined geographical areas and, of particular importance to advertisers, the effectiveness of their advertising messages. In 1991, 13 regional publishers formed the Alliance of Regional Publishers for Effective Advertising (AREA) in an attempt to offer advertisers nationally coordinated local packages that could compete more effectively with national media. The 'Mosaic' system for identifying readers and analysing their consumption characteristics was employed.[34] Under the auspices of the Regional Daily Advertising Council, 73 regional dailies combined to launch themselves as a 'national' medium with a single rate card. The package offered advertisers access to a total circulation of about 5.3 million. In these ways, by the early 1990s the regional press was, from the advertisers' viewpoint, steadily improving its product.

Underpinning the strategies described thus far was that of exploiting the regionals' key competitive advantage: their very 'regionalness' or 'localness'. We began this chapter by noting that the demand for local news and information – in all media – is fundamentally healthy. It has also been argued that the news audience is fragmenting into groups divided not only by geography, but also by demography and lifestyle. This cultural shift is one which the regional newspapers are optimally equipped to exploit. On the one hand readerships are becoming more narrowly focused, while on the other new technologies allow publishers to target them more precisely. Huw Stevenson of Westminster Press has argued that 'the UK's great regional dailies are mainly the product of an industrial revolution which turned our society from rural to urban living but now it's moving in the other direction. What I think this means for the prospects of the regional press is a proliferation of smaller communities which are now large enough to be viable publishing centres in their own right, some even on a daily basis'.[35]

Changing demographics are a double-edged sword for some regional newspapers, however. In 1988 the Henley Centre noted that the regional newspapers face 'a disintegration of their traditional urban markets. The self-contained city [is] changing into a network of inter-linked towns and cities as the middle class moves out to the surrounding villages and country towns'.[36]

For evening papers in particular, this development, combined with more recent long-term trends in lifestyle such as the increasing role of television and the internet in people's lives, presents a serious threat to their readership. The editor of the Glasgow *Evening Times* explained to this writer that 'evening papers were very strong in the days when we worked longer hours, and the only time that some people had to read was in the evening. Those days have gone, plus there are other ways of getting information.' The late Arnold Kemp, when editor of the *Evening Times*'s sister publication in Glasgow, *The Herald*, agreed that social change, alongside shifts in the nationals' marketing strategy, has created a potential crisis for the regional evenings:

> The tabloid morning papers have changed. They now sell throughout the day as entertainment packages – their reps top up supplies throughout the day. So the *Evening Times* is now competing with the *Daily Record*, the *Sun* and the other tabloids in a way that is quite new. Even five years ago, newsagents would have exhausted their morning supplies by lunchtime. Now the morning tabloids are still being sold at four o'clock in the afternoon, because they're less rooted in news. People buy them for showbiz chat and sport.
>
> In addition, the old industrial society is disappearing. The city centre is losing population. The bourgeois dormitory suburbs are growing, but the

old industrial parts are uniformly in rapid decline. Any paper which is targeted on that particular segment of the population is going to be in difficulties, whereas quality papers are targeted on the more affluent sectors of the economy – the growing professional classes.

Another editor observes that:

there is a long-term decline in the sales of evening newspapers. The major factor involved in that is cultural and social change; dramatic change in the jobs market; change in the reasons why people purchase an evening newspaper. At one time in this city you were selling about 400,000 copies of an evening newspaper. At the moment our circulation varies between 150,000 and 170,000, and that drop is in keeping with other evening newspapers elsewhere in the UK. Go round Glasgow and Edinburgh at six o'clock at night and see how quickly the city empties. At one time between 4:30 and 6:00 you had all these factories, shipyards, etc. spewing out people. They're not there anymore. Glasgow's population has fallen from 1.1 million just after the Second World War to just over 700,000, and it's predicted to go down even further. People don't use public transport to the same extent any more.

The evenings must respond to this challenge by turning their attention to the things they can do best, like 'need to know' news – what's on, where, when, what it costs – all the things which are difficult for the electronic media to do. People no longer buy evening papers to get the first bite of news, because they've probably heard it somewhere else – radio, TV – but to find out what that news means to them. The evening paper can best cover that.

In the 15 years since those comments were made, evening newspaper circulations have declined further, alongside those of regional newspapers in general. These worsened in 2008 as the 'credit crunch' and the financial crisis affecting most western countries worked its way into consumer spending and associated businesses such as advertising. As one observer put it in July 2008:

The media sector travails are symptomatic of the economic downturn as a whole. But the outlook is particularly grim for the print sector, facing as it does the double whammy of online competition and a falling market. The pressure on the newspaper industry in western European markets is both structural, because of disintermediation by the web [migration of audiences from print to online platforms], and cyclical because of slowing growth rates. The cyclical part will return, the structural one will not. The simple fact is that now people are reading newspapers or newspaper content online, rather than offline. Circulation among young people is down and regional newspapers and newspapers that depend on classified [advertising] are under tremendous pressure.[37]

The Henley Centre advised two decades ago that regional newspapers should 'focus their editorial and marketing policies more sharply on key groups – the newly affluent, the retired, working women, and the 'household formation group' in the 25–44 age group. There [is] a need for newspapers to cope with the shift towards 'communities of interest' and the relative decline of geographically based communities'.[38] The regionals, according to this view, had not only to 'cope' with these cultural changes but to embrace them as opportunities to hold and even increase their share of the newspaper-reading public. Today, the demographic trends may be different, but the advice is still good.

Devolution and the local press

Following the establishment of devolved assemblies in Scotland, Wales and Northern Ireland, it was recognised that local newspapers, like broadcasters (see above), would need to find extra resources to reflect the new political realities if they were to perform their important social functions adequately. While these countries have always had distinctive public spheres within the wider sphere of the UK, devolution was widely expected to give them greater definition and political relevance, as well as raising new issues for the ownership and control of local media. When the Scottish Media Group bought Caledonian Publishing for £120 million in 1996, for example, adding *The Herald* newspaper to its main businesses (the Scottish and Grampian TV companies), it was a relatively minor player in the UK media market. In a devolved Scotland, by contrast, it was by far the dominant commercial news provider (the *Herald* titles were later sold to a US-based company, Newsquest).

The local newspaper sector also faced a challenge in responding to the changing political environment of post-devolution Britain. In Scotland, with its historically rich and diverse public sphere of indigenous newspapers, the challenge was to negotiate the shifting allegiances of once-loyal Labour voters as more and more of them moved to the SNP. At the Scottish parliamentary election of 2007, for the first time, several self-proclaimedly unionist titles, such as the *Sunday Herald* and the *Scotsman*, editorialised in favour of the SNP (McNair, 2008c). As the promised referendum on independence approached in 2010, the role of the Scottish press would be crucial.

In Wales, on the other hand, there was no indigenous press on this scale, and a rising tide of Welsh nationalism seeking expression. How these emerging and evolving national identities would be mediated by the local press was one of the key issues for the future as this edition was completed.

Conclusions

For both print and broadcast news media, the demands of commerce have coincided in the past two decades with a cultural movement – seen throughout Europe – away from the nation-state towards identification with smaller communities and collectivities. What has led to war in post-communist eastern

Europe has its healthier manifestation in the desire of western European populations to view events and processes from their own local perspective, rather than that of a dominant metropolitan centre. In Britain, these communities include the nations of England, Northern Ireland, Scotland and Wales, and within them smaller communities shaped by such factors as industrial history and political culture. As we have seen, concern about the quantity and quality of regional journalism in broadcasting has grown, and the BBC has committed itself to addressing these.

The trend towards localisation is also impinging on the British press. For print journalists, like the broadcasters, audiences are fragmenting and markets are becoming smaller. This was true even before the rise of the internet and its growing share of advertising revenue. While, as I have argued, local news retains its core use value, and local newspapers have a solid basis for future development, circulations are falling (as they are at UK level). In Scotland, for example, there has been a 50 per cent decline in newspaper readership over 30 years, aggravated in the view of one former editor by the fact that the market is 'crowded with 16 morning papers [17, including *Metro*]'.[39]

Some sections of the local press – in particular the regional evening papers – continue to suffer from the emergence of the post-industrial city and the dispersal of populations to the suburbs – a process that has occurred throughout Britain, but is most evident in the huge industrial conurbations such as Glasgow. In London, where a captive commuter market will continue to exist for the foreseeable future, the *Evening Standard* is secure, but many in the industry doubt that the institution of the evening regional paper will survive for very long. What will survive is the 'free sheet', that curious hybrid of advertising and journalism now dominated by the phenomenon of the *Metro*.

Further reading

For recent work on the fortunes of the local press and broadcast media in the UK, see Bob Franklin's edited collection on *Local Journalism and Local Media* (2006). For recent essays on Scotland, see Blain and Hutchison's *The Media In Scotland* (2008). Reports cited in this chapter by the BBC Trust, Ofcom, the IPPC and others can be downloaded by readers wishing to pursue the issues raised in greater detail.

10 Conclusions

As this edition went t⌐
UK, and indeed th⌐
reaching structu⌐
around journ⌐
this perio⌐

- ⌐

ı.
dev
emerg⌐
an issue
devolved eı⌐
   More imme⌐
nalism, declining⌐
time when the glou⌐
time since the early ⌐.
analogue broadcasting a⌐
had made the traditional ⌐
was having an impact on both
mobile platforms for the cons⌐
PDAs). These trends, as we have ⌐
managers and editorial teams as the⌐
media integration, new ways of working⌐
sphere of crisis in the journalism industry.

   As we have also seen, however, the emerᵬ
offered opportunities as well as challenges and tı⌐
and ways of doing things. By 2008, British journa⌐
within a globalised public sphere comprising not jı⌐

agenda – focused on the relationship between journalism and public perceptions of risk, be it financial, environmental or terrorist risk – will continue to
grow in importance in the years ahead.
   For now, however, and apart from the big sociological and cultural questions which some of the trends I have described inevitably raise for scholars,
policy-makers and journalists themselves, let me end on a positive note.
Demand for news and journalism, in the UK as elsewhere in our increasingly
interdependent and connected world, is increasing, not falling. Journalists are
an expanding breed, and news is going nowhere except up in the cultural
landscape. The physical forms of our news media are changing, and may
change further, but the journalistic content of those media will continue to be
a central feature of British life.

Notes

Chapter One

1 For the full text of the report, see www.wan-press.org.
2 Confusingly, perhaps, *Metro* is also an international free newspaper brand owned by the Swedish company Metro International. As of 2006, Metro International published 70-plus editions of *Metro*, in 83 cities worldwide, and claimed more than 15 million readers.
3 Silver, J., 'Pressed for cash', the *Guardian*, 17 October 2005.
4 For a full list of regional newspaper companies see www.wrx.zen.co.uk/regions2.htm.
5 Greenslade, R., 'Return of the local heroes', the *Guardian*, 23 March 1998.
6 Gadher, D., 'BBC rings changes with news revamp', the *Sunday Times*, 13 April 2008.
7 *Application for Channel 3 Licence for Central Scotland: Summary*, Scottish Television, 1991.
8 See Chippindale and Franks (1991) for an account of the brief life of BSB. An account of the merger negotiations is contained in Chippindale, P. and Franks, S., 'How Sky fell on BSB', the *Guardian*, 11 November 1991.
9 Shamoon, S., 'BSkyB in the black by March', the *Observer*, 26 January 1992.
10 Neilsen/Net research, reported in *Press Gazette* (formerly *UK Press Gazette*), 9 August 2002.
11 For a short analysis by the author of UK satellite news coverage of the Iraqi invasion, see www.tbsjournal.com/Archives/Spring03/nair.html.
12 Dowell, B., 'Disillusioned of Doha', the *Guardian*, 31 March 2008.
13 Higham, N., 'Fine tuning radio's future', *Broadcast*, 24 April 1992.
14 *BBC Guide 1991*.
15 Kavanagh, M., 'World Service put under the microscope', *Broadcast*, 10 July 1992.
16 Reported in the *Guardian*, 15 April 1992.
17 Research conducted by Media Center for the BBC and Reuters, reported in May 2006: www.globescan.com/news_archives/bbcreut.html.
18 Editorial, *British Journalism Review* 2(1): 4. The study in question was undertaken by MORI and published in Jacobs and Worcester (1990)
19 Reported in *Press Gazette*, 14 March 2003. However, if it is true that audiences, when asked, tend to cite TV as the most important journalistic medium, some evidence suggests that its centrality as an information source has been exaggerated. Robinson and Levy describe as a 'myth' the belief, based largely on public opinion data, 'that the public receives most of its information from television' (Robinson and Levy 1986: 15). While viewers may *believe* that they do so, and repeat this belief to researchers, a number of studies have shown that the efficacy of television as an information source is limited by its very nature as a medium. Televised information,

and news in particular, is characteristically 'thin' in content. Many more 'bits' of information can be contained on the front page of a broadsheet newspaper than can be broadcast in a 20-minute TV news bulletin. Furthermore, television viewing may (although not necessarily every case) be a relatively passive experience – a 'domestic ritual', to use Morley's phrase (1990: 126), carried out in parallel with other activities such as talking, eating and reading. Gunter notes that television journalism 'constantly introduces new material before the viewer has been given a chance to grasp properly the visual and auditory material that has just been presented' (Gunter 1987: 47). He argues further that TV viewers do not have especially high levels of recall or comprehension of the news stories to which they have been exposed, and that 'the largest gains in news information are associated with newspaper usage' (*ibid.*).

Some research has suggested that interpersonal communication may be just as important to an individual's absorption of information as exposure to any mass medium, be it TV, radio or the press. Robinson and Levy do not deny that 'the public may be made aware of news stories more quickly from television, but [research] suggests that subsequent exposure, by reading in newspapers or magazines, or by interpersonal discussion may be required for the point of those news stories to make a lasting impression on the viewers' memory' (Robinson and Levy 1986: 130).

Chapter Two

1 William DeGeorge identifies three levels at which agenda-setting might work (if it works): first, the level of audience awareness, whereby 'the public is primarily aware of those issues or topics which are reported by the media'; second, the level of priorities, where 'the [media's] agenda of events, in proper-rank, will be transferred to the public largely intact'; and third, the level of salience, where 'the public assigns high or low importance to topics as held by the media' (DeGeorge, 1981: 222).

2 For a fierce critique of Chomsky's work see Cohen (2007), in which he argues that 'it is obviously true that much of what appears in the media is nonsense, and on occasion self-serving nonsense. Chomsky's mistake was to confuse corporate interests with political interests. Corporate bias is everywhere ... [but] Chomsky's notion of media propaganda went way beyond the usual critiques of media folly and bias and revived the old notions of false consciousness'(*ibid.*: 158).

Chapter Three

1 Noam Chomsky quotes a recent restatement of the liberal pluralist principle by US Supreme Court Justice Powell: 'no individual can obtain for himself the information needed for the intelligent discharge of his political responsibilities. ... By enabling the public to assert meaningful control over the political process, the press performs a crucial function' (Chomsky, 1989: 13).

2 Burkeman, O., 'Fox on the run', the *Guardian*, 25 November 2002.

3 Rusbridger, A., 'Taming the beast', the *Guardian*, 18 February 2002.

4 From the *BBC Guide 1990*, London: BBC.

5 Sullivan, A., 'Let's hear it for prejudiced television news', the *Sunday Times*, 17 November 2002.

6 The commercial channels' public service obligations in respect of due impartiality are set out in Ofcom's Broadcasting Code, Section 5 (www.ofcom.org.uk).

7 Grade, M., 'The digital challenge', *MediaGuardian*, 21 September 2006, www.guardian.co.uk/media/2006/sep/21/comment.broadcasting.

8 For a detailed discussion of Soviet news values, see McNair (1991).

9 For a recent book-length study of news values in the British media, see Brighton and Foy (2007).

10 See Lichtenberg (1991) for a defence of objectivity as seen from the journalists' perspective.

11 See Harrison (1985) and Philo (1987) for further discussion of the methodological issues raised by the GUMG's work.

12 For a recent appraisal of the work of the Glasgow group, see Quinn (2007).

13 Report of the Independent Panel for the BBC Governors on Impartiality of BBC Coverage of the Israeli–Palestinian Conflict, London, BBC, April 2006, www.bbcgovernorsarchive.co.uk/docs/rev_israelipalestinian.html.

Chapter Four

1 Morgan, R., 'Disease that's all in the minders', the *Guardian*, 15 July 1991.

2 Reported in the *Guardian*, 5 March 1990.

3 Stothard, P., 'Chinese whispers', the *Guardian*, 23 March 1998.

4 www.guardian.co.uk/media/2008/jan/23/sun.rupertmurdoch?gusrc=rss&feed=media.

5 Reported in Wray, R., 'Telegraph Media Group chairman refuses to speak to Lords committee', the *Guardian*, 27 June 2008.

6 Wolff, M., 'Tailored news', *Vanity Fair*, November 2004.

7 Buford, B., 'Money makes the words go round', the *Guardian*, 6 December 1997.

8 Whittam Smith, A., 'The secret of this newspaper lies in its title', the *Independent*, 7 October 1996.

9 Sutton Trust (2006), www.suttontrust.com/reports/Journalists-Backgrounds-final-report.pdf.

10 Simon, S., 'BBC launches new Labour channels', *The Spectator*, 7 February 1998, p. 9.

11 The author's own study of news coverage of the USSR in the 1980s argues that the 'ideological bias' of individual journalists was less important in explaining Western news images of the Soviet Union than the professional constraints routinely faced by Moscow correspondents (McNair, 1988).

12 For a discussion of British television news coverage of the KAL 007 incident, see McNair (1988).

13 McNair, B., 'Accidents don't just happen', *New Statesman and Society*, 15 July 1988.

14 Quoted by Greenslade, R., 'I may seem like a dandy now', the *Guardian*, 20 May 2002.

Chapter Five

1 Kronig, J., 'A crisis in the fourth estate', the *Guardian*, 16 August 2004.

2 Pilger, J., 'What a carve up!', the *Guardian*, 16 March 1998.

3 Sampson, A., 'The fourth estate under fire', the *Guardian*, 10 January 2005.

4 See Fallows (1996) and Bourdieu (1998) for discussions of tabloidisation in relation to the USA and France, respectively.

5 For a journalistic statement of the 'braining up' position, see Freedland, J., 'Dumbing down? Nonsense – the whole British nation is "braining up"', the *Guardian*, 11 March 1998.

6 Humphrys, J., 'Don't shoot the messenger, the press is doing its job', the *Sunday Times*, 17 November 2002.

7 Greenslade, R., 'How the broadsheets brightened up', the *Guardian*, 20 October 2003.

8 Liddiment, D., 'The Day of the Jacko', the *Guardian*, 10 February 2003.

9 Barnett, S., 'The way we watched', the *Guardian*, 21 March 2005.

10 Sieghart, M., 'Women's work', the *Guardian*, 30 June 1997.

11 Dugdale, J., 'Seeing and believing', the *Guardian*, 4 September 1995.

12 Dugdale, J., 'All the news you may need', the *Guardian*, 13 April 1998.

13 For a female-authored assessment of this phenomenon, see McAlpine, J., 'Girl power', the *Sunday Times*, 7 December 1997.

14 Sieghart, M., 'Women's work', the *Guardian*, 30 June 1997.

15 'The cheaper sex: how women lose out in journalism', *Women in Journalism*, July 1998.

16 Barnett, S., 'The age of contempt', the *Guardian*, 28 October 2002.

17 From text supplied by the BBC. The speech was delivered in 1997, so there is no online archive.

18 Lloyd, J., 'Scotland's media love tearing people to bits', the *Sunday Herald*, 6 March 2005.

19 For an entertaining and frank account of the New Labour spin apparatus as seen from the inside, see Campbell's volume of diaries, *The Blair Years* (2007).

20 Reported in Wells, M., 'Study deals a blow to claims of anti-war bias in BBC news', the *Guardian*, 4 July 2003.

21 the *Sunday Times*, 31 August 2003.

22 Grade, M., 'Making the important interesting: BBC journalism in the 21st century', Cudlipp Lecture, 24 January 2005, www.bbc.co.uk/pressoffice/speeches/stories/grade_cudlipp.shtml.

23 Toynbee, P., 'Breaking news', the *Guardian*, 5 September 2003.

24 Allan, T., 'Puffed up punks', the *Guardian*, 8 December 2004.

25 Sampson, A., 'The fourth estate under fire', the *Guardian*, 10 January 2005.

26 For the full text of the speech, delivered at the London offices of Reuters on 12 June 2007, see http://news.bbc.co.uk/1/hi/uk_politics/6744581.stm.

27 Toynbee, P., 'The BBC must not be led by the shock tactics of the *Mail*', the *Guardian*, August 11 2004.

28 *Self-regulation of the Press*, Report of the Select Committee on Culture, Media and Sport, July 2007.

29 Hewlett, S., 'Who is to blame for TV fakery?', the *Guardian*, 23 July 2007.

30 For the full text of Paxman's MacTaggart lecture, see www.telegraph.co.uk/news/main.jhtml?xml = /news/2007/08/25/npaxspeech125.xml.

Chapter Six

1 Wintour, P., 'Life at the longest funeral', the *Guardian*, 26 June 1987.

2 Reported in the UK *Press Gazette*, 23 September 1991.

3 Linton, M., '*Sun*-powered politics', the *Guardian*, 30 October 1995. For further discussion of the press deficit and its impact, see McNair (2007).

4 Porter, H., 'Thunderer versus the blunderer', the *Guardian*, 28 June 1993.

5 *Ibid.*

6 'It's War', the *Guardian*, 17 January 1994.

7 McKie, R., 'Five heads with a single mind', the *Guardian*, 15 August 1994.

8 Porter, H., 'The Murdoch Wooing Game', the *Guardian*, 26 September 1994.

9 *The Power of the Press*, CARMA International, 1997.

10 Goodman, A., 'Tradition and talent in an age of transition', the UK *Press Gazette*, 13 June 1988.

11 The *Guardian*, 10 November 1988.

12 Horsley, N., 'News that didn't fit', the *Guardian*, 26 June 1987.

13 Chippindale, P., 'Mercy killing', *Press Gazette*, 30 November 1987.

14 Whittaker, B., 'Will the cactus flower!', the *Guardian*, 7 September 1987.

15 Sutton, K., 'Rounded corner logos are politically Tory', *Press Gazette*, 15 June 1987.

16 Whittaker, B., *op. cit.*

17 Minogue, T., 'Sleazy does it', the *Guardian*, 25 January 1989.

18 Curran, J., 'Fleet Street: No Entry', the *Guardian*, 11 April 1988.

19 Foot, P., 'Never has so much been owned by so few', *Press Gazette*, 21–28 December 1987.

20 *Ibid.*

21 Goodman, A., 'Tradition and talent in an age of transition', *Press Gazette*, 13 June 1988.

22 See *Guardian* editor Alan Rusbridger's recent article on the virtues of the iRex and iPhone platforms, 'We're all doomed to be surprised', the *Guardian*, 20 August 2007.

23 The same can be said of magazines, as argued by the editor of Northern & Shell's US edition of *OK!* magazine. In a recent press item on the success of the title in the US market (850,000 weekly sales in August 2007, up 54 per cent on 2006), Sarah Ivens observes that 'women want this magazine to read on the subway home, to read in bed after a shitty day in the office, to read in the bath. You can't do that online' (Rushe, D., 'All fired up over America's *OK!*', the *Sunday Times*, 26 August 2007).

24 *Trust In Media*, conducted jointly by the BBC, Reuters and the Media Centre and published in May 2006.

25 For the WAN report in full, see www.wan-press.org.

26 Cole, P., 'The paradox of the pops', the *Guardian*, 27 August 2007.

27 Fletcher, K., 'Can Sundays survive the digital age', the *Guardian*, 16 October 2006.

28 13 April 2005. For the full text of the speech see the News Corporation website, www.newscorp.com.

29 Fletcher, K., 'A bright future for newspapers', the *Guardian*, 19 December 2005.

30 Rusbridger, A., 'We're all doomed to be surprised', the *Guardian*, 20 August 2007.

31 Durgan, P., 'Publisher puts its finger on the pulse', the *Sunday Times*, 22 October 2006.

32 Allen, K., 'Murdoch buys into "what it means" journalism', the *Guardian*, 6 August 2007.

Chapter Seven

1 See Leapman (1987) and Milne (1988).

 2 For an account of the making of the programme and its aftermath, see Bolton (1990).

 3 See *Index on Censorship* 16 (3): 1987 for the documents.

 4 From a speech to the Institute of Directors delivered on 23 February 1986.

 5 Birt I., 'Bias: where TV is guilty', reprinted in *The Times*, 23 March 1987.

 6 Hall, T., 'A voice worth listening to', *Broadcast*, 16 August 1991.

 7 Cox, B., 'Journalism without ceremony', *Broadcast*, 26 July 1991.

 8 Barnett, S., 'The BBC after the cold war', the *Guardian*, 8 April 1991.

 9 Quoted by Henry, G., 'Gameplan for a Beeb team spirit', the *Guardian*, 7 October 1991.

10 *The Future of the BBC*, Cm 2098, November 1992, London: HMSO.

11 Reported in the the *Guardian*, 11 July 1994.

12 Lloyd, J., 'What's on after the news?', *New Statesman*, 28 November 1997.

13 Beavis, S., 'Chris gets across', the *Guardian*, 6 April 1998.

14 Quoted in Brooks, R., 'Shows under threat as BBC losing ratings war', the *Sunday Times*, 21 March 1999.

15 Edwards, A., 'News moves fail to make a splash', *Broadcast*, 13 April 2001.

16 Richardson, I., 'A new golden age?', *Press Gazette*, 15 February 2002.

17 Stoddart, P., 'Breakfast for Four', *Broadcast*, 19 June 1992.

18 Tim Gardam, Head of News and Current Affairs at Channel 5, quoted by Ahmed, K., 'News from the battle fronts', the *Guardian*, 6 November 1997.

19 *Ibid.*
20 See Gardam, T., 'Television news you can use', *New Statesman*, 14 November 1997, where he again attacks 'establishment news for the news elite'.
21 Mulholland, J., 'Dawn's patrol', the *Guardian*, 23 March 1998.
22 Brown, M., 'What news from the front?', the *Guardian*, 2 February 1998.
23 Eyre, R., 'No tears for the bongs', *Press Gazette*, 17 September 1999.
24 Purvis, S., 'In search of the perfect revamp', the *Guardian*, 1 March 1999.
25 Reported in *Broadcast*, 19 June 1992.
26 Bolton, R., 'Year zero shouldn't mean zero confidence', *The Listener*, 3 March 1988.
27 Goodhart, D., 'Who are the masters now?', *Prospect*, May 1997.
28 Dugdale, J., 'Hour of truth', the *Guardian*, 6 July 1998.
29 Reported in the *Guardian*, 29 January 1990.
30 Reported in *Broadcast*, 21 June 1991. The importance of Sky News to Murdoch is observed in Chippindale and Franks's account of British Satellite Broadcasting. In 1990, when Murdoch employed Australian media manager Sam Chisholm to carry out a major cost-cutting exercise at Sky, it was suggested that Sky News be closed down. 'Murdoch disagreed. Not only was he pleased with its achievements but he told Chisholm there were overriding reasons of prestige and politics for keeping it. The final hurdle of the Broadcasting Bill had still to be overcome and the case being mounted in the Lords for the acceptability of Sky would collapse if suddenly there was no News Channel' (Chippindale and Franks, 1991: 262).
31 Howell, L., 'Broadcast news dues', the *Guardian*, 2 March 1992.
32 Here, and elsewhere, unless otherwise indicated, quotations from media practitioners are drawn from interviews conducted by the author.
33 *Ibid.*
34 *Time*, 6 January 1992.
35 the *Guardian*, 9 September 1986.
36 *The Future of Broadcasting*, HC 262, 1988, London: HMSO.
37 *Ibid.*: xli.
38 Tusa added: 'This market is so vital for the global flow of information that I believe it should not be the prerogative of the two existing players. Cultural and political pluralism demands that there should be at least a third competitor in this field, in the interests of diversity of opinion and information. Who will it be?' Few in his audience doubted that Rupert Murdoch's Sky News would be a serious contender.
39 Burnett, C., 'Sky faces BBC challenge', *Broadcast*, 21 February 1992.
40 Purvis, S., 'Ground control', *Press Gazette*, 3 March 2000.
41 *Choices and Opportunities*, Cm 92, 1987, London: HMSO.
42 Reported in the *Guardian*, 13 June 1988.
43 *Broadcast*, 8 June 1990.
44 *Press Gazette*, 30 September 1991.
45 Andrew Joynes, then head of English-language current affairs at the World Service, argued further in 1992 that 'with the barriers coming down, with new definitions of what constitutes an appropriate world order, with the emphasis upon the individual's rights as a citizen of the world as much as a citizen of a country, with new global threats to the environment, what is going to be needed above all is information. The new emphasis will be upon putting different parts of the world in touch with each other. Just as there's been a rebirth of the idea of the United Nations and its potential, so I think we're at the threshold of a new awareness of the potential of international broadcasting as a means of putting people in touch with each other.
46 Byford, M., 'Brave new world', the *Guardian*, 25 January 1999.
47 *Ibid.*

Chapter Eight

1 For a readable oral history of the internet, featuring many of its key players, see Mayo, K. and Newcomb, P., 'How the web was won', *Vanity Fair*, July 2008.
2 Sullivan, A., 'The Blogging Revolution', *Wired*, 10 (5), May 2002.
3 Useful research on *OhmyNews* has been conducted and published in English by Shaun Sutton (2006).
4 For a chapter-length account of the role of online media in this event, see Allan (2006).
5 *Next On 4*, Channel 4, March 2008.
6 Sabbagh, D., 'Now British bloggers are hogging the headlines', *The Times*, 1 January 2005.
7 Johnson, B., 'Ignore bloggers at your peril, say researchers', the *Guardian*, 18 April 2006.
8 Reported in the *Guardian*, 15 August 2007.
9 25 April, 2005, quoted by Allan (2006: 1).
10 Heidi Dawson quoted in *Press Gazette*, 25 June 2007. For a recent interview-based study of how journalists in three countries – the UK, the USA and Germany – are responding to the online challenge, and UGC in particular, see Heinrich (2008).
11 Butcher, M., 'Mail's rise reopens questions about target audiences', the *Guardian*, 23 June 2008.
12 Vass, S., 'I want the BBC to be the premier source for politics', the *Sunday Herald*, 21 January 2007.
13 For a full text of the speech, go to www.bbc.co.uk/blogs/theeditors/2008/01/ value_of_citizen_journalism.html.
14 'The Next Six Years', *Ariel*, 18 October 2007.
15 *Ibid.*
16 Newland, M., 'The formidable task facing the Telegraph', the *Guardian*, 23 October 2006.
17 Paul Holleran, quoted in *Press Gazette*, 25 June 2007. In December 2008, further radical restructuring was announced at Newsquest in Glasgow.
18 Gibson, O., 'Have you got news for us?', the *Guardian*, 6 November 2006.
19 Preston, P., 'Paperless newspapers are virtually a reality', the *Observer*, 29 July 2007.
20 *The Ownership of News*, House of Lords Select Committee on Communications, two volumes, HL Paper 122-I, HL Paper 122-II, www.publications.parliament.uk/ pa/ld/ldcomuni.htm.
21 *Ibid.*
22 Pilkington, E., 'The human search engines', the *Guardian*, 1 July 2008.
23 *Ibid.*
24 Major, J., 'We're hurting ourselves as well as Charles', the *Sunday Times*, 16 November 2003.
25 Berger, N., 'The "barking" of Doris Kearns Goodwin', *The American Prospect*, 7 March 2002.
26 Jones, A., 'Bloggers are the sizzle, not the steak', *Los Angeles Times*, 18 July 2004.
27 Kurtz, H., 'Boston's bloggers, filling in the margins', *The Washington Post*, 26 July 2004.
28 Barkham, P., 'How the net closed on Prescott', the *Guardian*, 10 July 2006.
29 Brown, A., 'The inner world of Joe Blogs', the *Sunday Times*, 13 March 2005.
30 Gardam, T., 'A bridge between parallel universes', the *Guardian*, 23 January 2006.
31 *The Amateur Computerist*, 15 (1), Winter 2007, www.ais.org/~jrh/acn/ACn15-1.pdf.
32 *Ibid.*, editorial.
33 Burkeman, O., 'The new commentariat', the *Guardian*, 17 November 2005.
34 *Ibid.*

35 Reynolds, G., 'Marxist is toast of the neocons', the *Sunday Times*, 6 February 2005.
36 Smith, I.D., 'Bloggers will rescue the right', the *Guardian*, 19 February 2005.
37 Sullivan, A., 'The Blogging Revolution', *Wired*, 10 (5): May 2002. Around the same time, Sullivan spoke of blogging as 'the most significant media revolution since the arrival of television' (Sullivan, A., 'An honest blogger will never make a quick buck', the *Sunday Times*, 13 October 2002).
38 Quoted by McIntosh, N., 'Spread the gospel', the *Guardian*, 3 July 2003.
39 Kamm, O., 'A parody of democracy', the *Guardian*, 2 April 2007.

Chapter Nine

 1 Oliver, L., 'BBC plans for £68m local video network go public', 24 June 2008, www.journalism.co.uk/2/articles/531810.php.
 2 *The Ownership of News*, House of Lords Select Committee on Communications, two volumes, HL Paper 122-I, HL Paper 122-II, www.publications.parliament.uk/pa/ld/ldcomuni.htm.
 3 All unreferenced speakers from this point on are from interviews with the author.
 4 As Donald Waters of Grampian TV puts it, referring to Scotland in particular, 'people get fed up about ITN's being too metropolitan, too English-oriented. Our market research shows it.'
 5 For a discussion of globalisation and its implications for television journalism, see Gurevitch and Levy (1990) and Gurevitch (1991).
 6 Scottish Television Application for Channel 3 licence, Summary.
 7 *The Ownership of News*, op. cit.
 8 Hewlett, S., 'It's only a matter of time for ITV', the *Guardian*, 7 July 2008.
 9 At the same time, however, companies such as Scottish continued to seek ways of providing as much local journalism as possible, and to exploit the niche-targeting potential of online and digital technology. By July 2008, Scottish had launched its own online video player, embedded in a beefed-up website.
10 For a more detailed discussion of the impact of devolution on the Scottish media, see Schlesinger (1998).
11 Martin, I., 'Tartan at ten', the *Sunday Times*, 1 June 1997.
12 *Ibid.*
13 *The BBC Trust Impartiality Report: BBC network news and current affairs coverage of the four UK nations*, June 2008.
14 King, A., 'BBC network news and current affairs coverage of the four UK nations', London, BBC, May 2008.
15 McCrone, A., 'Private sector tells BBC: get off our turf, you're distorting the market', the *Sunday Times*, 14 May 2006.
16 McNair, B., 'Scotland's devolution debate', the *Guardian*, 17 August 2007.
17 Wainwright, M., 'Local heroes', the *Guardian*, 3 March 2008.
18 Tryhorn, C., Sweeney, M., 'Press the panic button', the *Guardian*, 7 July 2008.
19 Marriner, C., 'Pelle the conqueror', the *Guardian*, 28 November 2005.
20 Garner, S., 'Free and proud of it: the new establishment line', *Press Gazette*, 15 September 1986.
21 Ward, M., '*Daily News*: up and running well', *Press Gazette*, 5 October 1987.
22 Radburn, P., 'On the road to a community press', *Press Gazette*, 5 October 1987.
23 Garner, S., 'Free and proud of it: the new establishment line', *Press Gazette*, 15 September 1986.
24 Garth, A., 'The free concept which paid off, *Press Gazette*, 15 August 1988.
25 *Press Gazette*, 25 February 1991.
26 Greenslade, R., 'Community service', the *Guardian*, 18 July 1994.
27 Barkham, P., 'Giving it all away', the *Guardian*, 22 September 2006.
28 *Ibid.*

29 Ruddock, A., ' Will the standard survive the freebie onslaught', the *Guardian*, 27 August 2007.

30 Quoted by Lawrence, C., 'Frees for all', *Press Gazette*, 15 September 1989.

31 Marks, N., 'Distilling the community spirit', *Press Gazette*, 12 March 1990.

32 Morgan, J., 'It's so bonny to be working in Scotland', *Press Gazette*, 14 March 1988.

33 *Press Gazette* has observed that 'more and more [regional] newspapers are being concentrated in fewer and fewer hands' (6 June 1988).

34 Morris, R., 'Hitting the right target', *Press Gazette*, 5 November 1990.

35 Quoted in Slattery, J., 'Regional press prospects are good, says Stevenson', *Press Gazette*, 18 June 1990.

36 Slattery, J., 'Regionals warned of threat from specialists', *Press Gazette*, 5 September 1988.

37 Tryhorn, C., Sweney, M., 'Press the panic button', the *Guardian*, 7 July 2008.

38 Slattery, J., 'Regionals warned of threat from specialists', *Press Gazette*, 5 September 1988.

39 Neil, A., 'The slide towards probable extinction', the *Guardian*, 11 February 2008.

Chapter Ten

1 Gardam, T., 'A bridge between parallel universes', the *Guardian*, 23 January 2006.

Bibliography

Alexander, J. (1981) 'The mass news media in systemic, historical and comparative perspective', in E. Katz and T. Szecsko (eds) *Mass Media and Social Change*, London: Sage, pp. 17–51.

Allan, S. (2004) *News Culture*, Milton Keynes: Open University Press.

——(2006) *Online News*, Maidenhead: Open University Press.

Allan, S. and Zelizer, B. (eds) (2002) *Journalism After September 11*, London: Routledge.

——(2004) *Reporting War: Journalism in Wartime*, London: Routledge.

Altschull, H. (1984) *Agents of Power*, New York: Longman.

Anderson, D. and Sharrock, W. (1979) 'Biasing the news: technical issues in media studies', *British Journal of Sociology* 13(3): 367–85.

Anderson, P.J., Ward, G. (eds) (2007) *The Future of Journalism in the Advanced Democracies*, Aldershot: Ashgate.

Baistow, T. (1985) *Fourth-rate Estate: An Anatomy of Fleet Street*, London: Comedia.

——(1989) 'The predator's press', in N. Buchan and T. Sumner (eds) *Glasnost in Britain?*, London: Macmillan, pp. 53–69.

Barnett, S. (1989) 'Broadcast News', *British Journalism Review* 1(1): 49–56.

Barnett, S., Seymour, E. and Gaber, I. (2000) *From Callaghan to Kosovo: Changing Trends in British TV News, 1975–1999*, London: University of Westminster.

——(2001) *Westminster Tales*, London: Continuum.

Belfield, R., Hird, C. and Kelly, S. (1991) *Murdoch: The Decline of an Empire*, London: Macdonald.

Bevins, A. (1990) 'The crippling of the scribes', *British Journalism Review* 1(2): 13–17.

Blain, N. and Hutchison, D. (eds) (2008) *The Media in Scotland*, Edinburgh: Edinburgh University Press.

Blanchard, S. (ed.) (1990) *The Challenge of Channel Five*, London: BFI.

Blom-Cooper, L. (1991) 'The last days of the Press Council', *British Journalism Review* 2(3): 34–39.

Bolton, R. (1990) *Death on the Rock and Other Stories*, London: W.H. Allen.

Bourdieu, P. (1998) *On Television and Journalism*, London: Pluto.

Boyd-Barrett, O. 'Positioning the News Audience as Idiot' in Maltby, S. and Keeble, R. (eds) (2007).

Briggs, A. and Cobley, P. (eds) (1998) *The Media: An Introduction*, Harlow: Longman.

Bridcut, J. (2007) *From Seesaw to Wagon Wheel: Safeguarding Impartiality in the 21st Century*, London: BBC Trust.

Brighton, D. and Foy, P. (2007) *News Values*, London: Sage.

Bruhn-Jensen, K. (1986) *Making Sense of the News*, Aarhus: Aarhus University Press.

Calcutt, D. (1990) *Report of the Committee on Privacy and Related Matters*, London: HMSO.

——(1993) *Review of Press Self-Regulation*, London: HMSO.

Carey, J. (1992) *The Intellectuals and the Masses*, London: Faber & Faber.

Chippindale, P. and Franks, S. (1991) *Dished! The Rise and Fall of British Satellite Broadcasting*, London: Simon & Schuster.

Chippindale, R. and Horrie, C. (1988) *Disaster*, London: Sphere.

——(1990) *Stick it up Your Punter*, London: Heinemann.

Chomsky, N. (1989) *Necessary Illusions*, London: Pluto.

Chomsky, N. and Herman, E. (1979) *The Political Economy of Human Rights, Vol. 1: The Washington Connection and Third World Fascism*, Boston: South End Press.

Cohen, N. (2007) *What's Left?*, London: Fourth Estate.

Cohen, S. (ed.) (1971) *Images of Deviance*, Harmondsworth: Penguin.

——(2004) *Folk Devils and Moral Panics*, 3rd edn, London: Routledge.

Cohen, S. and Young, J. (eds) (1973) *The Manufacture of News*, London: Constable.

Collins, R. (1976) *Television News*, London: BFI.

——(1990) *Television: Policy and Culture*, London: Unwin & Hyman.

Conboy, M. (2002) *The Press and Popular Culture*, London: Sage.

——(2004) *Journalism: A Critical History*, London: Sage.

Cornford, J. and Robins, K. (1990) 'Questions of geography', in S. Blanchard (ed.) *The Challenge of Channel Five*, London: BFI, pp. 3–21.

Cranfield, G. A. (1978) *The Press and Society*, London: Longman.

Crisell, A. (1994) *Understanding Radio*, 2nd edn, London: Routledge.

Critcher, C. (2003) *Moral Panics and the Media*, Milton Keynes: Open University Press.

Crozier, E. (1988) *The Making of the Independent*, London: Gordon Fraser.

Cumberbatch, G., McGregor, R., Brown, B. and Morrison, D. (1986) *Television and the Miners' Strike*, London: Broadcasting Research Unit.

Curran, J. (1989) 'Culturalist perspectives of news organizations: a reappraisal and a case study', in M. Ferguson (ed.) *Public Communication*, London: Sage, pp. 114–34.

——(1990) 'The new revisionism in mass communication research: a reappraisal', *European Journal of Communication* 5: 135–64.

Curran, J. and Gurevitch, M. (eds) (1991) *Mass Media and Society*, London: Edward Arnold.

Curran, J. and Seaton, J. (1991) *Power Without Responsibility*, 4th edn, London: Routledge.

——*Power Without Responsibility*, 5th edn, London: Routledge.

Dahlgren, P. and Sparks, C. (eds) (1992) *Journalism and Popular Culture*, London: Sage.

Davies, A. (2002) *Public Relations Democracy*, London: Routledge.

——(2007) *The Mediation of Power*, London: Routledge.

Davies, D. (1990) 'News and politics', in D. Swanson and D. Nimmo (eds) *New Directions in Political Communication*, London: Sage, pp. 147–84.

Davies, N. (2008) *Flat Earth News*, London: rBooks.

De Burgh, H. (2008) *Investigative Journalism*, London: Routledge.

DeGeorge, W. (1981) 'Conceptualisation and measurement of audience agenda', in G. Wilhoit and H. de Bock (eds) *Mass Communication Review Yearbook*, Vol. 2, London: Sage, pp. 219–24.

Deuze, M. (2007) *Media Work*, Cambridge: Polity.

Duff, A. (2008) 'Powers in the Land: British Political Columnists in the Information Era', *Journalism Practice* 2 (2): 230–44.

Dunnett, P. (1990) *The World Television Industry: An Economic Analysis*, London: Routledge.

Elliot, P., Halloran J. and Murdock, G. (1970) *Demonstrations and Communication*, Harmondsworth: Penguin.

Engel, M. (1996) *Tickle the Public*, London: Victor Gollancz.

Ericson, R. V., Baranek, P. M. and Chan, J. B. L. (1990) *Representing Order*, Toronto: Open University Press.

Evans, H. (1983) *Good Times, Bad Times*, London: Weidenfeld & Nicolson.

Fallows, J. (1996) *Breaking the News*, New York: Pantheon.

Ferguson, M. (ed.) (1989) *Public Communication*, London: Sage.

Fiske, J. (1987) *Television Culture*, London: Methuen.

Fowler, R. (1991) *Language in the News*, London: Routledge.

Franklin, B. (1997) *Newszak and News Media*, London: Arnold.

——(2006) 'Local journalism and local media: contested perceptions, rocket science and parallel universes', in Franklin, B. (ed.) *Local Journalism and Local Media: Making the Local News*, London: Routledge, pp. xvii–xxii.

——(ed.) (2006) *Local Journalism and Local Media: Making the Local News*, London: Routledge.

——(ed.) (2008) *Pulling Newspapers Apart*, London: Routledge.

Fraser, N. (1990) 'The grand design for ITN', *British Journalism Review* 2(1): 17–21.

Galtung, J. and Ruge, M. (1973) 'Structuring and selecting news', in S. Cohen and J. Young (eds) *The Manufacture of News*, London: Constable, pp. 62–72.

Garnham, N. (1986) 'The media and the public sphere', in P. Golding, G. Murdock and P. Schlesinger (eds) *Communicating Politics*, Leicester: Leicester University Press. pp. 37–54.

——(1989) 'Has public service broadcasting failed?' in N. Millar and C. Morris (eds) *Life After the Broadcasting Bill*, Manchester: Manchester Monographs, 7–35.

Glasgow University Media Group (1976) *Bad News*, London: Routledge & Kegan Paul.

——(1980) *More Bad News*, London: Routledge & Kegan Paul.

——(1986) *War and Peace News*, Milton Keynes: Open University Press

Golding, P., Murdock, G. and Schlesinger, P. (eds) (1986) *Communicating Politics*, Leicester: Leicester University Press.

Goodman, A. *Tradition and Talent in an Age of Transition*, UK Press Gazette, 13th June 1988.

Gowing, N. (1994) *Real-time Television Coverage of Armed Conflicts and Diplomatic Crises*, Harvard: Harvard University Press.

Gunter, B. (1987) *Poor Reception*, New Jersey: Lawrence Erlbaum Associates.

Gurevitch, M. (1991) 'The globalisation of electronic journalism', in J. Curran and M. Gurevitch (eds) *Mass Media and Society*, London: Edward Arnold, pp. 178–93.

Gurevitch, M. and Levy, M. (1990) 'The global newsroom', *British Journalism Review* 2(1): 27–37.

Hall, S., Critcher, S., Jefferson, T., Clarke, J. and Roberts, B. (1978) *Policing the Crisis*, London: Macmillan.

Hallin, D. (1986) *The Uncensored War*, Oxford: Oxford University Press.

Hargreaves, I., Thomas, J. (2002) *New News, Old News*, London: Independent Television Commission/Broadcasting Standards Council.

Hargreaves, I., Thomas J., Speers T. (2003) *Science and the Media: Towards a Better Map*, London: ESRC

Harrison, M. (1985) *TV News: Whose Bias?*, Hermitage: Policy Journals.

Hartley, J. (1982) *Understanding News*, London: Routledge.

Heinrich, A. (2008) 'Network journalism: journalistic practice in interactive spheres', PhD thesis, Dunedin: University of Otago.

Herman, E. (1982) *The Real Terror Network: Terrorism in Fact and Fiction*, Boston: South End Press.

——(1986) 'Gatekeeper versus propaganda models: a critical American perspective', in P. Golding, G. Murdock and P. Schlesinger (eds) *Communicating Politics*, Leicester: Leicester University Press, pp. 171–95.

Hetherington, A. (1989) *News in the Regions*, London: Macmillan.

Hill, A. (2005) *Reality TV*, London Routledge.

——(2007) *Popular Factual Television*, London: Routledge.

Horrie, C. and Clarke, S. (2001) *Citizen Greg*, London: Pocket Books.

Hoskins, A. and O'Loughlin, B. (2008) *Television and Terror: Conflicting Times and the Crisis of News Discourse*, Houndmills: Palgrave Macmillan.

Iyengar, S. and Kinder, D. R. (1987) *News that Matters*, Chicago: University of Chicago Press.

Jacobs, E., Worcester, R.M. (1990) *We British: Britain under the MORIscope*, London, Weidenfeld and Nicholson.

Jewkes, Y *Media and Crime* (2004) London: Sage.

Johnson, S. (2005) *Everything Bad Is Good For You*, London: Penguin.

Katz, E. and Szecsko, T. (eds) (1981) *Mass Media and Social Change*, London: Sage.

Keane, J. (1991) *The Media and Democracy*, Oxford: Polity Press.

Kuhn, R. and Neveu, E. (eds) (2002) *Political Journalism: New Challenges, New Practices*, London: Routledge.

Leapman, M. (1987) *The Last Days of the Beeb*, London: Coronet.

Lewis, J., Inthorn, S. and Wahl-Jorgensen, K. (2005) *Citizens or Consumers? What the Media Tell Us about Political Participation*, Milton Keynes: Open University Press.

Lichtenberg, J. (1991) 'In defence of objectivity', in J. Curran and M. Gurevitch (eds) *Mass Media and Society*, London: Edward Arnold, pp. 216–31.

Lloyd, J. (2004) *What the Media are Doing to Our Politics*, London: Constable.

Loffelholz, M. (2008) 'Heterogeneous – multidimensional – competing', in Loffelholz and Weaver (eds) *Global Journalism Research: Theories, Methods, Findings, Future*, Oxford: Blackwell, pp. 15–27.

Lowe, G.F. and Bardoel, J. (eds) (2008) *From Public Service Broadcasting to Public Service Media*, Goteborg: Nordicom.

Luhman, N. (2000) *The Reality of Mass Media*, Cambridge: Polity Press.

Lumby, C. (1999) *Gotcha: Life in a Tabloid World*, St Leonards: Allen & Unwin.

Lustig, R. (1990) 'Promises are no longer enough', *British Journalism Review* 1(2): 44–48.

MacArthur, B. (1988) *Eddie Shah: Today and the Newspaper Revolution*, London: David & Charles.

MacCabe, C. and Stewart, O. (eds) (1986) *The BBC and Public Service Broadcasting*, Manchester: Manchester University Press.

McCombs, M. (1981) 'Setting the agenda for agenda-setting research', in G. Wilhoit and H. de Bock (eds) *Mass Communication Review Yearbook*, Vol. 2, London: Sage, pp. 209–19.

MacGregor, B. (1997) *Live, Direct and Biased*, London: Arnold.

McGregor, O. R. (1977) *Royal Commission on the Press*, Final Report, Cmnd. 6810, London: HMSO.

McLaughlin, G. (2002) *The War Correspondent*, London: Pluto.

McKnight, d. (2005) *Beyond Right and Left: new Politics and the Culture Wars*, Sydney: Allen & Unwin.

McNair, B. (1988) *Images of the Enemy*, London: Routledge.

——(1991) *Glasnost, Perestroika and the Soviet Media*, London: Routledge.

——(1998a) 'New technology and the media', in A. Briggs and P. Cobley (eds) *The Media: An Introduction*, Harlow: Longman: pp. 173–85.

——(1998b) *The Sociology of Journalism*, London: Arnold.

——(2000) *Journalism and Democracy: an evaluation of the political public sphere*, London: Routledge.

——(2002) 'Journalism and democracy in contemporary Britain', in Kuhn, R. and Neveu, E. (eds) *Political Journalism: New Challenges, New Practices*, London: Routledge, pp. 189–202.

——(2006a) *Cultural Chaos: News, Journalism and Power in a Globalised World*, London: Routledge.

——(2006b) 'News from a small country: the media in Scotland', in Franklin, B. (ed.) *Local Journalism and Local Media: Making the Local News*, London: Routledge, pp. 37–48;

——(2007) *An Introduction to Political Communication*, 4th edn, London: Routledge.

——(2008a) 'Current affairs in British public service broadcasting: challenges and opportunities', in Lowe, G.F. and Bardoel, J. (eds) *From Public Service Broadcasting to Public Service Media*, Goteborg: Nordicom, pp. 151–65.

——(2008b) 'I, columnist', in Franklin, B. (ed.) *Pulling Newspapers Apart*, London: Routledge.

——(2008c) 'The Scottish media and politics', in Blain, N. and Hutchison, D. (eds) *The Media in Scotland*, Edinburgh: Edinburgh University Press, pp. 227–42.

McNair, B., Hibberd, M. and Schlesinger, P. (2003) *Mediated Access: Broadcasting and Democratic Participation in the Age of Mediated Politics*, Luton: University of Luton Press.

McQuail, D. (1987) *Mass Communication Theory*, London: Sage.

Maltby, S. and Keeble, R. (eds) (2007) *Communicating War: Memory, Media and Military*, London: Arima.

Melvern, L. (1988) *The End of the Street*, London: Methuen.

Miliband, R. (1972) *The State in Capitalist Society*, London: Quartet.

Millar, N. and Morris, C. (eds) (1989) *Life After the Broadcasting Bill*, Manchester: Manchester Monographs.

Miller, D. (ed.) (2004) *Tell Me Lies: Propaganda and Media Distortion in the Attack on Iraq*, London: Pluto.

Miller, W. (1991) *Media and Voters*, London: Clarendon Press.

Milne, A. (1988) *D.G.: Memoirs of a British Broadcaster*, London: Hodder & Stoughton.

Montgomery, M. (2007) *The Discourse of Broadcast News*, London: Routledge.

Morley, D. (1990) 'The construction of everyday life', in D. Swanson and D. Nimmo (eds) *New Directions in Political Communication*, London: Sage, pp. 123–26.

Murdock, G. (1973) 'Political deviance: the press presentation of a militant mass demonstration', in S. Cohen and J. Young (eds) *The Manufacture of News*, London: Constable, pp. 156–75.

Naughton, J. (1999) *A Brief History of the Future: The Origins of the Internet*, London: Weidenfeld & Nicolson.

Nguyen, A., Ferrier L., Western M., McKay S. (2005) 'Online News in Australia: Patterns of Uses and Gratifciations', *Australian Studies in Journalism*, 15: 5–34.

Ofcom (2007) *New News, Future News: The Challenges for Television News after Digital Switchover*, London: Office of Communications.

O'Malley, T. and Soley, C. (2000) *Regulating the Press*, London: Pluto.

Pax, Salam (2003) *The Baghdad Blogger*, London: Atlantic.

Peacock, A. (1986) *Broadcasting in the 1990s*, London: HMSO.

Philo, G. (1987) 'Whose news?', *Media, Culture and Society* 9(4): 397–406.

——(1990) *Seeing and Believing*, London: Routledge.

Philo, G., Berry, M. (2004) *Bad News Out of Israel*, London: Pluto.

Pudlowski, T. (ed.) (2007) *How the World's News Media Reacted to 9/11*, New York: Marquette.

Quinn, A. (2007) 'Contrary to claims, convention and culture: an apologia for the Glasgow University Media Group', *International Journal of Media and Cultural Politics*, 3(1): 5–24.

Ranney, A. (1983) *Channels of Power*, New York: Basic Books.

Raymond, J. (1996) *The Invention of the Newspaper*, Oxford: Clarendon Press.

Reid, H. (2006) *Deadline: The History of the Scottish Press*, Edinburgh: Mainstream.

Robinson, J. P. and Levy, M. R. (1986) *The Main Source*, London: Sage.

Rock, P. (1973) 'News as eternal recurrence', in S. Cohen and J. Young (eds) *The Manufacture of News*, London: Constable, pp. 73–80.

Scannell, P. (1989) 'Public service broadcasting and modern public life', *Media, Culture and Society* 11(2): 136–64.

Scannell, P. and Cardiff, D. (1991) *A Social History of British Broadcasting, Vol. I*, Oxford: Basil Blackwell.

Schiller, D. (1981) *Objectivity and the News*, Philadelphia: University of Pennsylvania Press.

Schlesinger, P. (1978) *Putting Reality Together*, London: Constable.

——(1989) 'From production to propaganda', *Media, Culture and Society* 11(3): 283–306.

——(1991) *Media, State and Nation*, London: Sage.

——(1998) 'Scotland's Parliament: devolution, the media and political culture', in J. Seaton (ed.) *The Media and Politics in Britain*, Oxford: Blackwell, pp. 56–76.

Schlesinger, P., Murdock, G. and Elliot, P. (1983) *Televising Terrorism*, London: Comedia.

Schudson, M. (1978) *Discovering News*, New York: Basic Books.

——(1989) 'The sociology of news production', *Media, Culture and Society* 11(3): 263–82.

Seaton, J. (ed.) (1998) *The Media and Politics in Britain*, Oxford: Blackwell.

Seymour, C., Barnett, S. (2006) *Bringing the World to the UK*, London: University of Westminster/3WE.

Siebert, F. (1956) *Four Theories of the Press*, Urbana: University of Illinois Press.

Sutton, S. (2006) 'The Oh My in Ohmynews: a uses and gratifications investigation into the motivations of journalists in South Korea', unpublished research paper, University of Leeds.

Sutton Trust (2006) *The Educational Background of Leading Journalists*, London: The Sutton Trust, www.suttontrust.com/reports/Journalists-Backgrounds-final-report.pdf.

Swanson, D. and Nimmo, D. (eds) (1990) *New Directions in Political Communication*, London: Sage.

Taylor, S. J. (1991) *Shock! Horror! The Tabloids in Action*, London: Bantam.

Tiffen, R. (1989) *News and Power*, Sydney: Allen & Unwin.

Tuchman, G. (1972) 'Objectivity as strategic ritual: an examination of newsmen's notions of objectivity', *American Journal of Sociology* 77(4): 660–70.

Tumber, H., Palmer, J. (2004) *The Media At War*, London: Palgrave.

Tumber, H. and Webster, F. (2007) 'Information War: encountering a chaotic information environment', in Maltby, S. and Keeble (2007).

Tunstall, J. (1996) *Newspaper Power*, Oxford: Clarendon Press.

Tunstall, J. and Dunford, M. (1991) *The ITC and the Future of Regional and National Television News*, London: Communications Policy Research Centre.

Tusa, J. (1990) *Conversations with the World*, London: BBC Books.

Van Dijk, T. A. (1988) *News Analysis. Case Studies of International and National News in the Press*, Hillsdale, NJ: Lawrence Erlbaum.

Veljanovski, C. (1990) *The Media in Britain Today*, London: News International.

Whittemore, H. (1990) *CNN: The Inside Story*, Boston: Little, Brown.

Wilhoit, G. and de Bock, H. (eds) (1981) *Mass Communication Review Yearbook*, Vol. 2, London: Sage.

Willis, P. (1971) 'What is news?', *Working Papers in Cultural Studies* 1(1).

Windlesham, Lord, Rampton R. (1989) *The Windlesham/Ramport Report on Death on the Rock*, London: Faber & Faber.

Young, J. (1971) 'The Role of the Police as Amplifiers of Deviance', *Images of Deviance*, ed. Cohen S, London: Faber & Faber, 27–61.

Index

An Introduction to Political Communication
Fourth Edition
Brian McNair

In this classic textbook, Brian McNair examines how politicians, trade unions, pressure groups, NGOs and terrorist organisations make use of the media. Separate chapters look at the theory of political communication and its role in a democracy; the political media and their effects; political advertising, marketing and public relations; and the communication practices of organisations at all levels. This fourth edition is revised and updated to include:

- The re-election of George W. Bush in 2004
- Developments in the war on terror since 2003, including the invasion of Iraq
- The re-election of New Labour in 2005
- The Gilligan affair, and changes in UK government communication since the Hutton report
- The growing role of the internet in political communication

Communication and Society

Series Editor: James Curran

ISBN13: 978-0-415-41070-0 (hbk)
ISBN13: 978-0-415-41069-4 (pbk)

Available at all good bookshops
For ordering and further information please visit:
www.routledge.com